COLONIAL SURRY

BY

JOHN B. BODDIE

CLEARFIELD

Originally Published
Richmond, 1948

Reprinted
Southern Book Company
Baltimore, 1959

Reissued
Genealogical Publishing Co., Inc.
Baltimore, 1974

Reprinted for
Clearfield Company by
Genealogical Publishing Cò.
Baltimore, Maryland
1992, 1997, 2000, 2004, 2007

Library of Congress Catalogue Card Number 66-22144
ISBN-13: 978-0-8063-0026-9
ISBN-10: 0-8063-0026-4

PREFACE

THIS book was begun in 1938 soon after *Seventeenth Century Isle of Wight County* was published. The first eight chapters were written in 1938-39. The outbreak of the war caused the removal of the writer to the Hawaiian Islands and brought about a temporary suspension. Work was resumed in 1943.

The manuscript reached such proportions that it seemed too large to publish in one volume. *Seventeenth Century* bulked too large and had too many pages. So it was decided to separate this work into two or three volumes. The next one, which is nearly complete, will contain about seven hundred pages and will be entitled *Colonial Families of Surry and Sussex.*

Many thanks are due to the Librarian of Newberry Library who granted the writer a shelf permit to roam at will through the book stacks and also to Mr. Joseph Wolf, head of the Genealogical Department, for their very great assistance.

Mrs. Charles E. Davis of Smithfield, Virginia, kindly furnished the list of Surry land grants dating from 1666 to 1740.

Miss Lorine Wilkins of Honolulu kindly re-typed many of the pages herein. Miss Yoshiko Kobashigawa of Honolulu also typed some of the chapters. Miss Elizabeth Bass of the Virginia State Library rendered invaluable aid in deciphering some of the early records.

Dr. B. C. Holtzclaw kindly contributed the chapter on "Bacon's Rebellion" from original sources as the writer was unable to go to Surry County.

Mr. W. A. Graham Clark of Washington, D. C. contributed the "list of Tithables" and Mr. James G. W. MacClamroch of Greensboro, N. C. contributed the documents from which the chapter entitled "The Warren House" was compiled.

All three of these gentlemen also furnished many of the family accounts which will appear in the next volume. Many thanks are due to them, and to others who will be mentioned hereafter for their very able assistance.

The next volume will contain the early records of more than a hundred Surry and Sussex families, descendants of persons who were granted land in the two counties and held all of the offices during the Colonial period.

It is seemingly the prevalent idea that we won our freedom from Great Britain at a single stroke. From these pages it will be seen that the colonists began their slow march toward the "Four Freedoms" at an early date and had achieved them in a great measure before the Revolution.

JOHN B. BODDIE.

Honolulu, T. H.,
January 2, 1946.

EXPLANATION OF ABBREVIATIONS

B or Bk	—Book.
Boddie	—References used by Dr. Holtzclaw for the book *17th Century Isle of Wight*, by the author.
C.P.	—*Cavaliers and Pioneers*, by Nell M. Nugent.
D.B.	—Deed Book.
D.N.B.	—*Dictionary of National Biography.*
Hen.	—*Hening's Statutes at Large.*
Hotten	—*Original Lists of Emigrants to America*, by J. C. Hotten.
M.C.G.C.	—*Minutes of the Council and the General Court.*
O.B.	—Order Book.
R.V.C.	—*Records of the Virginia Co. of London.*
17c	—*Seventeenth Century Isle of Wight, Va.*, by John B. Boddie.
Va. Co. Rec.	—*Records of the Virginia Co. of London.*
V.M.	—*Virginia Magazine*, by the Virginia Historical Society.
Waters	—*Genealogical Gleanings*, by H. Waters.
W.B.	—Will Book.
W.M.	—*William and Mary Quarterly*, by the College of William and Mary.

CONTENTS

Contents

Chapter I

THE KIND OF MEN WHO FOUNDED JAMESTOWN

IT has been the general belief that Jamestown was founded by English gentlemen who disdained to work and consequently nearly starved to death. Contrary to this idea, among the leaders of the Jamestown expedition were some of the hardest bitten men of Queen Elizabeth's time. Captain Newport, the admiral of the first expedition, was one of Elizabeth's greatest sea-captains. Sailors of his kind were not afraid of either the perils of the deep or of the Spaniards.

The boldest and most venturesome men of their day were the sea-captains of Queen Elizabeth. They were the terror of the Spaniards upon the high seas and had victoriously led many a forlorn hope against their great fleets. In a short time they made English naval power supreme upon the seas and thus enabled England to colonize far off lands like Virginia.

These sea-captains created a new style of fighting which changed the character of naval warfare and with it the history of the world.

Spanish war-vessels had been built with the idea that had come down through the ages which was that they were only carriers of men and their value as ships was measured mainly by the number of soldiers they could carry on board. Hence, the great galleons of the Spanish which were built to throw an overwhelming force upon the decks of smaller enemy ships. It was soldiers and not sailors they depended upon to win their naval fights.

Spanish ships, since the days of Columbus, had sailed the warm Southern waters, bringing back to Spain the treasures of the West Indies, Central and South America. This wealth had made Spain the mightiest nation of its day.

English sailors had been forced away from the Southern seas and had been trying to find a Northwest passage to the East Indies through the icebergs of the North Atlantic. Of necessity they had to build smaller and stauncher ships than the Spaniards. Their efforts to find a Northwest passage were futile. Baffled in their endeavor to escape by way of the North they timidly ventured towards the South and wherever they encountered the Spaniards they were surprised and even elated by their success.

Their small ships were better designed for sailing and were far

superior in maneuvering. They could literally sail "rings around" the
Spaniards. Ships themselves and their guns became the offensive
weapons and not the number of men aboard them. Of what value was
a great ship if it could be sunk before its land soldiers could be used
as boarders. Gunnery became of prime importance, and in our time
Dewey at Manila only repeated with ease the master-gunnery Elizabeth's
sea-captains had used against The Armada.

Chasing the Spaniards soon became a sport and a commercial venture
as well. "Let the Spaniards have the trouble of gathering in the
treasures," said the English merchant adventurers, "and we will gather
the treasure from the gatherers." Fleets began to sail from English
ports with the sole object of preying upon the great treasure-coffers
which were being wafted lazily from the Indies.

In 1591 some merchants of the City of London equipped and sent
forth a fleet of four vessels, under the command of Captain Christopher
Newport, to prey upon the treasure ships and rich cities in the West
Indies. John Twitt, a corporal on board the Golden Dragon on this
voyage, wrote an account of the expedition entitled, "A True Report of
a Voyage undertaken by M. Christopher Newport, General of a Fleet
of Three Ships and a Pinnace, viz., the Golden Dragon, Admiral thereof was Captain Newport himself; the Prudence Vice Admiral, under the
conduct of Captain Hugh Merrick; the Margaret under Captain Robert
Freed; and the Virgin, our Pinnace under Captain Henry Kidgil."[1]

Twitt says, "Having a favorable wind, the 4th of April, 1592, we
fell with Dominica in the West Indies, * * * where we bartered with
savages for tobacco. * * * Passing from thence to a watering place on
the other side of the cliff we took a Portugal ship of Lisbon of 300
tons, which came from Guinea and was bound for Cartegena, wherein
were 300 negroes."[2]

They then set sail for San Juan de Puerto Rico where they landed
the Portuguese captain in the hope he would raise some money to ransom his negroes. Upon his failure to do so Newport set the negroes
free on the island.

On the 15th of April, Newport sacked a town in Hispaniola called
Ocoa and found a great quantity of sugar. The Spaniards fled to the
mountains and later brought in "much cattle and two wagon loads of

---

[1] *Hakluyt's Voyages,* (Maclehose), Vol. X, pp. 184-191. (E.L. 910, H 12.)

[2] Twitt was related to Christopher Jones, Captain of the Mayflower of the Pilgrims.
See chart at page 46, *Master of the Mayflower,* by Henry Justin Smith.

sugar to ransom the town." While this was going on Captain Freed fought and captured two Spanish frigates which had sailed into the bay.

The English next "stood along for Cape Tiburon" and rounding it on the 27th of April at about two in the morning came to a town called Yaguana in the northwestern part of Hispaniola. They were discovered and the town aroused. "We marched notwithstanding along to the town, having a Spaniard for our guide, where by that time the day brake and we were before the town, where upon a fair green making a stand, we were encountered by horsemen who charged us very fiercely, but seeing they could not prevail, brought in a drove of two hundred beasts or more: and so forcibly thinking to have broken our array, it pleased God to cause their cattle to return back upon themselves: and thus by their own device sorted out their own detriment. In this skirmish we slew their Governor, a man very hardy and of great valor."

The town was burnt and they sailed away for Honduras where Newport captured the town of Puerto de Cavallos. They fought three frigates which "rode before the town, the castle playing upon us with their ordnance." In the harbor were "four rich ships laden from thence." * * * "We took three bells out of their church and destroyed their images." * * * "The town is of two hundred houses and wealthy, * * * we spared it because we found other contentment. And having taken our pleasure of the town as foresaid we returned aboard our ships standing for Truxillo."

The weather was so calm they were twenty-two days sailing back to Truxillo, "that which we had sailed in six days." The Spaniards were amply prepared and succeeded in preventing the capture of the town, whereupon Captain Newport decided to sail homeward with his heavily laden vessels. The ships were dispersed in a storm only the Golden Dragon and the Prudence remaining in consort.

Finally they reached the Island of Flores in the Azores where Newport met Sir John Burgh and his squadron awaiting the arrival of some treasure ships. It was here that Christopher Newport took part in capturing the greatest treasure ship known to history.

Sir John Burgh wished to strengthen his squadron and he made the following agreement with Newport. "I, Sir John Burgh, Knighte, and by vertue of her Majestie's commission, Generall of a fleete appoynted for the seas, have consorted, covenaunted, and agreed, * * * to and with Chrystopher Newporte, capitayne of The Goulden Dragon of

London, a shippe of the burthen of 180 tonne, for himself and one
ship more of his consortship, called The Prudence, of the sayde city of
London, being of the burthen of 100 tonne, to have possesse, and
enjoy, and to be partaker with me and my fleete, and I with them, of
all such lawful pryse and pryses as shall be taken by me or them, or
any of us jointlie or severally, in sighte or out of sighte; tunne for tunne
and man for man; from the daye of the date hereof untill the tenth
daye of September next."[3]

This agreement was made the 28th of July and the next day, Sir
John Burgh, from his ship The Roebuck, sighted a Portuguese carrack,
The Santa Cruz. The crew of this ship, rather than surrender its
valuable cargo, set fire to the vessel and swam ashore. Sir John Burgh
ordered 100 of his men to swim after the Portuguese. "Here was taken
among others Vincent Fonseca, a Portuguese, purser of the carrack, with
two others, one an Almaine and the second a Low-dutchman, canoniers,
who refusing to make a voluntary report of those things which were
demanded of them, had the torture threatened, the fear whereof at last
wrested from them the intelligence that within 15 days three other
great carracks would arrive, there being five carracks in the fleet upon
their departure from Goa."[4] the greatest of which was The Madre de
Dios.

On the 3rd of August Captain Thomas Thompson in The Dainty
had the first sight of this huge carrack.[5] She was of 1,600 tons burden
and had seven decks, her length over all was 165 feet. She carried 800
men, among them being several Spanish Governors going home to
retire with the fruits of their spoils from the Indies.

"The Dainty being of excellent saile got the start of the rest of our
fleet and began the conflict somewhat to her cost with the slaughter and
hurt of divers of her men. Within a while after, Sir John Burgh in
the Roebucke of Sir W. Raleigh's, was at hand to second her, who
saluted her with shot of great ordnance, and continued the fight within
musket shot assisted by Captain Thompson and Captain Newport till
Sir R. Crosse, Vice-admiral of the fleet came up being to leeward, at
whose arrival Sir J. Burgh demanded of him what was best to be done,

---

[3] Edward Edwards, *Life of Sir Walter Raleigh*, Vol. I, t. 61.

[4] Quoted from, "The Taking of the Madre de Dios," *Hakluyt's Voyages*, Vol. III,
p. iii.

[5] A daughter of Captain Thomas Thompson was the second wife of Captain
Christopher Jones of the Mayflower. Henry Justin Smith, *The Master of the Mayflower*, p. 22.

who answered, that if the carrack were not boarded she would recover the shore and fire herself as the other had done."

Thereupon Sir John Burgh decided to entangle the carrack and Sir Robert Cross also promised to fasten his ship to her at the same time. This was done, but Sir John Burgh's ship received a cannon shot below the water line and Sir John desired Sir Robert Cross to fall off so that he might clear himself and save his ship from sinking which he did with difficulty.

That same evening, Sir Robert Cross, after he had fought the treasure ship some three hours and finding her drawing nearer to the island decided to board the ship. Fortunately, as he did, three ships, one of which was the Golden Dragon commanded by Captain Newport (but wrongfully said to be of the Earl of Cumberland's fleet) came up in time to make the assault, and at last the great carrack was taken after a sixteen hours fight.

Captain Christopher Newport was given command of the great ship. "No man could but step upon a dead carcase or a bloody floor, but specially about the helm, where very many of them fell suddenly from steering to dying. For the greatness of this sterrage required the labor of twelve or fourteen men at once, and some of our ships beating her in at the stern with their ordnance often times with one shot slew four or five labouring on either side of the helm; whose rooms being still furnished with fresh supplies, and our artillery still playing upon them with continual volleys, it could not but be that much blood should be shed at that place."[6]

The rich treasure found in the Madre de Dios surpassed expectations. The cargo is said to have been valued at £500.000. The news of such unheard wealth on a single ship spread far and wide in England. Of the booty, the Queen who had contributed but £1,800 to the expedition took one-half, and the London merchants who had sent out Captain Christopher Newport and who had ventured £6,000, got only £12,000.[7]

It was fifteen years later that Captain Newport sailed as admiral of the first fleet to Jamestown and although he continued to follow the sea in the interim he seems to have remained unknown and unrewarded. Edwards in his "Successors of Drake," when referring to the

[6] Quoted from *Hakluyt's Voyages*, Vol. VII, p. 111.
[7] Edward Thompson's *Sir Walter Raleigh*, p. 99. Edward Edward's *Life of Raleigh*, p. 67.

vast wealth Elizabeth's reign had produced, said, "Even as the Queen lay dying (1603) a rumour spread that an obscure skipper called Newport whom no one had ever heard of, had captured between Nombre de Dios and Havanna, two or three of the Carthagena Treasure ships."[8]

Queen Elizabeth rarely advanced any one not of gentle birth. Maybe it was caused by a feeling of inferiority, for she was the granddaughter of a country knight and the Tudors had only recently risen from the gentry by a fortunate royal marriage.

Newport was not a letter writer and he probably had "no friend at court." Other men of greater position but of lesser worth seem to have taken credit for many of his feats. Newport News, on the James, was even named for another man.[9]

It seems that his companions in the Virginia venture, Thomas Gates and George Somers, fared better (for doing less), for they were knighted for their deeds. However, Gates was a writer and thereby advertised his adventures.

Gates sailed with Sir Francis Drake on his famous voyage to the West Indies and published an account of it, entitled, "A summarie and true discourse of Sir Francis Drake's West Indian voyage begun in the year 1585. Wherein were taken the cities of Saint Iago, Santo Domingo, Cartagena, and the town of Saint Augustine in Florida. Published by M. Thomas Gates."[10]

Drake sailed from Plymouth in his home county of Devon with 25 ships and 2,300 soldiers and mariners. One of his sea-captains was John Martin of the Benjamin who later sailed with Newport to Virginia in 1607 and lived longer in the Old Dominion than any other of the first voyagers.

Thomas Gates was a land captain. His narrative is interesting, but long, so we can relate only a few incidents. According to Gates, the fleet, after sacking and burning several towns in the West Indies, appeared before the city of San Domingo on New Years day, 1586. Drake, the night before, had put ashore the whole of his troops, landing them about ten miles from the city. Then at dawn he made a feint with his ships against the castle guarding the narrow entrance to the harbor. All eyes in the town were on the fleet with its crowd of small

---

[8] P. 401.

[9] *W. & M. Quarterly*, Vol. IX, p. 233-237. He needs a Henry Justin Smith.

[10] *Hakluyt's Voyages* (Macklehose), Vol. X, p. 97.

craft being made ready for landing. About noon they perceived the English troops advancing on the town from the rear. They wheeled the guns which had been pointing seaward but could only fire one round when the English were upon them. And so the town fell and the Spaniards fled to the mountains.

Gates relates that the General sent out one morning a small negro servant to meet an officer who was advancing with a white flag. Contrary to accustomed usage the officer thrust his pike through the little negro who crawled back to Drake's feet and died. Drake, mad with rage, took two Spanish Friars to the spot where the boy had been wounded and there hanged them. Then he sent a message advising that two more of his most distinguished captives would be hanged every morning at that place until the murderer was surrendered. They brought him to Drake next morning and Drake made his own countrymen hang him on the gallows.

After many other adventures Drake finally took Cartagena, the capital of the Spanish Main. From remaining there some six weeks in that notoriously unhealthy place his forces became much depleted from sickness, so he called a council of his land-captains, among whom was Captain Thomas Gates. He put three questions before them. One was, "Should they attempt the rest of their program, on which the taking of Panama was the next item, or turn homeward?" The land-captains decided that their forces had been so weakened by sickness that they could not anticipate any further success, but said that they would cheerfully attempt any operations Drake ordered.

Drake decided to go home, so he made the Spaniards pay a ransom of 100,000 ducats for Cartagena and sailed homeward sacking St. Augustine in Florida on the way. Small events sometimes change the course of nations. Drake also visited the Colony of Governor Ralph Lane on Roanoke Island and offered him a ship, a pinnace, and a month's stores, for his colony of 103 persons if he wished to remain, otherwise he would take all of them back to England. Lane chose to stay but the ship on which the stores were laden foundered suddenly in a storm. Drake had no more stores to give so Lane chose to go home.

Thomas Gates was with Raleigh in his attack upon the Spanish fleet at Cadiz in 1596 and was knighted for distinguished services along with about thirty other sea and land-captains.[11]

---

[11] *Hakluyt's Voyages*, Vol. IV, p. 259.

Captain George Somers was also a sea-captain of Queen Elizabeth's, and one worthy enough to have his exploits recorded in *Hakluyt's Voyages*. Somers, with Captain Amias Preston, (both afterwards knighted) described as "valiant and discreet commanders, lying ready with two tall ships, the Ascension and the Gift, at Plymouth, on March 12th, 1595 set forward their voyage to the West Indies."[12]

On this expedition, with the well known tactics and luck of the English heretofore described, they sacked and burned the stately city of San Jago de Leon, ransomed the town of Cumna, and captured the town of Coros.

Captain Somers was a good sailor, for our narrator (Robert Davis, one of the company) says, "Having gotten the town, they found nothing in it at all, for the Spaniards had intelligence from San Iago how we had used them before, which caused them to convey all their goods into the mountains and woods. Our Generall caused it to be set on fire, thinking it not good to remaine there, but to return again backe to the ships: and the greatest cause was by reason of the departure of Captain Somers; who the day before in a most furious tempest, being in the pinnace with some 50 men, at anchor, had his cables broken and lost all his anchors, and was faine to put to sea to save himself, otherwise they had been in danger of perishing. * * * The 13th towards night (after putting to sea) the General came to where Captain Somers was, and found him riding but not by any anchors, but by two bases which he had made to stay his barke by; at which meeting the company was very glad."[13]

Captain Prowse died, Captain Jones fell in combat, this left only Captain Somers. At Jamaica they met "with the honorable knight, Sir Walter Raleigh, returning from his painful but happy discovery of Guiana, and his surprise of the Isle of Trinidad. So with glad hearts we kept him and his fleet company till the twentieth day at night (July), at which time we lost him."[14] Then they set their course for home by way of the Grand Banks of Newfoundland.

It was more than a decade after the last described voyage of Captain Somers that he and Captain Gates, now "Sir George Somers and Sir

---

[12] The victorious voyage of Captain Amias Preston now knighted, and Captaine George Somers, to West India, March 1595, etc., *Hakluyt's Voyages* (Macklehose), Vol. X, p. 213.

[13] Do, Vol. X, p. 224.

[14] Do, Do, p. 225.

Thomas Gates", petitioned King James for permission to colonize Virginia.

That they were the prime movers in the colonization is proven by the fact that their names are mentioned first in the Charter of King James the preamble of which is as follows: "Letters Patent to Sir Thomas Gates, Sir George Somers and others, for two several Colonies and Plantations, to be made in Virginia, and other parts and Territories of America, dated April 10, 1606.

"I. James, by the grace of God, King of England, Scotland, France, and Ireland, Defender of the Faith, etc. Whereas our loving and well disposed subjects, Sir Thomas Gates, and Sir George Somers, Knights, Richard Hakluyt, clerk, Prebendary of Westminster, and Edward-Maria Wingfield, * * *[15] and divers others of our loving subjects, have been humble suitors unto us, that we vouch safe unto them our licence, to make habitation, plantation, and to deduce a colony of sundry of our people into that part of America commonly called Virginia, etc."

This company was known to history as the "London Company" and much credit for founding Virginia has been given to noblemen and knights who sat in comfortably cushioned arm chairs in stately offices in London and never saw Virginia. They may have ventured some of their fortunes in the Virginia undertaking but not their carcasses to the perils of the deep. The subscribers to shares in the London Company of Virginia are entitled "Adventurers to Virginia",[16] but it does seem that there should be a distinction between the "Adventurers" who stayed behind and those who "ventured" over.

Of the four men mentioned in the first charter, three of them came to Virginia. Besides Gates and Somers, Captain Edward-Maria Wingfield came over arriving with the first fleet. Gates and Somers arrived with the Third Supply in 1609 and the voyage of this great fleet will be mentioned later.

Sometimes, however, a man may have an adventurous spirit and yet

---

[15] The names of "Thomas Hanham, and Raleigh Gilbert, Esqrs., William Parker, and George Popham, gentlemen," have been omitted here as they and other adventurers of Bristol, Exeter and Plymouth, were given leave to colonize between 38 and 45 degrees north latitude. They established the colony of Sagadahoc on the Kennebec River, in New England in 1607, which was afterwards abandoned. Gates, Somers and their associates were granted leave to plant between 34 and 41 degrees north latitude. See Alexander Brown, *Genesis of the United States*, Vol. I, pp. 52-63, for complete charter of King James. The charter, however, provided that the two colonies were not to plant within 100 miles of each other.

[16] *Records of the Virginia Company*, Vol. III, p. 79.

be unable to exercise it in actual undertakings. Who has not longed for scenes more stirring than the drab ones we see out of high office windows? Such a spirit had Richard Hakluyt, the third person mentioned in the charter.

It is said of Hakluyt that he once paid a chance visit to a cousin of his, a student in law at the Middle Temple, who bore his own name. A map of the world lay on the table and this cousin took the occasion to give him a lecture in geography. He pointed out the far off places of the world and dwelt on the application of geography to the growing commerce of England. "From the map," says Hakluyt, "he brought me to the Bible, and turning to the 107th Psalm, directed me to the twenty-third and twenty-fourth verses, where I read that 'they which go down to the sea in ships, and occupy by the great waters, they see the works of the Lord and His wonders in the deep!'"[17]

Hakluyt was much impressed with his cousin's talk, and soon afterwards went to Oxford to prepare for the ministry, where in his spare time he endeavored to read all the Travels and Voyages extant in Greek Latin, Italian, French, English, Spanish and Portuguese. He quickly acquired the mastery of most of these languages and began a collection of the voyages of all nations which he continued throughout his life, and published from time to time.

The capture of the huge Madre de Dios, he confessed, yielded him some profit, for Sir Robert Cross presented him with a Latin treatise on China found among the spoils. It was given to Hakluyt "enclosed in a case of sweet cedarwood, and lapped up almost an hundred fold in fine calicut-cloth, as though it had been some incomparable jewel."[18]

Hakluyt was keenly interested in the Virginia venture. His last work was "Virginia Richly Valued, etc.", which appeared in 1609. It was translated from a Portuguese account of De Soto's expedition to Florida. Hakluyt was the propagandist for the Virginia enterprise.

It was nearly a year after King James granted the charter to Gates and Somers before an expedition "for the First Colony in Virginia" actually set forth.[19] The veteran sailor, Captain Christopher Newport, was placed in sole command of this first fleet to Virginia as evidenced by the following order of the Council for the London Company of

[17] *Hakluyt's Voyages*, Vol. XII, p. 78.
[18] *Hakluyt's Voyages*, Vol. XII, p. 84.
[19] In the charter the colony for South Virginia was called "The First Colony" and that for North Virginia was called "The Second Colony". *Brown's Genesis*, p. 59.

Virginia. "First, whereas the good ship called the Sarah Constant and the ship called the Goodspeed, with a pinnace called the Discovery are now ready Victualed, rigged and furnished for the said voyage; we think it fit and so do ordain and appoint that Captain Christopher Newport shall have the sole charge to appoint such captains, soldiers, sailors and mariners, as shall either command, or be shipped to pass in the said ships or pinnace," etc.[20] The order further provided that Captain Newport was also to have sole charge and command of all hereof until such time as they shall fortune to land upon the said coast persons on board the ships from captains to cabin boy, "from the date of Virginia," so there is no question but what the well tried Christopher Newport was the actual leader of the expedition.

Captain John Smith, most prolific writer on the Virginia "Venture", who rarely gave credit to any one but himself, says, "Captain Bartholomew Gosnold, one of the first movers of this plantation, having many years solicited many of his friends, but found small assistance; at last prevailed with some Gentlemen, as Captain John Smith, Master Edward-Maria Wingfield, Master Robert Hunt, and divers others, who depended a year upon his projects, but nothing could be effected, till by their great charge and industry, it came to be apprehended by certain of the Nobility, Gentry, and Merchants, so that his Majesty, by his letters patent (10 April 1606), gave commission for establishing Councils, to direct here; and govern and to execute there.[21] To effect this was spent another year, and by that three ships were provided, one of 100 tons, another of 40, and a pinnace of 20."[22]

Captain Newport selected the largest vessel, the Sarah Constant, as his flag-ship. Captain Bartholomew Gosnold was appointed captain of the Goodspeed and Captain John Ratcliffe sailed the Discovery. Those ships were comparatively small even for those days. The Sarah Constant

---

[20] Alexander Brown, *Genesis of the U. S.*, p. 52.

[21] The charter provided for the appointment of a Council in London to direct affairs and for another in Virginia to govern. Each was supposed to consist of thirteen members but the early Councils in Virginia rarely had that many, the first Council only having six.

[22] *Travels and Works of Captain John Smith*, edited by Edward Arber and A. G. Bradley (2 vols., Edinburgh, John Grant, 1910), p. 385, hereafter referred to as "Smith's Works".

carried 71 persons, the Goodspeed, 52, and the Discovery, 20, making
a total of 143 persons on the expedition.[23]

Captain Bartholomew Gosnold was another Elizabethan sea-captain,
who served under Raleigh. He also had made a voyage to the "North
Part of Virginia" in 1602, about which an account had been written by
Captain Gabriel Archer who accompanied him on that voyage in the
Concord and was with him in the Goodspeed on this voyage.[24]

Captain Gabriel Archer, a former student in law at Gray's Inn, was
also an able sailor and will be met with on another voyage.

Captain Edward-Maria Wingfield, also mentioned by Smith, was a
grandson of Sir Richard Wingfield and a son of Thomas-Maria Wingfield, the last named being a godson of Queen Mary, hence the second
Christian name "Maria", which ran in the family for several generations. Wingfield, destined to be the first Governor of Virginia, was
seemingly pompous and puffed up by his superior birth and position
and was unable to coöperate with common men. He was America's
first "Stuffed Shirt".

Another leader of note was Captain John Martin, also an Elizabethan
sea-captain, who had sailed as Captain of the Benjamin on Drake's
expedition to the West Indies in 1585, as heretofore related. This was
not his first voyage to the shores of North America, for on his way
back to England, in 1585, he had aided in the sacking of St. Augustine
in Florida and helped bring back Lane's colony from Roanoke Island.
Captain Martin was a son of Sir Richard Martin of the East Indian
company and lived longer in Virginia than any other colonist of the
first expedition.

Two other men of note, who by virtue of being elected Presidents of
the Council became "Governors of Virginia", were Captains George
Percy and John Smith. Captain Percy was the eighth son of the eighth
Earl of Northumberland. He was a land-captain of experience having
twice served in campaigns against the Spaniards in the Low Countries.
Captain John Smith was destined to be the most famous of all because
of his "General History", most of which concerned his own doings.

---

[23] The quoted orders of the Council would seem to make the names of the ships
official. However, there are very good authorities for the names "Susan Constant"
and "God Speed". "Goodspeed" and "God Speed" were probably synonymous. See
article by Mrs. Minnie G. Cook, *William and Mary Quarterly*, Vol. 17 (2), p. 229,
and another one by Gregory Robinson and Robin R. Goodison, W.M. 16, (2), pp.
519-521. The "Sarah" should be "Susan".

[24] *Old South Leaflets*, Vol. V, pp. 405-416. (Chicago Library #B 2112.5.)

Some one has said of this remarkable work, "That what is historical is not his, and what is his is not historical." Every one is familiar with his story of the taking of three Turk's heads. The College of Heralds seemingly placed the stamp of authenticity upon this story by granting to Smith a coat-of-arms bearing the three heads.[25]

Smith, regardless of whether or not his boastful adventures are but Arabian Nights Tales was really a man of ability and strong physical courage, and in his term of office as president of the Council restored order to the infant colony.

The fleet of three small vessels dropped down the Thames from London on December 30th, 1606, but on account of contrary winds, they anchored in the Downs, the 15th of January, where Captain Percy says, "We suffered great storms, but by the skilfulness of the Captain we suffered no great loss or danger."[26] The voyagers were delayed for more than a month when at last they departed and touched first at the Canaries. Then sailing due west they arrived at Dominica on March 24th. (O.S.) Among the sights mentioned at Dominica were some natives who painted their bodies "all red to keep away the biting of mosquitoes."

On the way across the Atlantic there was an attempt at mutiny and one Stephen Galthrop, destined to die early in Virginia, made a confession implicating the redoubtable Captain John Smith with the result that Smith was held a prisoner and not freed until June 20th in Virginia.[27]

"The sixth and twentieth day of April, 1607," Percy says, "about four a clock in the morning, we descried the land of Virginia. The same day we entered the Bay of Chesapeake." Here Captain Newport, Archer, and others landed on the South side of the entrance to the Bay which they named "Cape Henry" after the Prince of Wales. The Northern cape they called "Charles" in honor of his brother.[28]

---

[25] Foster's Grantees of Arms. See page 842 of Smith's Works, (1910, Edinburgh Edition) for a copy of Prince Sigismund's grant of arms of the three Turk's heads.

[26] Percy's Relation, Smith's Works, p. lvii. Edinburgh 1910.

[27] Smith's own explanation of the charges are shown in Smith's Works, page 388, in which he says, "Now Captain Smith, who all this time from their departure from the Canaries was restrained as a prisoner upon the scandalous suggestions of some of the chiefs (envying his repute) who feigned he intended to usurp the government, murder the Council, and make himself King."

[28] May 6th, 1607. (N.S.).

Chapter II

THE ENGLISH REACH SURRY COUNTY

THE English proceeded leisurely on their way up the James River and on the fourth of May, 1607 (O.S.) came to the country of the Pashbahayes. The Chief or Werowance of that tribe entertained them "with much welcome"[1]. This tribe was seated on the north side of the river in what is now Charles City County, and while the English were in the company of the Pashbahayes the Werowance of Rapahanna in his canoe came from the other side of the river. He was displeased with their being with the Pashbahayes and promised them better entertainment in his country.

The next day, the fifth of May, Smith and his stout-hearted companion set out for the "Rapahanna" country and landed in what is now Surry County not far from the present town of Claremont. Captain George Percy relates that "when we landed the Werowance came down to the water side with all his train, as goodly men as I have seen of Savages or Christians." The Werowance, playing on a flute made of reeds, led his band of Savages. He wore a crown of deer's hair colored red with two long feathers fashioned like a pair of horns placed in the middle of his crown and his body was painted crimson with a chain of beads about his neck, etc.

Percy speaks of the character of his entertainment and the fertility of the soil of Surry. He says, "He entertained us in so modest yet proud fashion as though he had been a Prince of civil government, holding his countenance without laughter or any such ill behavior. He caused his mat to be spread on the ground where he sat down with great majesty, taking a pipe of tobacco, the rest of his company standing about him."

"After he had rested a while, he rose, made sign to us to come to his town. He went foremost and all the rest of his people and our selves followed him up a steep hill where his palace was settled. We passed through the woods in fine paths, that had most pleasant springs which issued from the mountains. We went through the goodliest corn fields that were seen in any country."[2]

---

[1] Travels and works of Captain John Smith (Arber Edition, Edinburgh, 1910), *Percy's Narrative*, p. LXIV.
[2] Smith Works, p. LXV.

The voyagers on their return down the James landed May 13, 1607 (O.S.) at the historic spot later called "Jamestown" but the King of the Rapahanna evidently did not maintain his friendly relations with the English after they settled near him. Although no friction with this particular tribe is mentioned by Smith and his chroniclers yet it appears that Powhatan was the means of restoring peace between the two, for on June 25, a messenger came from him to Jamestown "with worde of peace". He said that Powhatan "greatly desired their friendship and that unless the Werowances of Paspahegh and Tapahanna became our friends he would make war on them with us. This message fell true, for both these Werowances have ever since remained in peace and trade with us. We rewarded the messenger with many trifles which were great wonders to him."[3]

At the time of the landing of the English at Jamestown, Sir John Popham, Lord Chief Justice of England, had obtained a charter to colonize Northern Virginia, and the Earl of Salisbury was then the leading man in the Virginia, or southern company. This led to the settlers calling the south side of the James "the Salisbury side" and the north side "the Popham side". So, President Wingfield in his further narrative concerning the Indians dwelling in Surry says, "The 7th of July, Tapahanna, a Werowance, dweller on the Salisbury side, hailed us with the word of peace. The President (Wingfield), with a shallop well manned, went to him. He found him sitting on the ground cross legged, as is their custom, with one attending on him, who did often say, 'This is the Werowance, Tapahanna, which he did likewise confirm with stroking his breast. He was well enough known; for the President had seen him divers times before. His countenance was nothing cheerful; for we had not seen him since he was in the field against us, but the President would take no knowledge thereof, and used him kindly, giving him a red waistcoat he did desire."[4]

About three weeks later the "King of the Rapahanna" came to demand a canoe which was restored to him. He then "lifted up his hand to the sun which they worship as their God, and laid his hand on his heart that he would be our special friend."[5]

The Jamestown colonist besides calling the south side the "Salisbury

[3] Quoted from *Wingfield's Narrative*, Smith Works, pp. LXXV-LXXVI.
[4] *Wingfield's Narrative*, Smith Works, LXXVI, Wingfield was the president and refers to himself here in the third person.
[5] *Ibid.*, p. LXXI.

side" spoke of the country of the "Rapahanna" as the country or plantations "over the river" or "over against James City".[6] It was also called the "Territory of the Tappahannock over against James City" and "The Plantations across the waters". The names "Rapahanna" and "Tappahanock" were erroneously applied to the south side Indians opposite Jamestown for the tribe bearing that name was then living on the banks of what is now the Rappahannock River.

The correct name of the tribe living across the river on the south bank of the James was "Quicyoughanocks". Captain John Smith, in describing the James River region says "From the South there falls into this river, first the pleasant river of Appamatuck, next more to the east are the two rivers of the Quicyoughanocks. * * * The Appamatucks have 60 fighting men, the Quicyoughanocks 25.[7]

The colonists probably for better security, kept their hogs on an island on the south side of the James which they called the "Isle of Hogges." It was on January 7, 1609 (O.S.) that the small colony suffered a grievous loss. Amos Todkill, one of the early chroniclers, says that on that day "Master Scrivener would need visit the Isle of Hogges and took with him Captain Waldo, Master Anthony Gosnold and eight others, but so violent was the wind (that extreme frozen time) that the boat sank; but where, or how, none doth know, for they were all drowned. * * * The savages were the first that found their bodies, which so much the more encouraged them to their projects."[8]

Todkill relates the diligence of the settlers in the cold winter and spring of 1608-09. He says, "30 or 40 acres of ground we digged and planted, of 3 sows, in one year increased 60 odd pigs; and near 500 chickens brought up themselves without having any meat given them. The hogs were transported to Hog Isle where also we built a block house with a garrison to give us notice of any shipping.

We also built a fort for a retreat near a convenient river, upon a high commanding hill, very hard to be assaulted, and easy to be defended, but ere it was half finished, this defect caused a stay."[9]

This fort was built in what is now Surry County about two miles from the mouth of Gray's Creek, and the defect that "caused a stay" was the consuming of their stored corn by "many thousands of rats

[6] Hottens' Emigrants, pp. 178, 190.
[7] Smith Works, pp. 50-51.
[8] Smith's Works, pp. 143-144.
[9] Smith's Works, pp. 154-155.

increased from the first ships." This nearly reduced them to starvation.[10]

The fort is shown as "the new fort" on Captain Smith's map of Virginia.[11] It was the site of "Smith's Fort Plantation", often referred to in the Surry records and should not be confused with the fort erected by Captain Roger Smith in Isle of Wight County near the mouth of Lawne's Creek.

---

[10] Smith's Works, opposite page 384.
[11] Smith's Works, opposite page 384.

Chapter III

AN EPIC OF THE SEA

IN the Spring of 1609, four members of the Virginia Council were in London organizing another expedition for that far off land. One of them was Captain Christopher Newport, admiral of the original expedition and commander of both the First and Second Supply, the first one arriving January 1608 and the second in October of the same year. Now he was valiantly engaged in equipping the Third Supply. For his energy in leading and navigating these first four fleets across the stormy Atlantic, the infant colony seems to owe more to him than to any other one man.

The other Councillors, all seasoned from the first voyage, were Captain John Martin, who had returned with a gold nugget and a quantity of fool's gold; Captain Gabriel Archer of "Archer's Hope" fame, and Captain John Ratcliffe, former captain of the Discovery. The last named was fated to die horribly under Indian torture.

Somewhere or somehow, John Rolfe, John Proctor, Captain William Powell, and Captain William Peirce, destined to be early Surry land owners, were brought into the orbit of their influence and decided to adventure to Virginia. An adventure it was in those days sailing in frail ships across stormy water. Well fitted by name was the sturdy ship on which they sailed, the Sea-Adventure, better known to history by its shorter name, the "Sea-Venture", the largest and strongest of the entire fleet.

The group of adventurers under a new charter granted in 1609 consisted of many wealthy noblemen and London merchants. The London Council for the Virginia Company appointed Thomas West, Lord Delaware, Governor and Captain General of Virginia; Sir Thomas Gates, Lieutenant General; Sir George Somers, Admiral, and Christopher Newport, Vice Admiral.

With renewed enthusiasm the Virginia Company put forth its mightiest effort in behalf of its infant colony. On the 15th of May, 1609, the greatest fleet ever sent out by the company sailed down the Thames from Woolwich.

According to his commission as governor, Sir Thomas Gates was to be in command of the expedition and was required "with all convenient speed to take charge of our fleets consisting of eight good shipes and one pinnace and of six hundred land men to be transported under your command, and with the first wind to set sail for Virginia."[1]

The ships in the fleet were commanded by experienced sailors. The voyage was not to be one of mere novices. Every captain had previously sailed the Atlantic. The flagship, the Sea-Venture, was under the command of Captain Christopher Newport. The ill-fated Captain Radcliffe, with Captain King as his master, flew the flag of Vice Admiral on the Diamond. The Falcon, The Blessing, and the Unity were commanded respectively by Captain John Martin, Rear Admiral; Captain Gabriel Archer and Captain Wood. Their masters were Captain Francis Nelson, Captain Adams, and Captain Robert Pitt. The last named was of the noted Pitt family of ship masters of Bristol, a branch of the house of the Earl of Chatham. Captain Robert Pitt later settled in Isle of Wight County, Virginia.[2] The Lion was commanded by Captain George Webb and the Catch by Master Matthew Fitch who had been with Newport on his first voyage as also had been Captain Nelson.[3]

On May 20th the fleet arrived at Plymouth where Sir George Somers joined them with two small ships. One was the Swallow commanded by Captain John Moone[4] with Captain Mathew Somers, nephew of Sir George, as Master, and the other was the Virginia commanded by Captain James Davis.

The last named vessel had been built in New England during the Winter of 1607 by a colony which had settled on the Kennebec River at Sagdahoc, and in it those weary settlers had returned to England in 1608. This was Captain James Davis' third trip to America and the master of his vessel was Robert Davis, probably his brother.

Captain James Davis settled in Virginia and fell in the great massacre of 1622. He has many descendants in the southern states.[5]

---

[1] *Records of the Va. Co.*, Vol. III, p. 12. Strachey says the fleet consisted of "seven good ships and two pinnaces." Sir George Somers, upon leaving the island erected a cross on which the fleet was described as seven vessels besides the Sea-Venture. Wesley Frank Craven, 17 (2) W. & M., p. 74. Sir J. H. Lefroy's *Memorials of the Discovery of the Bermudas*, Vol. I, pp. 15, 22, 49.

[2] Boddie, *17th Century Isle of Wight County, Virginia.* p. 510.

[3] Brown, *Genesis of the U. S.*, p. 92.

[4] Captain John Moone later settled in Isle of Wight County. *17th Century, etc.*, p. 100. Captain Wood may have been the Captain Abraham Wood who later patented land on the Appomattox River in what is now Prince George County in 1638 (C.P. 88).

[5] *17th Century, etc.*, p. 438.

Captain Robert Davis continued to sail the seas and was the captain of
the Plough which brought Governor Richard Moore to the Bermudas
in 1612.[6]

When Englishmen get together the first thing that concerns them
is precedence. Admiral Somers did not wish to concede precedence to
General Gates, at least not while on the sea, so he embarked also in
the flagship, the Sea-Venture. The Surry settlers before mentioned were
thus in the congenial company of the leaders of the expedition.

The fleet of nine vessels finally departed on the 8th of June 1609
headed straight for Virginia. In the event that the fleet became scattered
it was to rendezvous at Bermuda, with instructions to wait there seven
days for the admiral before resuming the voyage.

Several accounts of this voyage have been written. Captain Gabriel
Archer wrote one upon his arrival in Virginia. He said "We ran a
Southerly course for the Tropic of Cancer, where having the sun
within six or seven degrees right over our head in July, we bore away
West; so that by the fervent heat and loose breezes, many of our men
fell sick of the Calenture, and out of two ships were thrown overboard
thirty two persons. The Vice-Admirall was said to have the plague in
her; but in the Blessing we had not any sick, although we had twenty
women and children."

"Upon Saint James Day, being about one hundred and fifty leagues
distant from the West Indies, in cross the Gulf of Bahama (Gulf
Stream) there happened a most terrible and vehement storm, which
was a tail of a West Indian Hurricane, this tempest separated all of
our fleet one from another, and it was so violent that men could scarce
stand upon the decks, neither could any man hear another speak, being
thus divided every man steered his own course, and as it fell out about
five or six days after the storm ceased (which endured forty four hours
in extremity) The Lion first, and after the Falcon and the Unity got
sight of our ship, so we lay directly away from Virginia, finding neither
current or wind opposing, as some have reported to the great charge of
our Council and Adventurers.

"The Unity was sore distressed when she came up with us, for of
seventy land men, she had not ten sound, and all her seamen were
down, but only the Master and his Boy, with some poor sailor, but we
relieved them, and we four consorting haply fell into the King's River

---

[6] W. & M., 17 (2), p. 77.

the eleventh of August. In the Unity were born two children at sea but both died, being both boys."

The calenture was the dreaded yellow fever of modern days and from this account it seems that both yellow fever and the plague were taken to Virginia by the fleet. The mortality there was very large shortly after the arrival of these new immigrants.

Rolfe and his companions on the Sea-Venture were not as fortunate as Captain Archer. One of Rolfe's fellow passengers was William Strachey, later Secretary and Recorder General of Virginia, whom Rolfe was to succeed in office. Strachey wrote an account of the storm which was immortalized by the world's greatest playwright in The Tempest. It therefore may be interesting to read Strachey's own words. He says "in the height of 30 degrees of northerly latitude, or thereabouts, we were taken with a most sharpe and cruel storm upon the fifth and twentieth day of July, anno 1609, which doth not only separate us from the rest of the fleet but with the violent working of the seas our ship became so shaken, torne and leaky, that she received so much water as covered two tiers of hogsheads above the ballast; that our men stood up to the middles with buckets, baricos and kettles, to bail out the water and continually pumped for 3 days and three nights together without an intermission; and yet the water seemed rather to increase than to diminish, in so much that all our men, being utterly spent, tired, and disabled for longer labor, were even resolved without any hope of their lives to shut up the hatches, and to have committed themselves to the mercie of the sea * * * It pleased God out of his most gracious and merciful providence so to direct and guide our ship (being left to the mercy of the sea) for her most advantage; that Sir George Somers sitting upon the poope of the ship, (where he sat three days and three nights together, without meals, meat, and little or no sleep) conning the ship to keep her upright as he could (for otherwise she must have instantly have foundered) most wishedly and happily descried land * * *"

"And there neither did our ship sink, but more fortunately in so great a misfortune fell in between two rocks, where she was fast lodged and locked from further budging: whereby we gained not only sufficient time, with the present help of our boat and skiffe, safely to set and convey our men ashore, (which were 150 in number) but afterwards had time and leisure to save some good part of our goods and provisions, which the water had not spoiled, with all the tackling of our ship and much of the iron about her, which were necessaries not a little available for the building and furnishing of a new ship and pinnace which we made there for the transporting and carrying of us to Virginia"

Strachey's story of the wreck upon the rocks of Bermuda may be said to be the source from which Shakespeare derived his idea of The Tempest. This account was sent from Jamestown by Strachey and it was addressed to an "Excellent Lady". According to Professor Charles Mills Gayley, in his *Shakespeare and the Founders of Liberty in America,* this "Excellent Lady" was Elizabeth Hume, daughter of the Earl of Dunbar and the widow of Theophilius Howard of the London Company. The Earl of Southampton, Shakespeare's first patron, was president of the Company.[7]

In his further writing of the storm, Strachey says that it was so violent that a man could scarce stand upon the deck, neither could he hear another speak. He tells the "Excellent Lady" how the storm came "dreadful and hideous, * * * at length did beat out all light from the heavens" and "created a hell of darkness. * * * Fury was added to fury. * * * The sea swelled above the clouds and gave battle unto heaven. It could not be said to rain, the waters like whole rivers did flood in the air. And this I did still observe, that whereas upon the land, when a storm hath poured itself forth in drifts of rain, the wind, as beaten down and vanquished therewith, not long after endureth; here the glut of water (as if throttling the wind ere while) was no sooner a little emptied and qualified, but instantly the winds * * * grew more tumoultous and malignant."[8]

Those English sailors in bringing their small ships through such a semi-tropical hurricane must have used incomparable skill for even now great liners are buffeted about by North Atlantic storms. No seafaring men were ever more heroic than the sailors who brought over our first settlers.

From Strachey's account there seems to have been a panic among the passengers, especially the women "not used to such burly and discomforts". Picture their distress cooped up below deck in close and unsanitary confinement and in terror lest the creaking timbers give way at any moment.

---

[7] Andrews, *Virginia, the Old Dominion,* p. 49.
[8] Strachey, *A True Reportory of the Wracke etc.,* Purchas' Works, Vol. IV, Book IX, p. 1737, quoted by Henry Justin Smith in *Master of the Mayflower,* p. 137.

Sometimes six and eight men were not enough to hold "the whip-staffe in the steerage. * * * A wave "once broke upon the poop and quartered upon us as it covered our ship from stem to stern; like a garment of vast clouds it filled her brim full, from the hatches up to the sparre deck. It carried the helmsman from the helm and wrested the whipstaffe out of his hand, which so flew from side to side that it so tossed him from starboard to larboard as it was God's mercy it had not split him." But a relief helmsman sprang to the whipstaff "and by main strength bearing somewhat up, made good his place." The wave so "stunned the ship in her full face that she stirred no more than if she had been caught in a net."

Strachey's picturesque description may have inspired the following lines from Shakespeare's play, "The Tempest", first produced on the stage November 1st, 1611. There seems to be a parallel between the lines from that play and this shipwreck.

"Scene II. Miranda to Prospero

If by your art, my dearest father, you have
Put the wild waters in this roar, allay them.
The sky, it seems, would pour down stinking pitch,
But that the sea, mounting to the welkin's check,
Dashes the fire out. O, I have suffer'd
With those that I saw suffer! A brave vessel,
Who had, no doubt, some noble creature in her,
Dash'd all to pieces. O, the cry did knock
Against my very heart! Poor souls, they perish'd!
Had I been any god of power, I would
Have sunk the sea within the earth, or ere
It should the good ship so have swallow'd and
The fraughting souls within her.

Prospero

Be collected:
No more amazement: tell your piteous heart
There's no harm done.

* * * * * *

Prospero

But are they, Ariel, safe?

Ariel

>   Not a hair perish'd;
> On their sustaining garments not a blemish,
> But fresher than before: and, as thou badest me,
> in troops I have dispersed them 'bout the Isle.

* * * *

>   Safely in harbour
> Is the king's ship: in the deep nook, where once
> Thou call'dst me up at midnight to fetch dew
> From the still-vex'd Bermoothes,[9] there she's hid."

---

[9] Bermuda.

Chapter IV

EARLY SETTLEMENTS IN SURRY

THAT part of London which lies on the south side of the Thames is in the county or shire of Surrey and the Jamestown settlers often referred to the south side of the James River as "over on the Surrey side". This name spelled without the "e" later became the name of the county. This has a counterpart in our saying "over on the Brooklyn side", or "over on the Jersey side". London, south of the Thames, was then in the Parish of Southwark, and this name also was later given to the parish on the south side of the river.

Surry was first considered a part of the Jamestown settlement. Many inhabitants of Jamestown had land on the "Surry Side" and some of the settlers living in Surry owned property in Jamestown. In 1619, Governor Argall defined the limits of Jamestown, saying that on the south side it included "Hog Island, and from thence to the four mile tree (four miles from Jamestown proper) on the south usually called by the name of 'Tappahannock'."

Later, what is now Surry County, became part of James City County when that county was formed in 1634. Surry was not detached from James City until 1652.

The Charter granted the London Company in 1606 provided that every citizen of Virginia should enjoy "the liberties, franchises, and immunities" of native born Englishmen, and the colony was to be under the immediate control of the King. In 1609 the London Company was reorganized and the control of the colony was delegated to this company whose shareholders consisted of six hundred and fifty-nine of the wealthiest persons in England. This company as reorganized was to be a perpetual corporation.

Sir Thomas Smythe, a wealthy London merchant, became treasurer of the company and endeavored to manage the company from a purely commercial point of view. In his opinion the success of the company was to be measured by the extent of its financial rewards to the stockholders. In 1619 Sir Thomas Smythe was succeeded in the office of Treasurer by Sir Edwin Sandys. John Bargrave, of the well-known Kent family of ship captains, accused Sir Thomas Smythe of "exercising absolute power in administering the affairs of both the company and the Colony, of depriving the settler of all reasonable assurance as to the safety of his estate, of the preservation of his freedom, and of laying the hand of oppression on the small planter and large associations of adventurers alike." (Bruce, *Inst. History of Va.*, Vol. II, p. 243.) On the other hand, he said that Sir Edwin Sandys had declared "that his purpose was to erect a free popular state, in which the inhabitants should have no government put on them but by their own consent." (Brown, *English Politics in Early Va. History*, p. 47.)

This well states the difference between the two factions in the London Company.

The liberal faction came into control in 1618 and at the quarter court of the company convening in London, November 18, 1618, the right of representation in an assembly of their own choice was given to the people of Virginia. The new Governor, Sir George Yeardley, was authorized to call together a General Assembly consisting of the Governor, Council, and Burgesses. The Burgesses were to be elected by the inhabitants of each town, hundred, or group of plantations. This resulted in the calling of the First General Assembly of Virginia which convened at Jamestown, Friday, July 30, 1619.

Sir Edwin Sandys was treasurer only a single term of twelve months as the King strongly objected to his continuance in office, so Sandys did not permit his name to be used. (Bruce I.H., Vol. II, p. 246.)

The Earl of Southampton, a liberal, was then elected treasurer and he selected as his deputy, George Sandys, brother of Sir Edwin, who later came over to Virginia and was designated as the "Treasurer of Virginia".

King James, wearied by the contention of the two factions in the London Company, revoked its letters patent in January 1624 and Virginia became a Royal Province subject only to his control. The King intended to revoke all the popular rights granted in 1618 but died before he could issue a proclamation. (Bruce, I.H., Vol. II, p. 255.)

When the first colonists arrived in Virginia the London Company decreed that no planters or adventurers were to have land assigned to them until seven years had elapsed.[1] Many years more than seven expired before these early adventurers received land, for it was not until November 18, 1618 that the London Company provided for them in the "Great Charter" heretofore mentioned. On that day the Quarter

---

[1] Nugent's, *Cavalier and Pioneers*, p. XXI, hereafter designated "C.P."

Court in London made provisions for three different classes of settlers and these provisions were followed thereafter.

The first class of settlers provided for were the "Ancient Planters" who came over before the going away of Sir Thomas Dale in 1616. The Court ordered "that for all such planters as were brought thither at the company's charge to inhabit there before the coming away of Sir Thomas Dale (1616) after their time of service to the Company on the common land shall be expired, there shall be set out 100 acres of land for each of them, their heirs and assigne forever."[2]

In January 1620, John Rolfe, wrote Sir Edwin Sandys, treasurer of the Company, "that all the Ancient Planters, being set free, have chosen places for their dividends according to the Commission. Which gives all great content, for now knowing their own land, they strive and are prepared to build houses and to clear their ground ready to plant, which giveth the greatest encouragement than anything ever yet happened."[3]

The second class of persons were those who came over at their own costs "since the going away of Sir Thomas Dale". As to these the company did "ordain that all such persons as since the coming away of the said Sir Thomas Dale have at their own charges been transported thither to inhabit and so continued as aforesaid there be allotted and set out at first Division 50 acres of land to them and theirs forever."

The third class of persons were those who were brought over at the company's charges. It was decreed that they should "be placed as tenants on the company's lands for the time of seven years to occupy the same and to have a half part of the profits."[4]

Company stockholders, called "Adventurers", were allowed 100 acres of land for each share of stock costing 12 pounds 10 shillings each. Very few grants were issued to such stockholders and in most cases they appear to have been given to persons who actually settled on the land.

In order to stimulate immigration, later on, the company granted 50 acres to every person who transported himself to Virginia "at his own costs" and 50 additional acres for each person whose passage he paid. These transported persons were called "Head rights" in the

---

[2] C.P., p. XXVI. A few individuals grants may have been made before this time but only one is found in the Virginia Patents (C.P., p. XXVII).
[3] C.P., p. XVII.
[4] C.P., p. XVII.

patents—and this headright system was the only method by which an immigrant could obtain a grant of land from the colony.

The "Headrights" were in the main "servants" who were indentured to their "masters" for varying lengths of time up to seven years in order to reimburse him for his expense. Oftentimes among the headrights were persons of all classes of society. Many a settler brought over his wife, children, friends and relatives, receiving 50 acres of land for each one of them. This was the system in use in Surry for obtaining land grants during the seventeenth century. ..

The first "Plantations across the water" were probably company lands worked by tenants and managed from Jamestown.

When the First General Assembly met in 1619, the Burgesses from James City were Captain William Powell and Ensign William Spence. Captain William Powell held land on the Surry side of James City. John Rolfe, a member of the Council, or Upper House of the Assembly, better known to romantic historians as the husband of Pocahontas, also owned land on the Surry Side.

After the Virginia Company was dissolved and was succeeded by Royal Governors appointed by the Crown, it became the custom to issue patents several years after the arrival of the patentees. Whether this delay was caused by "red tape", or because the Governors waited for the new settlers "to prove up" does not seem to be known.

Even after the granting of the Great Charter of 1618 the Company seemed reluctant to grant land to individuals for such reason as were set out in their answer to a petition of Captain William Powell and John Smith, February 2, 1620, as follows: "The Petition of Captain Powell and Mr. Smith being presented by their brother, Provost Marshall of Middlesex, to have grant of the Company 400 acres of land for fifty pounds adventure betwixt them, viz., one hundred lying in one parcel between the Sunken Marsh on the other side of the River against James City and Chippokes Creek, and one parcel of marsh land containing 300 acres called Hogg Island. The Court held it inconvenient to grant land in that kind, picked out by the Planters themselves not knowing who already may lay claim thereunto or otherwise how necessary it may be for the public, but Mr. Treasurer (George Sandys) in regard of the good affection declared by their brother to the Companies service hath promised to write to the Governor that the said 400 acres

shall be well set out for them and their content with reason."[5] The
Treasurer's appeal was evidently effective, for Captain William Powell
received his land, as his name appears in the list of persons granted
patents in 1626. (See Post.)

On Good Friday, March 22, 1622, there occurred the Great Massacre
by the Indians under Opecanough. Richard Pace was then residing at
his plantation called "Paces Paines" on the banks of the James on the
Surry side near the Four Mile Tree and Mount Pleasant plantations.
Pace, who had been living at his plantation since December 5, 1620,
was instrumental in saving the lives of the Jamestown settlers.

His story is known to every school child, yet it might be well to
quote from the original account published in the records of the Virginia
Company, as follows:[6] "The slaughter would have been universal if
God had not put it into the heart of an Indian belonging to one Perry,
to disclose it, who living in the house of one Pace, was urged by
another Indian his brother (who came in the night and lay with him)
to kill Pace, (so commanded by their King as he declared) as he would
kill Perry: telling further by such an hour in the morning a number
would come from divers places to finish the Execution, (who failed
not at the time). Perry's Indian rose out of his bed and revealed it to
Pace who had used him as a son: And thus the rest of the Colony that
had warning given them, by this means was saved. * * *"

"Pace upon this discovery, securing his house, before day rowed
over the river to James City (in that place near three miles in breadth)
and gave notice thereof to the Governor, by which means they were
prevented there, and at such other plantations as was possible for a
timely intelligence to be given; for where they saw us standing upon our
guard, at the sight of a Piece they all ran away."

Pace was forced to leave his plantation and reside in Jamestown for
safety. In the Winter of 1622, he petitioned the Governor to allow
him to return to the plantation promising "to fortify and strengthen the
place with a good company of able men."[8]

The petition was granted but the brave Pace died not long afterwards, for George Pace, "son and heir apparent to Richard Pace, decd.,"
on 1 September, 1628 received a patent "to the plantation called 'Pace's

[5] *Records of the Virginia Company*, Vol. I, p. 308.
[6] *Records of the Virginia Company*, Vol. III, p. 555.
[7] ____
[8] *Va. Co. Rec.*, Vol. III, p. 682.

Paines', granted his father 5 December, 1620; westward on land of his mother Isabella Perry; East on land of Francis Chapman now in the tenure of William Perry, gent., his father in law, and north upon the main river; 100 acres due for the personal adventure of his father Richard Pace and 300 acres for the transportation of four persons."[9]

George Pace married Sarah, a daughter of Captain Samuel Maycock, a member of the Council, who was killed in the massacre. Decendants of the Pace family have spread throughout the South.

In the Massacre there were 347 persons killed out of a total population of 1,240 in Virginia. This is known because a census of the inhabitants. "The Living and the Dead", was taken afterwards on February 16th, 1623.

There were thirty-three persons shown in the census of 1623 as living on the Surry side of the river at that time. They were as follows:[10]

"John Smith, his wife and infant; John Pergo, Richard Fenn, William Richardson, Robert Lindsey, Richard Dolphenby, John Botnam, John Elliot, Susan Barber, Thomas Gates and wife, Percivall Wood, Anthony Burrni, William Bidford, William Sandys, John Proctor, Mrs. Proctor, Phetteplace Clause, Henry Horne, Richard Horun, Thomas Flower, William Bullocke, Elias Hinton, John Foxen, Edward Smith, John Skinner, Martin Moore, William Naile, Thomas Fitts, Alice Fitts, Elizabeth Abbott."

Living at Hog Island at this time were 31 persons, as follows:[11]

"David Sandys, minister; John Utie, Mrs. Utie, John Utie, infant; William Tyler, Elizabeth Tyler, Richard Whitby, William Ramshaw, Richard Watkins, Thomas Foskew, lost; Henry Elsword, Thomas Causey, George Vinon, Henry Woodward, Roger Webster, John Dounston, Joseph Johnson, Richard Croker, child; William Hitchcock, lost; George Prowse, Robert Paramore, John Forvice alias Glover, John Brown, William Burcher, John Burcher, John Fulwood, Thomas Bransby, Thomas Colly, Thomas Simpson, Thomas Powell, Nicholas Long."

---

[9] C.P., p. 10.
[10] List of Immigrants to America, Hotten, p. 178.
[11] List of Immigrants to America, Hotten, p. 178.

Another general "Muster of the Inhabitants of Virginia" was taken January and February 1624-25 (O.S.) and the data shown therein is very interesting for not only were the names of the persons given but also their ages and the ships on which they came. The muster for the "Surry Side" was taken February 4, 1624-25 as follows:

Burrow's Hill, James City

Mr. Burrows and six of his men which are planted here are returned with their arms at James City.

John Smith came in the Elizabeth 1611.
Susanna, his wife, in the Bona Nova, 1619.
Francis Smith, his son, aged 1 year.

Servant

John Elliott, aged 15 years in the Margaret and John, 1621.

— — — —

George Pelton came in the *Furtherance*, 1622.
Richard Richards, came in the *London Merchant*, 1620.
Richard Dolphenby, came in the *Guift*, 1618.

Paces Paines, James City

John Proctor, came in the *Seaventure*, 1607 (1610).
Allis, his wife, in the *George*, 1621.

Servants

Richard Grove, aged 30, in the *George*, 1623.
Edward Smith, aged 20, in the *George*, 1621.
William Nayle, aged 15, in the *Ann*, 1623.
Phetteplace Clause, came in the *Star*, 1608.
Daniel Watkins, in the *Charles*, 1621.
John Skinner, in the *Marmaduke*, 1621.

— — — —

Thomas Gates, in the *Swan*, 1609.
Elizabeth, his wife, in the *Warwick*, 1620.

Smith's Plantation, James City

The MUSTER of Captain Roger Smith's men over the water.
Francis Fowler aged 23

— — — —

Christopher Lawson
Alice, his wife

Christopher Redhead, aged 24 years
Stephen Webb, " 25 "
John Butterfield, " 23 "
William Baker, " 24 "
Richard Alford, " 26 "
Thomas Harvie, " 24 "
Thomas Molton, " 25 "

Mr. Blaney's Plantation, James City

The MUSTER of Mr. Edward Blaney's men over the water.
Rice Watkins, aged 30 years, came in the *Francis Bonaventure*.
Nathaniel Floid, aged 24, in the *Bona Nova*.
George Rogers, 23, in the *Bona Nova*.
John Shelley, 23 " " " "
Thomas Ottowell, 40 " " " "
Thomas Crouch, 40 " " " "
Robert Sheppard, 20, in the *Hopewell*.
William Sawyer, 18, in the *Hopewell*.
Robert Chambrie, 19, in the *George*.
William Harley, 23, in the *Charles*.
Lawley Damfort, 29, in the *Duty*.
William Ward, 20, in the *Jonathan*.
Jeremy White, 20, in the *Tyger*.
John Hatker, 17, in the *Hopewell*.
Robert Whitmore, 22, in the *Duty*.

Hog Island 1624

Robert Martin in the *George*.
Katherine Davies in the *Southampton*.

John Uty came in the *Francis Bonaventure*.
Ann his wife in the *Seaflower*.
John his son in the *Seaflower*.

Servants

William Burt in the *Bonny Bess*.
William Stocker in the *Bonny Bess*.
Richard Bickley in the *Return*.

John Chew came in the *Charitie*.
Sarah his wife in the *Seaflower*.

Servants

Roger Delke in the *Southampton*.
Samuel Parson in the *Hopewell*.
Walter Haslewood in the *Due Return*.

Henry Elwood in the *Francis Bonaventure*.
William Ramshaw in the *Francis Bonaventure*.
John Stone in the *Swann*.
Sisly his wife in the *Seaflower*.
Henry Crocker in the *Marygold*.
Jane his wife in the *Swan*.
Henry Woodward in the *Diana*.
Jane his wife
Thomas Hitchkock in the *Marygold*
Alice his wife
Roger Webster
Joane his wife
Joane Davis

Hog Island

The MUSTER of Captain Ralph Hamor's Servants.
Jeffrey Hull, came in the *George*.
Mordecay Knight, in the *William and John*.
Thomas Doleman, in the *Return*.
Elkinton Ratliff, in the *Seaflower*.
Thomas Powell, in the *Seaflower*.
Thomas Cooper, in the *Return*.
John Davies, in the *Guifte*.

Hog Island

The MUSTER of Sir George Yeardley's men.
Maxmilian Stone, aged 36 years, came in the *Temperance*, 1620.
Elizabeth, his wife, in same ship.
Maxmilian, his son, aged 9 months.
Robert Guy, 22, in the *Swan*, 1619.
Edward Yates, 18, in the *Duty*, 1619.

Oscar Puggett, 20, in the *Diana,* 1619.
Alexander Saunders, 24, in the *Truelove.*
William Strathey, 17, in the *Temperance,* 1620.
George Whitehead, 24, in the *Temperance,* 1620.
Henry King, 22, in the *Jonathan,* 1620.
John Day, 24, in the *London Merchant,* 1620.
Wife of John Day, in the same ship.
John Root in the *Guift,* Dweller.
Walter Blake, in the *Swan,* Dweller.
Thomas Watts, in the *Treasurer,* Dweller.

David Hutton,   Dead
Richard Baker,   "

The rest of his servants are returned from James City.

Dead at the Plantations over the water:

John Filmer	John Foxen
William Plant	Elias Hinton
Thomas Rowlson	Thomas Fitch
Edward Jones	Enecha Fitch
John Dimisdale	John Sere
John Docker	William Sandys
Robert Aldridge	George Gurr, Slain by Indians
Richard Greene	William Comes, " " "
James Davis	Robert Evars
David Williams	Peaceble Sherewood
	William Hall

At Hog Island (1623)

William Barkley
Peter Dunn
John Long

Patents Granted to Settlers in Virginia in the Corporation of James City Published in 1626 The Territory of Tappahanna over against James City.[12]

Acres

John Dodd	150
John Burrows,	150 planted

[12] R.V.C., Vol. IV, pp. 555, 556.

Richard Pace,	200 planted
Francis Chapman,	100
Thomas Gates,	100
Mr. John Rolfe,	400 planted
Captain William Powell,	200 planted
Captain Samuel Mathews,	dividend, planted
Captain John Hurlestone,	,, ,,
John Bainham,	200 planted
Mr. George Sandys,	300 planted
Edward Grendon,	150 planted
William Ewens,	1000 planted
Captain William Powell,	550 planted
Ensign John Utie,	100 planted
Robert Evers,	100 planted

In Hog Island, Mary Baily, 500 acres planted by patent.

In Hog Island, Captain Ralph Hamor, by claim 250 A. planted.

Upon easterly side of Chippokes Creek is appointed 500 acres belonging to ye place of —— ?.

Chapter V

SOME EARLY LAND OWNERS

IN the list of patents granted to settlers on the Surry Side before and up to 1626, appears the name of "Mr. George Sandys, 300 acres, planted." Sandys received the first recorded grant of land in Surry. This grant appears in full on the first page of *Cavaliers and Pioneers* (Mrs. Nell Marion Nugent's Abstracts of Land Patents).

This patent was in part as follows: "Know yee that I Sr Francis Wyatt Kt. Governor and Capt. Generll. of Virginia by Vertue of the great charter of orders and lawes concluded on in a Generll. quarter Court by the Treasurer Councell and Company of Adventurers for this first Southerne Colony of Virginia according to the authoritie graunted them by his Majtie, under his great Seale and by them dated at London the Eighteenth day of November One Thowsand six hundred & Eighteene and directed to the Governor and Councell of State here resident doe with the approbacon and consent of the same Councell * * * give and graunt unto Georg Sandys Esqr. and Treasurer in Virginia and to his heires and assignes for ever in the nature and quality of his first devident to *bee augmented and doubled* by the Company to him his said heires or assignes when hee or they shall once sufficiently have peopled and planted the same three hundred acres of Land scituate & being on the other side of the river opposite agt. James Citty and abutting Westward on the land of John Baineham and Eastward on the land of Edward Grindon of both which devidents hee is now actually possessed &c * * * One hundred acres of the same being for a bill of Adventure of twelve pownds tenn shillings and the other two hundred in the right of his transportation into this Country of fower servants * * * Provided that the said three hundred acres doe extend in a right line along the banke of the said river not above one hundred & fifty pole at sixteene foote and a halfe the pole."

The patent provides that same is "to be augmented and doubled when * * * he (or his heirs) shall have peopled and planted the same three hundred acres of land." This accounts for the many second grants of land for the bringing over of the same persons who were named in the first grants.

It will be noted that this patent is issued by "Virtue of the Great Charter". Dr. Phillip Alexander Bruce, with reference to the Great

Charter, says "The noble series of Instructions ratified at the Quarter Court convening November 18, 1618, is a date which should be among the most celebrated in the History of the English speaking race."[1]

This grant of Sandys in Surry later came into possession of Montjoy Evelin, son of Captain George Evelin, who on behalf of Lord Baltimore captured Kent Island from Colonel William Claiborne. Mountjoy, on 20 June, 1651, received a patent to 650 acres of land which included Sandy's 300 acres. (C.P. 401) (See chapter V, following under "Edward Grendon", and "Binns family", post, for more details.)

George Sandys was the youngest son of Edwin Sandys, Archbishop of York, and a brother of Sir Edwin Sandys, the leader of the Liberal faction of the London Company. George's niece, Margaret Sandys, was married to Sir Francis Wyatt, Governor of Virginia.

Sandys never married. His father died a month after the defeat of the Spanish Armada (1588) George was then of the age of ten. He remained with his mother until her death, when he was thirty-two years of age. Then he decided to turn adventurer and see the world. In those days journeying through foreign lands, especially those of the Infidel, was a real danger and required courage. He left England in 1610 and visited Greece, Turkey, Syria, Palestine, Egypt, Cyprus, Crete, Malta, Sicily and Italy.

Sandys was often in danger in the Moslem countries and complained that when in Constantinople the Turks would not let a "Christian dog" ride a horse, but made him ride an "asse". He entered the Church of the Nativity at Bethlehem and the Holy Sepulchre at Jerusalem. While in Egypt he ventured into the Great Pyramid, but before doing so had his guides fire their arquebuses into the dark interior to scare away the thieves. He mentioned that the sands round the Pyramids were strewn with mummies and that "within their bellies were painted papers." These were ancient papyrus which were not interpreted until the finding of the famous Rosetta stone during Napoleon's invasion.

Sandys' journey lasted two years. When he returned he produced a book entitled *A Relation of a Journey begun An:Dom: 1610*, which was illustrated with a number of woodcuts. Sandys ended his book with the oft quoted paragraph, "now shape we our course for England. Beloved soil; as in sight wholly from the world disjointed; so in thy felicities the sun burns thee not, nor the winter benumbs thee; defended

---

[1] *Institutional History of Virginia*, Vol. II, p. 246.

by the sea from wasteful incursions, and by the valour of thy sons from
hostile invasions. All other countries are in some things defective;
when the, a provident parent, do'st administer unto thine whatsoever is
useful: foreign additions only tending to vanity and luxury. Virtue in
thee at the least is praised, and vices are branded with their names, if
not pursued with punishments."[2]

Soon after George Sandys returned to England his family became
actively involved in the colonizing of Virginia through their great
interest in the London Company. In 1621, his nephew, Sir Francis
Wyatt, probably because of the influence of Sir Edwin Sandys, was
elected Governor of Virginia and sailed for Virginia on the ship
"George" hereafter mentioned. He brought with him his brother the
Reverend Hawte Wyatt, of Queen's College, Oxford, as the new
minister at Jamestown. The Reverend Mr. Wyatt has numerous descendants living throughout the South. Also among those who came
with him were his uncles, George Sandys, as Treasurer, and the
Reverend David Sandys. "David Sandys, minister," is heretofore shown
as one of the thirty-one persons living at Hog Island in 1623 but he
soon succumbed to the pestilent diseases of the new world for he is
shown "among the dead" in 1625.

Sir Francis Wyatt, the kinsman of Sandys, had been educated at
St. Mary's Hall, Oxford and Gray's Inn. He came from a Kentish
family long distinguished in English history. Successive members of
this family gave a legend to the Tower of London, a poet to English
letters, and a martyr to the Protestant cause. Sir Henry Wyatt, bought
the castle of Allington, one of the seven chief castles in Kent, in 1492.
This was shortly after the Reign of Richard III. Sir Henry had been
imprisoned by the usurper in the Tower of London on account his
Tudor sympathies where he was fed on mustard and vinegar. Here he
was succoured by a cat which daily brought to the bars of his window
a pigeon from a neighbouring cote and so saved him from starvation.
Sir Henry became noted as a lover and protector of cats and was in
great favor with Henry VIII. (D.N.B.)

Sir Thomas Wyatt, the elder, son of the lover of cats, became am-
bassador to Italy and brought back to England the art of sonnet-writing.
Nothing from his pen was published during his lifetime but he is said
to be one of the first of those who corrected the roughness of English

---
[2] *I Saw Two Englands*, H. V. Morton, p. 58.

poetic style. In romantic legend he is said to have been the lover of the ill-fated Anne Boleyn before Henry VIII became her wooer. One of his poems ending with the following verse is said to have been addressed to the fair Anne who lived not far away in Hever Castle:

> Disdain me not that am your own
> Refuse me not that am so true
> Mistrust me not till all be known
> Forsake me not—me for no new.

The poet's son, Sir Thomas Wyatt, was the leader of the Kentish rebellion against the marriage of Queen Mary with Phillip of Spain.

For his part in the conspiracy he was beheaded in the Tower, suffering a death which he must have known would be the penalty of failure. It was from Allington Castle that he set out. His farewell is given in Tennyson's "Queen Mary".

> "Ah, Grey old castle of Allington, green field
> Beside the brimming Medway, it may chance
> That I shall never look upon you more."

Not far from Allington Castle was Boxley Hall, another possession of the Wyatts, which was the home of Sir Francis Wyatt, grandson of the Kentish Rebel and later the residence of George Sandys.

Sandys was due to encounter more dangerous and unlooked for adventures in Virginia, for within a year of his arrival in Virginia came the great massacre in which the Indians butchered more than 300 settlers. When the news reached Kent four months later, Margaret Wyatt decided at once to share her husband's and uncle's dangers and started for Virginia. When she arrived she found her uncle, to quote her own words, had written two books, "amongst the roaring of the seas" and "by the imperfect light which was snatched from the hours of night and repose." They were his translation of Ovid's *Metamorphoses* and the *First Book of Virgil's Ænid*. Sandys seems to have the distinction of being the first Englishman to write a book while in America. (D.N.B.)

Sandys actively entered colonial life, serving as a member of the Council from 1624 to 1628, attended to the office of Treasurer in Virginia, and managed his plantation in Surry. He was often quarreling with his fellow colonists and after ten years, wearied of continued strife, he returned to Kent where he spent his remaining years in writing at Boxley Abbey.

Sir Francis Wyatt, also at Boxley, returned to Virginia to again serve as Governor from 1638 to 1642. Sir Francis, returning to Boxley in the Spring of 1643, was just in time to reach the death bed of Sandys.

These former Virginians, all three of them died within a year. Margaret Wyatt died in March 1644 and Sir Francis a few months later. They were laid to rest in Boxley church where there is a tablet to the memory of:

> "George Sandys, Esq. eminent as a traveller, a divine poet and a good man, who died March 4, 1643, at Boxley Abbey, aged 66, and lies interred in the chancel of this church.

> "His life was throughout blameless and never unuseful. Its earlier part was sometimes pass'd in observing his fellow-men in foreign lands; and its latter years at home in celebrating the praises of his God and attuning the Songs of Zion to the British lyre."

CAPTAIN JOHN UTIE

The second recorded grant of land in Surry was issued to Ensign John Utie. This patent was dated November 3, 1624, one month and one day before the date of George Sandys' grant, but Sandys' was recorded in the Patent Book I, page 12, and Utie's on page 14. Utie was residing at Hog Island with his wife and infant son, John, when the census was taken on February 16, 1623.

The above patent describes Utie as "Ensign John Utie, gentleman, of Hog Island" and the land was located on the James River near the mouth of Lower Chippokes Creek. In 1629-30 Utie was Burgess for Hog Island, but later on December 20, 1631, became a member of the Council.

In 1635 Captain Utie made his appearance on the pages of Virginia history at the ousting of Governor Harvey. When at a meeting of the Council, Mr. Menifie, a member, was declaiming against Governor Harvey, the Governor struck Menifie on the shoulder and said "I arrest you for treason," Utie then took hold of the Governor and exclaimed, "And we the like to you Sir."

Utie with Menifie, Captain William Pierce, and others, were summoned to England to answer the charge of treason, but it seems that Utie died before he reached England.

About 1630 Utie had moved to his place called "Ultimara" in York County. He was dead before July 25, 1638 for on that day his son, John, as "son and heir" received a patent to this York plantation.

On April 8, 1640, "John Utie, gentleman, and Mary, his wife," assign to William Tayloe all their right in two patents granted unto Captain John Utie, father of said John, dated 15 March, 1630 and 4 March, 1638.[3]

John Utie, Jr., died before 15th of December, 1642, for on that date the County Court of Lower Norfolk commanded one, Richard Foster, to carry out a previous order dated October 4, 1641 and "pay unto Mrs. Marian Utie, now the wife of Richard Bennett, Esq., 114 lbs. tobacco."[4]

Richard Bennett became the Puritan governor of Virginia in 1652. Richard Bennett, Jr., and his half brother, Nathaniel Utie, entered Harvard College in 1655. They were probably the first Southerners to attend that famous institution.

CAPTAIN WILLIAM EWEN

The largest land owner in Surry in 1626 was William Ewen. In that year he had 1,000 acres "planted" in Surry and 400 acres more which he evidently had not yet cleared. This is shown in a patent granted to him as late as July 8, 1648 as follows: "William Ewen, merchant, 1400 acres * * * N. W. upon land of Mr. Grendon, N. E. upon the river, 400 acres by a patent granted him September 15, 1619 and 1000 acres by a patent granted January 1621 * * * for the transportation of 28 persons."

Ewen was a bold sea captain in his early days and brought many settlers to Virginia but evidently quit the sea in his later years and became a merchant and ship owner. From the records of the Public Record office in London we can reconstruct his life. His career well illustrates the hardihood of the navigators of those days and the great opportunities offered them for the making of fortunes.

He was captain and owner of the good ship "George" in its voyage to Virginia in 1617 and it seems to have been a "good ship" indeed for during the course of its voyages it was entrusted with the safety of two of Virginia's new governors. Among the 1617 arrivals were Mrs.

---

[3] C.P., p. 122.
[4] Norfolk Bk. 1637-46, Item 17.

Elizabeth Clements and her four children who were the captain's relatives by marriage. (C.P. 17) Mrs. Clements was the widow of Jeffry Clements of Oxford, a shareholder of the London Company, who died in 1609, and the niece of Sir Nicholas Fuller another company member. On February 9th, 1613-14, "William Ewen of Stepney, Middlesex, mariner, and Margery Clement of same, widow of John Clements were married." John Clements and Jeffrey Clements were brothers.

John Clements, Jr., son of Margery Clements—Ewen, died in 1620. His will was probated 17, May of that year. He bequeathed legacies to his father, William Ewen; mother, Margaret Ewen, and gave his uncle Clements' daughter (not named but evidently Mrs. Elizabeth Clements) his interest in the ship "George."[5]

Captain John Smith in his *General History Book* says that in 1617, "The Company having well furnished Captain Samuel Argall, the Lady Pocahontas, alias Rebecca, with her husband and others, in the 'good ship' called 'George', it pleased God at Gravesend to take this young lady to his mercy." It seems that the George waited both at Gravesend and Plymouth, for Smith says "This year (1617) having planted our fields, came a great drought and such a cruel storm of hail, which did spare so little of both the corn and tobacco, that we reaped but small profit: the magazine that came in the 'George', being five months in her passage was badly conditioned; but ere she had arrived, we had gathered up our tobacco. In 1619 Smith further relates the "George" was sent to New Foundland and there she bought fish which defrayed her charges and made a good voyage in seven weeks."[6]

In July 1621 William Ewen made a covenant with the Virginia Company "for 480Ll to see that the ship George 150 tons is staunch and strong and fitted out with furniture and with mariners and seaman, to take on passengers and to bring back tobacco from the plantation, with forfeit of 1000Ll." Also he made the same kind of a contract "to fit out the ship Charles 180 tons, and take same with freight and passengers to Virginia. He was to carry 80 persons in the George "at Vj Ll a man and 3Ll a ton for goods."[7]

A letter was "written on Mr. Ewen's behalf to the Governor and Council of State in Virginia who were entreated to procure for Mr.

[5] *P.C.C. Abstracts Soame Wills*, p. 180.
[6] *Tyler's Narratives*, pp. 330-31, 337.
[7] *Va. Co. Rec.*, Vol. I, pp. 149, 466, 497.

Ewens what freight they could homewards to recompense for the loss he sustained by carrying less freight outward in the George than is usual for a ship of such burden only to accomodate Sir Francis Wyatt and some other gentlemen the better in said ship."[8]

On April 20, 1623, William Ewen made a deposition in a law suit in which he stated "he had gone master of ships to Virginia four several times" and had lived there one whole year.[9]

Tobias Felgate, master of Williams Ewen's ship "Supply" also deposed at the same time that he had gone master and mate of ships five times to Virginia. Felgate was another hardy Virginia pilot. On one of his later voyages he died at Westover as shown by his will as follows, "I, Tobias Felgate, being in Westover in Virginia and having been for the space of eight days or thereabouts sick in body and so then continuing, but of sound and perfect memory, being requested by one Mr. Jeremy Blackman and others then present do make my will, April 1635."

Felgate's will was proven in Virginia 23 April, 1635, and later probated in England (P.C.C. 38 Sadler). He bequeathed monies to his eldest son William Felgate, daughter Sarah Felgate and wife Sarah; to Mrs. Elizabeth Menifie dwelling in Virginia he gave ten pounds.

William Ewen of Limehouse, mariner, on 17 Dec., 1624, bought a messuage and wharf on the south side of the Thames at East Greenwich in Kent from Martha, widow of Thomas Raynborowe for £600. He appears to have lived in Limehouse in Stepney until 1637 when he moved to Greenwich, for he was chosen a vestryman of Stepney Parish in 1627 and elected a churchwarden in 1632. In 1637 he presented an account of his wardenship and from that date onward appears in the records of Greenwich, Kent. This is known because William Ewen prospered and became the owner of a fleet of ships sailing to Virginia. Turkey, and the East Indies. In consequence of his enterprises he was often involved in chancery and maritime suits.

William Ewen made his will April 2, 1649, and same was probated 12 Aug. 1650 (P.C.C. 132 Pembroke). The will is that of a wealthy man and too long to quote. He appears to have had an only daughter Mary, but had numerous relatives to whom he bequeathed legacies. His lands in Surry were bequeathed as follows, "Lands, cattle, chattels,

---

[8] *Va. Co. Rec.*, Vol. I, p. 506.
[9] *Va. Co. Rec.*, Vol. II, p. 385.

and servants in Virginia to be sold, and the money I bequeath to Mary, my wife, one fourth, and to Mary, my daughter three fourths, To Mary, my daughter, two shares of land in the Somer Island Co."

On June 30, 1660, Mrs. Mary Ewen gave a power of attorney to Mr. Francis Newton, planter, to handle her affairs in Virginia, as a substitute for her well beloved brother Nicholas Newton since deceased and Richard Hopkin his attorney, 6 Dec., 1659. Mrs. Ewen held 1,400 acres of land, 7 negroes, 50 head of cattle, 15 hogs, etc.[10]

---

[10] Bk. I, p. 154. William Ewen's will and other information was kindly furnished by Mrs. Carolyn L. Bulkley of Shreveport, La.

Chapter VI

THE ANCIENT PLANTERS OF SURRY

FROM the musters given in a former chapter, it appears that in 1625 there were four plantations then existing "over the water". These were the plantations of "Burrows Hill", "Paces Paines", and those owned by Captain Roger Smith and Mr. Edward Blaney. In Hog Island were two more plantations, those of Captain Ralph Hamor and Sir George Yeardley.

The musters show that several of the inhabitants came over before 1616 and were therefore entitled to be called "Ancient Planters", for they had come over before "the coming away of Sir Thomas Dale" who left Virginia for England, November 1616. As Ancient Planters they were entitled to have 100 acres of free land. Other special legislation was enacted for their benefit, for the General Assembly of March 5, 1623/24, provided, "That all old planters that were here before or came in at the coming of Sir Thomas Gates, they and *their posterity* shall be exempted from personal service to the wars and any public charge (church duties excepted).[1] This act appears to literally mean that not only they—but their descendants—were exempt from service as soldiers and payment of taxes. One wonders if these privileges were ever claimed.

Ancient Planters, who either resided in or owned land in Surry, with the date of their arrivals, were, John Dodd, who came in the Susan or Sarah Constant, April 1607; William Spencer in the Sarah Constant, 1607; Phettiplace Clause, Starr, 1608; Francis Chapman, Starr, 1608; Thomas Gray, 1608; Thomas Gates, Swan, 1609; Captain William Peirce, Sea Venture, 1610; John Proctor, Sea Venture, 1610;[2] John Flood, Swann 1610; Captain William Perry, Starr, 1611; John Smith, 1611; John Bainham, Susan, 1616; Edward Grendon, called "Ancient Planter", date not known.

JOHN DODD

It will be noted that nearly all of the planters, shown as patent holders in 1626, were "Ancient Planters". John Dodd was first on this

---

[1] *Journals of the House of Burgess.*
[2] The Musters show he came on the Sea Venture 1607, but the Sea Venture arrived in 1610.

list as the holder of 150 acres. He and his wife were living at the Neck of Land in Charles City in 1624. He was aged 36 and his wife Jane was aged 40 at that time[3] When Captain John Smith went on his expedition at Pamunkey in 1608, John Dodd was one of his soldiers.[4]

John Dodd was living at the upper Neck of Land, now Chesterfield, in 1627.[5] The disposition of his Surry holdings is not known. He may have left descendants as persons bearing his name are later found in Henrico and Chesterfield.

PHETTIPLACE CLAUSE

Phettiplace Clause who came on the Starr in 1608 was living at Pace's Paines in February, 1624-25. He had previously patented land in Isle of Wight, May 2, 1619, but gave it up on account of the "great danger of planting". In October, 1629, he was a Burgess for Mulberry Island, and in 1632 for the plantations "from Denbigh to Waters Creek". On the 25th of February 1638, William Cloys patented 750 acres in Charles River County (York) "due in right of my father, Phettiplace Cloys."[6]

FRANCIS CHAPMAN

Francis Chapman came on the Starr with Phettiplace Clause. In 1626 Chapman was holding 100 acres by patent. This land was near Captain William Perry's plantation as Captain Perry was holding same in 1628.[7] Chapman married a daughter of Richard Pace, as he is called a son-in-law (step son) by Captain Perry who married Pace's widow. This place later became known as "Swan's Point". (See Swan Family.)

THOMAS GRAY

Thomas Gray also came in the Starr with the two above mentioned planters. On August 27, 1635, he received a patent for 550 acres of land "on the South side of the main river over against James City, adjacent on the East to the plantation now in his possession and to land of Captain Perry, running along by Rolfe's Creek and south into the woods upon Cross Creek, 100 acres due as an Ancient Planter at or before the time of Sir Thomas Dale, according to a charter of orders

---

[3] Hotten, p. 169.
[4] Smith's, p. 131.
[5] Minutes of Court and General Council, p. 166.
[6] C.P., p. 102.
[7] C.P., p. 10.

from the late Treasurer & Co., dated 18 November 1618; 50 acres for the personal adventurers of Annis Gray his first wife; 50 acres for the personal adventure of Rebecca Gray his now wife; 350 acres for transportation of his 2 sons, William Gray and Thomas Gray, and 5 servants: John Bishop, Robert Browne, Robert Welsh, Luke Mizell, John Bancker."[8]

The issuing of this patent in 1635 illustrates how long some of the planters waited to obtain patents for their land. It is probable, however, that Thomas Gray had been in possession of some of this land for many years. His descendants flourished long in Surry. (See Gray Family.*)

John Bishop who was transported by Thomas Gray as shown above, patented 150 acres, 9 November 1638 at the head of Tappahannock Creek. He was active in Bacon's Rebellion, was condemned to death by Berkeley, and died in prison. Administration upon his estate was granted Francis Mason, 14 June, 1676. (Bk. 2, p. 117.)

Luke Mizell, also transported, testified in court, on May 11, 1659, that he was "aged 45 or thereabouts" and that "when deponent was servant to Thomas Gray, Sr., deceased, he did often hear said Gray and his wife say that Thomas Gates had given 50 acres to their son Thomas and daughter Jane." (Bk. 1, p. 139.)

WILLIAM SPENCER

William Spencer, Ancient Planter, is noted as a member of the first expedition which arrived at Jamestown, for he came over on the "Sarah Constant" with Christopher Newport in 1607. Captain John Smith in referring to the men to whom Sir Thomas Dale had alloted farms for the raising of corn, said in 1614, "From all those Farmers whereof the first was William Spencer, an honest, valiant, and industrious man, (and hath continued from 1607 to this present) from those is expected such a contribution to the store, as we shall neither want for ourselves, nor entertain our supplies."[9] John Rolfe said "William Spencer and Thomas Barret a sergeant, with some others of the Ancient Planters being set free, were the first farmers that went forth; and have chosen

---

[8] C.P., p. 131.
[9] *Tyler's Narratives*, p. 312.

* The Gray family and families similarly mentioned will be shown in a subsequent volume.

places to their content: so that knowing their own land they strive who should exceed in building and planting."[10]

On August 14, 1624, William Spencer, "yeoman and ancient planter" received a grant of 12 acres on Jamestown Island "part of his first dividend within the Island, towards Goose Hill, near land of Sir Thomas Dale, due for his personal adventure." As William Spencer "of James Island" he patented 250 acres on the west side Lawne's Creek at the mouth, 9th September 1632.[11] This clearly identifies the Surry patentee as being William Spencer of Jamestown.[12]

He was living at Jamestown in 1624 with his wife, Alice, and daughter, Alice[13] and was Burgess for Mulberry Island 1624 and 1632-33. In 1635 he patented 1,100 acres on "Lawnes Creek and Westerly upon Hog Island Creek, Southerly upon a parcel of land he hath taken up near the mouth of the Creek."

In 1637 he further patented 550 and 1,350 acres "upon Lawnes Creek". This is the last reference to him in the patent books.

Two daughters, Elizabeth, wife of Major Robert Sheppard, and Anne, wife of Captain William Cockerham, survived. Major Robert Sheppard died in 1654 and his widow Elizabeth married Thomas Warren—one daughter, Elizabeth Warren, married John Hunnicutt. Elizabeth (Spencer) Sheppard also had a daughter, Anne Sheppard, who married first, Thomas Hart, secondly, William Newsom. Through these several families survive many descendants of this valiant Ancient Planter.

William Spencer has heretofore been identified in all biographies as a member of the First General Assembly of Virginia held in 1619. This is because his record has been confused with that of Ensign William Spence who was a member.

Ensign William Spence, with his wife and daughter, Sara, was residing in James Island (Jamestown) in 1623. (Hotten, p. 178.) In a "List of the names of the dead in Virginia since April last", dated February 16, 1623-24, appears the following entry:

William Spence ⎫
Mrs. Spence   ⎬ lost

---

[10] *Tyler's Narratives*, p. 337.

[11] C.P., pp. 4, 16. He is shown as an "Ancient Planter" in the patent but does not so appear in Mrs. Nugent's list of Ancient Planters.

[12] Hotten, p. 228.

[13] *Hotten's Emigrants*, p. 228.

They were therefore undoubtedly lost and considered deceased at the time this census was taken.

Ensign William Spence, Gent., was a member of the jury for the trial of Daniel Franks and George Clarke upon Tuesday, August 5, 1623. (M.C.G.C., p. 5.)

On January 10, 1624, Susan Bush of Elizabeth City was appointed guardian of Sarah Spence, orphan, and her lands and goods (M.C.G.C., p. 42). In the census of 1624 taken soon afterwards "Sara Spence, aged 4, born in Virginia" appears in the muster with Susan Bush. (Hotten, p. 249.)

On August 16, 1624, the General Court ordered that John Johnson shall "cover and repair the *late* dwelling house of Ensign William Spence." (*Ibid.,* p. 19.)

Contemporary with Sara Spence, orphan, and Susan Bush, in the same muster of 1624, William Spencer is shown as residing in James Island with his wife and daughter, both named Alice. So there appears to be no doubt that he was the survivor and later settled in Surry County.

THOMAS GATES

Thomas Gates, who came in 1609, held 100 acres in 1626 and was then living at Paces Paines with his wife, Elizabeth, who came in the Warwick in 1620. He was Burgess for Mulberry Island, October 1629. Owing to destruction of the James City records his fate is not known, but it appears that he gave away 50 of the above 100 acres to Thomas Gray, Jr. and his sister, Jane. This is shown by the testimony of Mrs. Dorothy Corker, aged 50, who testified in Surry Court, May 9, 1659, that Thomas Gates gave those two persons 50 acres of land on Gray's Creek. (Bk. I, p. 130.)

CAPTAIN WILLIAM PEIRCE

Captain William Peirce was a large land owner in Surry. He received a grant of 2,000 acres, 22 June 1635. This grant was to "Captain William Peirce, one of the Council of State" and was located on Lawne's Creek. It was bounded by land of Alice Delke, Widow, and William Spencer, and extended westward to Chippokes Creek. It was given for the transportation of 40 persons, one of whom was Thomas Rolfe.[14]

Captain Peirce came on the *Sea Venture* in 1610 with Sir Thomas Gates. Joan, his wife, came on the Blessing.[15] They were living at Jamestown, with four servants, at the time of the musters of 1624. In May 1623, Governor Wyatt appointed him Captain of the Guard and Governor of the City. In that same year as Lieutenant Governor of James City he led an expedition against the Chichahomines, in retaliation for the Massacre of 1622, falling on them July 23 with no small slaughter.[16] It was not long after that time that George Sandys, Treasurer of Virginia, wrote to England that Captain William Peirce, Governor of Jamestown" was inferior to none in experience, ability and capacity" and recommended him for appointment to the Council. His appointment was not made until 1631 at which time he was living in Surry.

In 1629 he was in England and while there prepared "A Relation of the Present State of the Colony of Virginia by Captain William Perse, an Ancient Planter of 20 years standing." He said there were then between four and five thousand English in Virginia. His wife, "Mrs. Jone Pearse", who accompanied him, was known in England as "An honest industrious woman, who, after passing 20 years in Virginia; on her return to England, reported that she had a garden at Jamestown containing 3 or 4 acres, where in one year she had gathered a hundred bushels of excellent figs, and that of her own provision she could keep a better home in Virginia than in London, for three or four hundred pounds a year, although she had gone there with little or nothing."[17]

Peirce and his wife returned to Virginia and while in the Council, December 20, he signed an amity agreement between that body and Governor Harvey. He was displeased with Harvey's government of the colony and was one of the Councilors who arrested and deposed him in 1635, he himself leading the musketeers who surrounded Harvey's home.

Harvey complained of this treatment and Peirce, with other Councilors, was ordered to England to answer Harvey's charge although

---

[14] C. P., p. 29.
[15] Hotten, p. 224.
[16] Va. Co. Rec., Vol. IV, pp. 111, 209, 250.
[17] V. M., I, p. 447.

same were never formally filed. He was present in Council in 1639 and was last mentioned there in February 1644-45.

Jane Peirce, his daughter, was the third wife of John Rolfe. Captain Peirce's final end is not known. He went on an expedition to the Northern Neck called "Chicoan", in 1645. From an item in the Surry records dated 21 January 1655, he, his son, Thomas Peirce, and his grandson, William Peirce, seem to have been living on Mulberry Island in Warwick County on that date. (Bk. I, p. 116.) The Warwick County records have been destroyed. The grandson, William Peirce, is probably the person of the same name who later appears in the Westmoreland records.

JOHN PROCTOR

John Proctor, another "Ancient Planter" who died in Surry, 1628, also came on the *Sea Venture* with Sir Thomas Gates.[18] His first plantation was in Henrico but he afterwards settled in Surry. During the Massacre he was in England, but his wife valiantly defended their house located on Proctor's Creek.

"Mrs. Alice Proctor, a proper gentlewoman, defended her place with great bravery in 1622 and refused to abandon her house and would not leave till officers threatened to burn it down."[19] That John Proctor was in England at the time of the Massacre is shown by the records of the Virginia Company, for on the 17th of July 1622, while present as a stockholder at a Court held on that day, was appointed on a committee to devise the best ways and means for aiding the Colonists in their distress. At a meeting held April 30, 1623, he stated he had lived "near 14 years in Virginia." In May 1625 he was granted 200 acres on S. Side of James River in Surry. This grant was evidently located at Pace's Paines where he was living at the time of the Muster previously shown.[20]

He was a brother of Thomas Proctor, "Citizen & Haberdasher of London", Mrs. Alice Proctor administered on his estate in Surry July 1627.[21]

---

[18] Muster shows that he came on the Sea Venture in 1607 but that ship did not arrive then. He came in 1610, C. & P., p. XXX.

[19] Tyler's *Narratives*.

[20] Va. Co. Rec., Vol. II, pp. 94, 385, 440, 457, 466.

[21] *Minutes of Council and General Court*, p. 150.

JOHN FLOOD

John Flood, "ancient planter", came over in the Swan in 1610. In 1616 he was one of the Reverend Alexander Whitaker's men at Charles City, and on January 6, 1625, he was shown as living at Jordan's Journey in that county where he made the following muster:

> John "Fludd" arrived in the Swan, 1610.
> Margaret, his wife, in the Supply, 1620.
> Frances Finch, her daughter, in the Supply, 1620.
> William "Fludd", his son, aged 3 weeks.

Margaret, his wife, was the widow of William Finche who brought her and his daughter, Frances, to Berkeley Hundred in January, 1620. They came over with a colony of 50 persons sent out by the historian, John Smith of Nibley, Richard Berkeley, William Tracy and others.[22]

In September 1620, William Finch and his wife were shown as the holders of 50 acres of land, each, but later William Finch was shown as "dead" and his wife as "remarried."[23]

John Flood was Burgess for Flowerdew Hundred in 1630 and for Westover, Flowerdew and Weyanoke in 1632.

John "Fludd", gentleman, patented 2,100 acres in Surry, 12 May, 1638, "North upon the maine river, east upon land of Captain Henry Browne, south into the woods, and west upon Benjamin Harrison's marked trees," for the transportation of 42 persons. Among the persons shown were John Flood; Margaret his wife, Frances Finch, her daughter, and John Flood, Jr. This place is still known as "Floods". John Flood, Jr., was aged 30 in 1652.

Surry was then part of James City and John Flood represented James City in the House of Burgesses in 1642, 45, 52, and 56. He was an Indian Interpreter in 1646, a captain of militia in 1652, a lieutenant colonel and also Speaker of the House of Burgesses in 1652. He died in 1661 and his son, (V.M. 5, p. 185) Captain Thomas Flood succeeded him as interpreter. (See Flood family.)

CAPTAIN WILLIAM PERRY

Captain William Perry came over in the Starr in 1611. He later

---

[22] Va. Co. Rec., Vol. III, p. 427. See an account of this colony under "Captain John Woodliffe", post.

[23] Va. Co. Rec., Vol. III, p. 397.

married Isabella, widow of Richard Pace, and came to live at Pace's
Paines. This is proven by a grant of land made to Isabella Perry, "Wife
of William Perry, gentleman". 20th September, 1628, for 200 acres
"At the south side of the Plantation called Pace's Paines, granted to
herself and her late husband, Richard Pace, deceased." She was an
"Ancient Planter" for the grant further described the land as situated
"west on the land of John Burrows now in the tenure of John Smith,
last granted to her son George Pace and north on the maine river:
100 acres for her owne personal adventure being an "Ancient
Planter."[24] Captain Perry represented Pace's Paines in the House of
Burgesses, October 1629 and March 1630. In February 1631-32 he
was Burgess for the territory "From Captain Perry's downward to Hog
Island." He was a member of the Council in 1632-34.

He later moved to Charles City County, where he died in 1637 and
was buried at the old Westover Church. His tomb is still there but the
epitaph is now illegible. It was copied by Campbell the Historian.

"Here lyeth the body of Captaine
William Perry who lived neire
Westover in the Collony
Who departed this life the 6th day of
August, Anno Domini 1637."

JOHN SMITH

John Smith, ancient planter, came over in the Elizabeth in 1611. He
later purchased or rented "Burrow's Hill" and called it "Smith's
Mount."[25] It lay next to Pace's Paines. In 1629 he was Burgess for
Pace's Paines and in 1630 for Smith's Mount. He and Captain William
Powell were brothers-in-law of the Provost Marshall of Middlesex
County, England, quite an influential gentleman in the Virginia Com-
pany.[26] This land was afterwards patented by Colonel Henry Browne.
(See Browne.)

JOHN BAINHAM

John Bainham, shown as the holder of a patent of 200 acres in

---

[24] C. P., p. 10.
[25] C. P., p. 10, 26, 32, 103.
[26] Rec. Va. Co., p. 308.

1626, came in the Susan in 1616. He was not identified with Surry but lived in Elizabeth City.

EDWARD GRENDON

Edward Grendon was called an "Ancient Planter" but the date of his arrival is not known. In 1626 he had 150 acres planted in Surry.

On December 4, 1624, George Sandys, Treasurer, received a grant of 300 acres of land in Surry, "on the other side of the river opposite James City and abutting westward on the land of John Bainham and eastward on the land of Edward Grendon." Grendon's and Bainham's patents are not shown in Mrs. Nugent's book but Edward Grendon's was called "Grindall's Hill". In 1628 Grendon was Burgess for James City (Surry) and died that same year.[27]

His place was located a mile from mouth of Gray's Creek and went to his heir Thomas Grendon, who sold same to Mountjoy Evelln in 1649. The patent issued to Evelin for this land shows that Grendon's and Bainham's land grants, although not now recorded in the Office in Richmond had been issued at very early dates. The patent was for 650 acres "200 acres granted unto John Bainham, 17 January 1619; 150 acres granted to Edward Grendon 5 December 1620; and 300 acres granted to Mr. George Sandys, 4 December 1624; purchased of Thomas Grendon by Captain George Evelin, 3 August, 1649, who gave same by deed to his son, the said Monjoy April 28, 1650."

Possibly many of the earliest grants were not recorded.

---

[27] M. C. G. C., p. 179.

Chapter VII

OTHER EARLY WORTHIES OF SURRY

CAPTAIN WILLIAM POWELL

CAPTAIN WILLIAM POWELL was another passenger on the Sea Venture in 1610. He was a large land owner in Surry. His heirs were holding two tracts of land in 1626, one of 200 and another of 550 acres. He and John Smith of "Smith's Mount" were brothers-in-law of the Provost Marshall of the County of Middlesex, England. In 1617 William Powell was made Captain of the Governor's Guards and Lieutenant Governor and Commander of Jamestown.

He was a representative in the First Assembly of Virginia, 1619, from James City[1] and commanded the Jamestown Guard when they repelled the Indians in March 1622.

Captain Powell led an expedition against the Chickahominies and was killed by them between January 20th and January 24th, 1623.

His land lay near Richard Pace's and Captain William Perry's. After Captain Powell's death there was a long dispute before the General Court concerning his rights to certain lands that he had cleared. Hugh Crowther, gentleman, testified "That in April 1622, Captain William Powell's men and divers others did clear a piece of ground which Captain Samuel Mathews now useth, out of which ground Captain Powell had 21 shares, Hugh Crother 11 shares, Richard Pace 10 shares, William Perry 3 shares, Thomas Gates 2 shares and Richard Richards had 1 share. Further he sayeth that the ground was not cleared for Captain Powell or any other man in particular—and that six of his family did help and had no share.[2]

All of the people mentioned here were prominent in early Surry history and the above testimony indicates that our early settlers cleared much of their land on shares.

Captain Powell's widow married Edward Blaney. He left a son, George Powell, who died in 1650. July 1, 1656, William Powell, brother of Captain William Powell, and heir of his son, George, "of Southwark Parish, Surrey England, baker, and William Parker of Leaden Hall St., London and Anne his wife, Anne being the grand-

---

[1] M. C. G. C., pp. 75, 153.
[2] M. C. G. C., p. 63.

child of the said Captain William Powell "sold to William Batt", 600 acres in Lower Chippokes on the James River, and 200 acres on Little Creek called Crouche's Creek."[3]

CAPTAIN ROGER SMITH

Captain Roger Smith's place in Surry was called "Smith's Plantation". The muster of 1625 shows that he had eight men, and two other persons, Christopher Lawson and Alice, his wife, at that place.

The place may have been managed by Christopher Lawson as the muster shows that at that time Captain Smith was residing at his plantation on James Island. Captain Smith's wife, shown in the Muster below, was the widow of John Rolfe and with them was Elizabeth Rolfe, his daughter.

THE MUSTER OF CAPTAIN ROGER SMITH

Captain Roger Smith, came in the Abigal, 1620.

Mrs. Joan Smith, came in the Blessinge.

Elizabeth Salter, aged 7 years, came in the Seaflower.

Elizabeth Rolfe, aged 4 years, born in Virginia

Sarah Macock, aged 2 years, born in Virginia.

Captain Smith had been in Virginia before he made the crossing on the Abigal. This is shown by an order of the London Company, December 1620, just before the Captain embarked on his voyage.

The Company decreed that "Captain Roger Smith being desirous to go this present voyage to Virginia, moved that he might have the charge of some of those people that were now sent to be the Company's Tenants. * * * Captain Smith was recommended to be a gentleman very sufficient for that employment, and in regard of his good experience already (having heretofore in Virginia about some three years) might thereby do the company great service. * * * It was ordered that he should have the command of 50 persons now transported to be tenants upon the Company's land."[4]

Captain Smith is mentioned in the records as commander of a company of Infantry under Sir Frances Vere in the Low Countries in 1592. In November 1619, after he had been in Virginia some three years he

---

[3] Surry, Bk. I, p. 93. Brothers sometimes had the same names.
[4] R.V.C., Vol. I, p. 433.

sailed back to England and made complaint to the Virginia Company
concerning his treatment by Sir George Yeardley.

On July 24, 1621, Captain Smith was appointed a member of the
Council. At the time of the Massacre in March, 1622, five men were
killed at his plantation. An entry in the company's records shows that
soon after this, every 20th man in the colony worked "under the
command of Captain Roger Smith, who had served 12 or 13 years in
the Wars in the Low Countries, to build a blockhouse upon the shore
where we might as well command shipping and withal will have a
strong Plantation the ground being rich and good."[5]

This fort was mentioned in a letter of the Council to the Company,
dated April 4, 1623 in which it was said that "a fort upon the shore
would fully command the channel, being not above musket shot over."
The exact location of this fort is not given but it appears to have been
in "Wariscoyke" (Isle of Wight), for in a proclamation by the Governor, dated April 29, 1623, it was ordered "for the safety * * * of the
colony" to begin fortifying "some place upon this river to defend the
same against the invasion of any foreign foe" and that every twentieth
man through the whole colony should be employed about the building
of a fort, at Warriscoyicke under the command of Captain Roger
Smith."

Whereupon Captain William Tucker was commissioned "to immediately levy upon every 20th man" and not to take newcomers but able
and sufficiently seasoned men from 20 years old up to 45.[6] Two later
entries in the company's records deal with the building of this fort in
"Warriscoyock"[7] (Isle of Wight) so there is no question but that the
fort was built in that county and not in Surry as has been supposed.
That this fort was in Isle of Wight County is further shown in a letter
written by Robert Bennett (uncle of Governor Richard Bennett) to
Edward Bennett, his brother, in London, dated at "Bennett's Welcome"
(Bennett's Plantation in Isle of Wight) June 9, 1623, in which he says
"The fort is building apace. * * * We purpose after we have weeded
our tobacco * * * with the help of Captain Smith to go upon the
Waresquokes and put them to the sword."[8]

On the 24th of January 1624, The Council ordered that "Captain

[5] R. V. C., Vol. IV, p. 229.
[6] R. V. C., Vol. IV, p. 129.
[7] R. V. C., Vol. IV, p. 188, 191.
[8] Boddie, 17th Cent.

Roger Smith shall have paid him by the treasurer in full satisfaction of his salary agreed upon for the undertaking of the Fort at Warescoyack twelve hundred pounds of tobacco and 12 barrels of Indian corn."[9]

From the description of the location of the Fort, it was "to fully command the channel" and not be above "musket shot over." It would therefore seem to have been located in Isle of Wight across from Mulberry Point and near the mouth of Lawne's Creek which is the narrowest part of the river. It should not be confused with Captain John Smith's fort on Gray's Creek, built in 1609, which is shown on Captain Smith's map as the "New Fort."[10]

The minutes of the Council and the General Court show that Captain Roger Smith was sitting in the General Court continuously from 1623 to 1629.

Captain Smith was an able and valiant soldier. Soon after the Indian Massacre of March 22, 1622, he was given absolute and sole command over the peoples of "Charles City, Henrico, Coxendale, Passbehay and the Maine." For better protection he compelled many persons to leave their homes and assemble at safer places—even against their violent protests.[11] Later on, nearly every year, he led expeditions against the Indians.

JOHN ROLFE

It is not known when John Rolfe first began to cultivate land in Surry. It may have been at a very early date. His heirs were holding 400 acres of planted land in Surry in 1626 and it was probably on this very land that he began his experiments and endeavored to sweeten the native tobacco. We have seen that he came over in the famous "Sea Venture" in 1610, and soon after his arrival he industriously began to cultivate the plant. Before he began experiments in 1612 Virginia tobacco had been found unpalatable by Europeans and Rolfe endeavored to cure this defect. According to Ralph Hamor, Rolfe succeeded in producing a leaf "as pleasant sweet and strong as any under the sun."[12] His scientific method of curing tobacco produced many important results in the country's history.

It stimulated the trade in servants and slaves, built the great planta-

---

[9] M. C. G. C., p. 45.
[10] Map faces page 38 and in Smith's Works.
[11] R. V. C., Vol. III, pp. 609, 611, 623.
[12] Hamor's *Narrative*, p. 34.

tions of the Tidewater and shaped the destiny of the colony until the Civil War.

Rolfe was Secretary and Recorder for the infant colony from 1614 to 1619. He married Pocahontas in 1614, thereby bringing about an ensuing peace with the Indians which lasted eight years. He went to England with her in 1616, where she died. He then returned to Virginia in May 1617.

It was the next month, June 8, 1617, that he wrote to Sir Edwin Sandys about his voyage and said "We found the Colony (God be thanked) in good estate and enjoying a firmer Peace and more plenty, however in buildings, fortifications and boats, much ruined and in great want. Our present Governor at Jamestown in repairing and making straight what he findeth decayed and crooked, to whose good endeavor and noble disposition our colony has been, is, and will be much indebted. All men cheerfully labor about their grounds, their hearts and hands not ceasing from worke to cover their naked bodies."[13]

In 1617-18 Rolfe was Secretary of State for Virginia and in 1619 he sat in the First General Assembly of Virginia as a member of the Council.

Rolfe was a true politician as his letters and statements in able language give fulsome praise and defense of the government of which he was a member.

While in the General Assembly, he complained against Captain John Martin for writing a letter to him which "casteth aspersions upon the present government, which is the most temperate and just that ever was in this country, too mild indeed, for many of this colony, whom unwanted liberty hath made insolent."[14]

From Rolfe also we have an account of the first slave ship. In a letter to Sir Edwin Sandys written January 1620 he says,[15] "About the latter end of August, a Dutch man of War of the burden of a 160 tons arrived at Point Comfort, the Commanders name, Captain Jope, his pilot from the West Indies, one Mr. Marmaduke an Englishman. They met with the Treasurer in the West Indies and determined to hold consort ship hetherward, but in their passage lost one the other. He brought not anything but 20 and odd negroes, which the Governor and Cape Merchant bought for victuals (whereof he was in great need as

---

[13] R. V. C., Vol. III, p. 71.
[14] R. V. C., Vol. III, p. 170.
[15] R. V. C., Vol. III, p. 243.

he pretended) at the best and easiest rates they could. He had a large and ample commission from his Excellency to range and take purchase in the West Indies."

About 1619 Rolfe married Jane, daughter of Captain William Peirce, heretofore mentioned, also a member of the Council, and had a daughter, Elizabeth, born 1620. He sat in Council, January 21, 1620, July 24, 1621, and November 30, 1621. This was his last appearance there, for notwithstanding his former marriage to the daughter of the great chief, Powhatan, he is said to have fallen under the tomahawk of the Indians in the Great Massacre of March 22, 1622.

John Rolfe's will was probated in England by Captain Peirce, his father-in-law. A copy was filed in Surry County more than a century later. (Bk. 15, p. 460.) It was as follows:

"In the name of God, amen, the tenth day of March, Anno domini, 1621 and in the year of the reign of our sovereign lord, James, by the grace of God, King of England, Scotland, France and Ireland, Defender of the faith etc., that is to say, of England, France and Ireland the nineteenth and of Scotland the —?—, I, John Rolfe of James City County in Virginia, Esquire, being sick in body but of perfect mind and memory, laud and praise be given to Almighty God therefor, do make and ordain this my last and final will and testament in form following, that is to say, first and principally, I do commend my soul into the hands of Almighty God, my maker and redeemer, assuredly trusting in the merits of Jesus Christ, my lord and only savior, to have full and ample remission of all my sins and to inherit with him a portion of the glorious kingdom of God with all the holy angels and archangels and blessed saints and elect of that eternal kingdom, and my body I commit to the earth in hope of a joyful resurrection to be buried at the discretion of my executor hereafter named in such decent and comely manner as unto my said executor shall be thought fit:

"Item, whereas Almighty God hath bestowed upon me two small children of very tender age, for whose bringing up and education in the faith and true fear of the same God I know myself obliged to be zealously careful, therefore I do commend and commit them unto the tuition of my dearly beloved friend and father-in-law, Lieutenant William Pyers, gentleman, upon whose love and favor in this behalf I do with great confidence depend, and for their better means of sustentation and education I do hereby devise and ordain that my said father-in-law shall and may have, hold, receive, take, order and dispose of all and all manner such estate and estates as unto them shall descend and come and of right belong and appertain during the time of their minorities.

"Item, whereas by certain letters under the common or general seal of the king's majesty's council for Virginia heretofore made and granted to me and my heirs I am and stand lawfully seised of a certain parcel or quantity of land situate in the country of Tappahannah between the two creeks over against James City County in the continent or country of Virginia, my will and desire is and I do hereby devise and ordain that said land or ground and all and singular profits, commodities, emoluments, rights, royalties, jurisdictions and hereditaments whatsoever thereunto belonging or in anywise appertaining shall be and shall any may remain and be unto my son Thomas and to the heirs of his body lawfully begotten, and I do hereby give, grant and confirm the same premises unto my said son accordingly by these presents and for default of such issue to the use and behoof of Elizabeth, my daughter, and to the heirs of her body lawfully to be begotten and for default of such issue to the use and behoof of the right heirs of me, said John Rolfe, forever.

"Item, my will is that if my said son shall happen to espouse and marry any wife by and with the consent of my said father-in-law within the time of his minority and before such time as he shall accomplish the age of 21 years, that then upon such espousal or marriage by and with such consent as aforesaid my said son shall or may enter into and upon the premises and every part thereof and receive, perceive and enjoy the rents, issues, revenues and profits thereof and thereby coming from thenceforth, to his and their own proper use and behoof forever, and in case my said son shall happen to die and depart this life on this side and before such time as he shall or may accomplish the full age of 21 years or be espoused and married as aforesaid, then my said daughter upon her accomplishment of the full age of 21 years or upon her espousal and marriage with the consent of my said father-in-law shall or may lawfully enter into and upon the premises, and receive, perceive and enjoy the rents, issues, revenues and profits thereof or thereby coming, growing or arising from thenceforth, to her own proper use and behoof forever.

"Item, whereas by certain other letters patent heretofore sufficiently passed and made there is given, granted and confirmed unto me and my heirs among others a certain quantity or portion of land or ground with the appurtenances situate, lying and being near Mulberry Island in the country or continent of Virginia, I do give, devise and dispose the same as followeth, viz: to the use and behoof of Joan, my wife, during the term of her natural life, and from and after her decease to the use and behoof of Elizabeth, my daughter, and to the heirs and assigns of said Elizabeth 'forever.

"Item, as touching and concerning all and singular such personal estate, goods, chattels, cattles and household stuff as God hath lent me, my debts and funeral charges being deducted and paid, my will and desire is that they shall or may be equally and proportionably shared, distributed and divided into three equal and indifferent parts and portions unto, between and among Joan, my said wife, Thomas, my son, and Elizabeth, my daughter, and that each of them shall or may have, hold and enjoy one full and entire third part of and in said goods, chattels, cattles and household stuff severally to their several uses and behoofs forever, provided always that if either of my said children shall happen to die or depart this present life before they shall accomplish the age of 21 years and before such their espousals and marriage with such consent as aforesaid, then my will and desire is that the part and portion of said child so deceasing of and in said goods, chattels, cattles and household stuff shall be and remain to the survivor of my said children. And also that if both of my said children shall happen to die and depart this present life before their accomplishment of their several ages or their marriages, then my will and desire is that the several parts and portions of my said children of and in said last mentioned premises shall be and remain unto my said wife (if she shall be then living). And if she shall happen to die or depart this present life before my said children, then the same last mentioned premises shall be and remain unto my said father-in-law to his own proper use and behoof forever.

"Item, my will and desire is, and I do hereby ordain and appoint, that my said father-in-law shall or may in the meantime have and take the several parts and portions of my said children of and in said goods, chattels, cattles and household stuff into his own hands and at his best discretion to dispose of them to their best advantage until they shall accomplish their several ages.

"Item, I give and bequeath unto my said father-in-law, William Pyers, my three bullocks or oxen which now are and heretofore have been usually yoked or put to draw in the yoke and also my best sword and girdle and hangers and my best armour.

"Item, I give and bequeath unto my said wife to her own proper use and behoof all the benefit, profit, commodity and advantage to be had, gotten or obtained for or by the labour, travail or painstaking of my three servants during all the residue of the time of their service due unto me by any covenant, promise or contract from them, or any of them, heretofore made unto me.

"Item, I give and bequeath unto my servant, Robert Davies, 20 pounds of lawful money of England to be paid him in such money or in good and merchantable wares amounting to such a value at the end and expiration of two years from hence next ensuing and fully to be complete.

"Item, I do make and ordain my said father-in-law to be the executor of this my will and testament.

"In witness whereof I have hereunto set my hand and seal the day and year first above written.

"Sealed, delivered, published and declared for and as the last will and testament of said John Rolfe in the presence of Temperance Yardley, Richard Buck, John Cartwright, Robert Davie, John Milwards.

"PROBATUM fuit testamentum supra scriptum apud London coram magro Thoma Bennett legum doctore surrogato venerabilis viri D—Henrici Marten militis legum etiam doctoris Curie Prerogative Cant' magri custodis sive Commissary cume constitut vice — simo primo die mensis May Anno domini millino Sexcentessimo tricesimo Juramento Willimi Pyers executoris in eodem testamento nominat Cui commissa fuit administratio omnia et singulorum bonorum *bonorum* iuvium et creditorum dict defunct de bene et fideliter administrando eadem ad sancta de Evangelia iuvat, &c."

Rolfe's will, written March 10, 1621/22 states that he was "sick in body". This was only twelve days before the great massacre of March 22, 1621/22.

Historians have charged that Rolfe fell under the tomahawk of the Indians. His death has been often commented upon as a horrible example of Indian perfidy, because Rolfe was a son-in-law of the great chief Powhatan.

It now seems that Rolfe did not fall before the savage fury but died peacefully in bed. One of the witnesses to his will was Temperance Yardley, wife of the Governor. She resided in Jamestown where Rolfe evidently died. Jamestown was warned by Pace in time and none of its inhabitants were massacred.

It will be noted from John Rolfe's will that during his time, Surry bore the Indian name of "Tappahanna".

According to the testimony of William Spencer, given March, 1626, in a suit before the General Council at Jamestown, Rolfe's plantation was in cultivation in 1622. Spencer said that "in March 1622, there planted over the water at Mr. Rolfe's Plantation 31 persons, whereof some belonged to Mr. Rolfe, some to Captain Pierce, some to Mr. Ewens and some to this deponent, each of which men had for their single share one hundred weight of tobacco and one barrel of corn, of which number of men before mentioned, two only belonged to Mr. Rolfe, viz., Robert Daves and William Rabnett."[16] This was the Rolfe plantation in Surry, part of which was afterwards purchased by Thomas Warren and on which now stands the Warren House.

John Rolfe's son Thomas to whom he gave this plantation in Tappahanna was born in Virginia in 1615. He had been taken to England by his parents about a year later. When Pocahontas died at Gravesend, Rolfe re-embarked with Thomas on the "George". The child became sick and it was feared that he would not be able to survive the voyage so Rolfe left him at Plymouth with Sir Louis Stukely afterwards notorious as an informer against Sir Walter Raleigh.

Thomas Rolfe later came into the care of his uncle Henry Rolfe of London who in October 1622 petitioned the Virginia Council that he be paid out of the estate of his brother John Rolfe for having brought up the son of his brother and Pocahontas.[17]

On June 22, 1635, Captain William Peirce received a grant of 2,000 acres on Lawne's Creek for the transportation of 40 persons among whom was Thomas Rolfe, so it appears that Thomas was brought to Virginia by his stepmother's father. In 1641 Thomas petitioned the governor for permission to visit his "Aunt, Cleopatra, and his kinsmen, Opecanough."[18] He was later, as "Lieutenant Thomas Rolfe", granted Fort Chickahominy and 600 acres of land conditioned on his keeping a guard at the fort. In 1656 he was granted 300 more acres on the Chickahominy.[19]

On June 10, 1654, he deeded William Corker 150 acres in Surry County lying between "Smith's Fort old field and the Devil's woodyard swamp * * * being due unto the said Rolfe by gift from the Indian King."[20]

---

[16] M. C. G. C., p. 99.
[17] V. C.R.
[18] C. P., p. 29.
[19] C. P., p. 328.
[20] Surry Bk. II, p. 54.

It was about 1643 that Thomas Rolfe sold to Thomas Warren the land on which the noted Warren House was built.

The date of Thomas Rolfe's death is not known, for if he made a will it perished in the destruction of the James City records at Richmond in 1865. Thomas Rolfe's daughter Jane married Robert Bolling. This is proven by the following deed:[21] "Indenture Oct. 1698, between John Bolling of County of Henrico and Parish of Varina, gent., son & heir of Jane late wife of Robert Bolling of Charles City County, gentl., which Jane was the only daughter of Thomas Rolfe, decd., and William Brown of Wilmington Parish, County of James City, for 1000 acres of land, commonly called the fort on Chickahominy River as per patent granted Thomas Rolfe."

On the fly-leaf of a volume, the *Purvis Collection of Virginia Laws* now in the Virginia State Library, is written by Robert Bolling, the emigrant, the date of his birth, "and in the year '75, married Jane, daughter of Thomas Rolfe, gent., by whom he had one son John Bolling, born 20th Day Jan., 1672."[22] (See chapters on "Warren House" and "Bolling Family", post.)

---

[21] V. M. 1, p. 447.
[22] V. M. 22, p. 104.

Chapter VIII

THE WARREN HOUSE

THE oldest brick house in Surry is the one which was built by young Thomas Warren in 1651-52 on land purchased by him from Thomas Rolfe. There is no doubt about the authenticity of its ownership and age as it is clearly proven by the records.

The house is located about a half mile from a high bluff on Gray's Creek. The bluff is situated at about the middle of a long bend in the creek, and on each side of the bluff are wide marshes and ravines. This makes the place something like a promontory. Across the rear of this promontory traces of trenches can be seen. (1904.) There is little doubt but that this is the remains of Captain John Smith's "New Fort" of 1609 which gave the name of "Smith's Fort" to the plantation.

Thomas Warren, in a marriage agreement made September 23, 1654, with Mrs. Elizabeth Shepard, daughter of Ancient William Spencer and widow of Major Robert Shepard, described himself as "Thomas Warren, gentleman, of Smith's Fort." (Bk. I, p. 56.) This plantation lay next to the 550 acres granted Thomas Gray in 1635, heretofore mentioned. The title to the plantation and therefore to the Warren house was clearly decided in favor of the Warrens in two law suits, one in 1677 and the other in 1712. The two suits give an interesting account of the purchase of the place. Thomas Warren stated that he was "aged 40 or thereabouts", in a deposition made in the County Court, May 3, 1661. (Bk. I, p. 161.) This should place his date of birth as having occurred in the year 1621, but the use of the word "thereabouts" makes the date uncertain. It seems to have been customary in those days to follow the decades and speak of persons as "about forty", "about fifty", "about sixty." Even now when one does not know of another person's exact age we follow the same pattern. John Hux of Surry in a deposition made in 1652 said he was about forty and in another one made seven years later in 1659 said he was about forty six. Martin Johnson was thirty in 1670 and thirty-three in 1672. Many other examples could be given. Rarely in those days where a person made more than one deposition did the ages agree. (See "Ages of Surry Settlers", post.) This may have been occasioned by the fact that the depositions were drawn by clerks, agents, or attorneys, and the exact age of the deponent was not material.

Thomas Warren seems to have settled on the eastern branch of Smith's Fort Creek in 1640. His original grant was for 450 acres and payment for the same was to be made seven years after entry. This is set forth in a grant for 290 acres made to him by William Berkeley 3rd July, 1648, as follows (Pat. Bk., p. 146): "grant unto Mr. Thomas Warren two hundred and ninety acres of land lyeing at the head of the Eastermost branch of Smith Fort Creeke being in the County of James City bounded as followeth (Vizt) from a poplar along the bounds of Goodman Spiltimber north by east half westerly seventy chaines along the bounds of Mr. John Corker * * * The said land being due unto the said Thomas Warren as followeth (Vizt.) being part of a patent of four hundred and fifty acres formerly granted unto the said Warren the 3rd of February 1640 to have and to hold &c. to be held &c. yielding &c. which payment is to be made seven years after the date of the 3rd of February 1640 and not before &c. Dated the 3rd of July 1648."

Thomas Warren served in the House of Burgesses in October 1, 1644, thus becoming a member at about the age of twenty-two which was exceptional but not unusual. Richard Bennett, afterwards Governor also became a member of the Assembly at the early age of twenty-one (17th Cent., p. 703). Thomas Warren was also a member of the House in the sessions of November 20, 1645; March 1, 1658-59; December 1662 to September 10, 1663, and October 23, 1666, (*Journals House of Burgesses*). On June 10, 1668, the list of tithables (taxpayers) living between the College and Smith's Fort was taken by Thomas Warren. His will was dated the 16th of March 1669. The original will in evidence in 1712 has been lost and apparently was not recorded or the original recording has been lost.

In the law suit of 1677, Richard Tyus, son of John Tyus who came on the *Bona Nova* in 1620, made deposition, "Sworn in Open Court held for the County of Surry, March 5, 1677," which was in part as follows: "Richard Tyus, aged about forty-nine years, Sworne saith: 'That Mr. Thomas Warren, his heirs and assigns have peaceably and quietly posest and enjoyed in their own rights that plantation commonly called Smith's Fort about 34 years, without any suits, troubles or molestations concerning the same, and further about twenty-five or twenty-six years since ye said Mr. Warren did begin to build ye fifty foot brick house which now stands upon ye said land and finished ye same without being forewarned or disturbed by any person, and that

Mr. Rolfe was then living and lived several yeares afterwards and was commonly at ye said Warren's house before, after and whilst the said house was building and further your deponent was present at a room of ye said Warren's house on ye said plantation with Mr. Warren, Mr. Thomas Rolfe aforesaid and Mr. Mason and several others some certaine time before the said Warren built ye said brick house where he saw ye said Mr. Rolfe write a bill of sale with his owne hands wherein he did make over and sell from him and his heires and assigns forever ye said plantation called Smith's Forte and further ye said Warren payd ye said Rolfe parte of ye consideration which he gave for ye said lands in Corne. . . .'"

Mr. Thomas Pittman, ancestor of a well-known North Carolina family also on the same day made a deposition as follows:

"The deposition of Thomas Pittman, sr., aged sixty-three years or thereabouts, Examined, sworn and saith: 'That Mr. Thomas Warren, his heirs and assignes have peaceably and quietly possessed and enjoyed in theire own right ye plantation called Smith's Forte which right has been held upwards of twenty and eight years without any suit or trouble or molestation concerning the same and further it is about five or six and twenty years since the said Mr. Warren did begin to build the fifty foot brick house which now stands upon ye said land and, without being forewarned or disturbed by any person, finished the same, and that Mr. Thomas Rolfe was then living and lived several years after, and was commonly at Mr. Warren's, his house, before and after whilst ye said house was abuilding. And did live awhile after, and that the said Captain Barrett did never claim that ever was known any right in any part of ye said land before expressed, and further your deponent hath seen a writing in Mr. Warren's possession signed and sealed sealed wherein Mr. Thomas Rolfe did make over all his right and title in ye said plantation called Smith's Fort to Mr. Warren, his heirs and assignees forever and that the writing was Mr. Rolfe's, his own hand. For your deponent in the year 1653 was at the house of Mr. Warren and Mr. Rolfe was present when Mr. Warren showed your deponent ye convaiance of Mr. Rolfe, and he did own it and tould ye said Warren that if it was not sufficient a convaiance he would make it new with a larger expression when he would have it, for he nor his heirs should ever be troubled by him or his and that there hath been no survey of this said land this twenty and eight years, your deponent having lived ever since in the same county and parish very neare to the said land. This is the best of your deponent's knowledge and further saith not.'"

Both of these deponents testify in 1677 that it was about twenty-five or twenty-six years ago that Mr. Warren began to build his fifty-foot brick house. This establishes the time in 1651-52 and the building therefore antedates Bacon's Castle by two or three years.

Richard Tyus says that Mr. Thomas Warren and his heirs have been in peaceable possession of the plantation for about thirty-four years which would make Mr. Warren's entry upon same about the year 1643. Mr. Pittman says it was about twenty-eight years which would make the time about 1648 or 49. The year 1648 was the date of Thomas Warren's patent.

The title of this property again came into question in 1712. Allen Warren, who testified in court, was born in 1663 and was then about fifty years of age. He was the third son of Thomas Warren. The verdict of the jury is somewhat long but because of its evident accuracy and interest is shown in full as follows:

"At a court held at Southwark for the
County of Surry December the 17th 1712:

"In action of ejections firmae (a common law action in ejectment in which farm lands are involved) between Solomon Saveell, plaintiff, and Samuel Thompson, defendant, for land and appurtenances lying and being in the Parish of Southwark in this county which *Henry Hart demised to the plaintiff* for a term not yet expired as is set forth in the declaration, Hinthia Guillum, Thomas Davis, Walter Lashly, John Clark, Charles Briggs, James Stanton, Walter Flood, Hugh Hunniford, Robert Pettiway, George Nicholson, William Gray and Christopher Moring were sworn to try the issue joined, who bringing in their verdict in these words, 'We of the jury do find as followeth:—for the plaintiff: We find that the land in question was granted to one *Thomas Hart,* son of Henry Hart, by patent dated the third day of July 1648, hereto annexed; that *Henry Hart,* the lessor of the plaintiff, is the eldest son and heir at law of said *Thomas Hart,* the patentee. For the defendant: We find by the oath of *Allen Warren* that he heard *John Clements,* now dead, oftentimes say that the land in question did formerly belong to the *Indian King, Powhatan,* who gave it to one *John Rolfe* in marriage with *Pocahontas,* daughter of said *Powhatan,* that when the son of said Rolfe was in England several tenants who lived upon the

land belonging to said son took out patents of said land in their own names, but that after when said son came into Virginia said tenants who had taken out patents did become tenants to said son; we find the depositions of *Richard Tyus* and *Thomas Pittman* dated the fifth day of March 1677 hereto annexed; *we find the will of Thomas Warren dated the sixteenth day of March, 1669 hereto annexed,* and said *Thomas Warren* died seised of the land in question: We find that *William Warren,* son of said Thomas Warren, died seised of the land in question without issue and that the land in question did descend to Alice, wife of Matthias Mariott and *sister of said William Warren;* we find a deed from said Matthias Mariott and said Alice Warren Mariott to *John Salway* dated the twenty-third day of July 1673, hereto annexed, by which the land in question is conveyed to said *John Salway* in fee; we find the will of said *John Salway* dated the tenth of April 1678 hereto annexed and that said *John Salway* died seised of the land in question; we find that *John Thompson,* brother of the defendant, married Elizabeth, widow of said John Salway, who died the wife of said *John Thompson,* and that said *John Thompson* and *Elizabeth,* his said wife, died seised of the land in question; we find the will of said *John Thompson,* dated the twenty-seventh day of January, 1698, hereto annexed by which the land in question is devised to the defendant; we find a patent dated the twentieth day of April 1687 hereto annexed by which the land in question is granted to *Henry Hartwell;* we find a deed from said Henry Hartwell dated the twenty-second day of May, 1688, hereto annexed by which the land in question is conveyed to said *John Thompson* in fee; we find the lessor of the plaintiff and those under whom he claims have lived near the place where the land in question lies ever since the year 1640. We do not find that the lessor of the plantiff or any of those under whom he claims ever were in possession of the land in question. And if upon the whole matter the law be with the plaintiff we find for the plaintiff one shilling damage; if not we find for the defendant. William Gray, Foreman. Which said verdict at the plaintiff's motion is recorded and the cause is continued till the next court to argue the matter of law arising from said verdict.' "
(Order Book 1691-1713, page 409.)

Thomas Warren was evidently a person of education and importance in his time and seemingly well-connected which is supported by the fact of his becoming a Burgess at the early age of twenty-one.

Many erroneous statements about him have crept into print which seems to necessitate a detailed explanation in order to disprove these errors.

It has been said that Thomas Warren was a son of Sir Edward Warren of Poynton Manor, Stockport, County Cheshire, England and this seems to be the prevailing belief in Surry today. (V. M. 6, p. 200 *et seq.*)

The printed records of the Lancaster Parish Register Society, Volume 27, page 1 (one) for the Parish Church of Woodplumpton, show that *Thomas Warren* and Edmund Warren, sons of Sir Edward Warren were christened the 10th of June 1604, "being 16 day olde". On page fifty-five (55) of the same volume is the following entry: "Sir Edward Warren of Poynton, Kt., and Baron of Stockport, deceased at Warren 13, Nov. 1609."

Omerod's *History of Cheshire,* Vol. 3, p. 683 shows that Sir Edward Warren born 1553, died at Poynton and was buried at Stockport, November 14, 1609. Also it is shown that *Thomas Warren,* son of Sir Edward, died at Sandbach and was buried at Prestbury, December 16, 1677.

Thomas Warren, being "about forty years of age" in Surry in 1661, therefore born about 1621 could not be the son of Sir Edward Warren who died in 1609.

Who therefore was Thomas Warren? He did not receive any grant for his own transportation which in a way tends to prove that he was either born in Virginia or was transported by someone else. Reference to the land patent books finds that Daniel Gookin received a grant of 1,400 acres of land, November 4th 1642, on the north side of the Rappahannock River for the transportation of twenty-eight persons among whom were "Himself, Daniel Gookin, twice; Mrs. Mary Gookin, Samuel Gookin, Thomas Warren," etc. (C. P., p. 138.)

Thomas Warren's name is shown in the patent right after the family where relatives are usually placed.

It is known that the Gookins came from Kent, England, and a reference to that family in the county histories of Kent show that the Warrens and Gookins were kin. William Warren, owned the manor of Ripple Court near the village of Ripple in Kent. He was a son of John Warren and his wife, Anna, daughter of Sir William Craford of Mongeham, nearby. William had married Catharine, daughter of Thomas Gookin of Ripple on June 4, 1619, and they had a son,

Thomas Warren, baptized at Ripple, January 30, 1624. Sir William Crayford (Crafford) had another daughter, Alice, who married John Meriwether of Sheperdswell, January 7, 1613.

In Surry we find these same families, well to do, prominent and intermarrying. Nicholas Meriwether, Clerk of Surry, married a daughter of David Crafford (Not Crawford) of James City.

Robert Crafford, founder of the Surry family, patented land in Surry. Edward Warren who died in Surry in 1676 was possibly a member of this Warren family of Kent. In his will he made his "loving friend", Nicholas Meriwether, his executor.

One bane of genealogical research is the desire to jump across the water and make noble connections.

The Meriwethers are said to have come from Wales, the Crayfords from a younger son of an Earl of Crawford in Scotland. (*Burgess, Virginia, Soldiers 1776*, Vol. I, p. 465.) Truth is often stranger than fiction. These Kent families not only seem more real and interesting, but they are about as ancient and well-connected as any of the English gentry. (See Warren, Crayford and Meriwether families.) (For Warren see Harleian Society, Vol. 42, pp. 38, 48; *Berry's Kent,* 113. For Craford see *Berry's Kent,* 109, 133; *Hasted's Kent,* Vol. 4, p. 137. For Meriwether, see Harleian 42, p. 193.)

Copies of documents used in this chapter were kindly furnished by Mr. James G. W. MacGlamroch of Greensboro, North Carolina, a descendant of Thomas Warren.

Chapter IX

SURRY PEOPLE BEFORE THE COUNCIL AND GENERAL COURT—1622-1632

THE Justices who sat in the General Court were also members of the Council. The General Court at the above time had jurisdiction over all petty crimes and misdemeanors including slander and libel. Many charges of disorderly and slanderous conduct were unproven. Therefore, some of our early settlers will appear in an unfavorable light but the customs and manners of the times can best be shown by narrating some of the events which occurred in this Court.

On the 19th of November 1624, John Burrows, gentleman, was sworn and examined before the General Court. Mr. Burrows owned "Burrows Hill" in Surry but at the Census taken in February, 1624-25, it was shown that "Mr. Burrows and 6 of his men which are planted here are returned with their arms at James City." David Sandys, a minister, and a relative of George Sandys was then living at Hog Island. John Burrows testified that on Whitson Monday last Thomas Allnut told him that he knew who it was who would try to steal away Maria Buck from him, that it was no small one but a great one. Upon which Burrows implored Mr. Allnut to tell him who it was and Mr. Allnut had said that it was none other than Mr. Sandys on the other side of the water and "that he would rather have Mr. Richards have her than he."

John Jackson was sworn and said that he had been at the house of Mr. Burrows, the provost marshall, who being put about that Maria Buck would be stolen away said that he would rather Mr. Richards would have her, "whereupon this examinat, walking in the Island with Mr. Richards" asked him whether he had any such intent to marry Maria Buck which Mr. Richards utterly denied.[1]

The Court found the charges unproven and "ordered that Mr. Thomas Allnut for giving out words of defamation against David Sandys, minister, that he shall ask him forgiveness before this court and shall likewise pay 100 lbs. of tobacco towards repairing the church at James City." (V. M. 19, p. 239.)

---

[1] V. M. 21, p. 50.

David Sandys did not long survive, he came in the *Bona Nova* 1620 and died August 1, 1625.[2]

When the census of 1624 was taken Maria Buck, then thirteen years of age, was living in the household of Mr. John Burrows at Jamestown. She was the daughter of the Reverend Richard Buck, deceased, who had come over on the *Sea Venture* in 1610. He officiated at the marriage of Pocahontas and John Rolfe.

At the same court Anne Cooper (wife of Justinian Cooper of Isle of Wight) complained that her late husband James Harrison did lend a shallop to Lt. George Harrison, deceased, which boat she had often demanded of the said Lieutenant but never could get satisfaction. That Ensign Harrison did lend the shallop to Lt. George Harrison was proven by the testimony of Captain Ralph Hamor and Captain Tucker.

The Court therefore ordered that George Menefie, administrator of Lt. George Harrison, pay the said Anna Cooper satisfaction for the Shallop.[3]

Lt. George Harrison was another early Surry land owner although his name does not appear in any Surry patents. His patent was granted by Sir George Yeardley, March 6, 1620-21, and was for 200 acres located upon the easterly side of Chippokes Creek.[4] This is the same locality where Benjamin Harrison, founder of the distinguished Harrison family, patented land in 1636.

Lieutenant Harrison became involved in a dispute with Captain Richard Stephens, Burgess from James City, 1623, and later a prominent member of the Council. This resulted in a duel which took place on James Island. George Harrison received a wound near the knee and died two weeks later. The verdict of the Coroner's jury, however, was that at the time of the duel Lieutenant Harrison was suffering from a fatal illness which had caused his death.

At a Court held March 20, 1625, it was "ordered that Randall Holt upon his petition preferred in court shall serve and remain with Doctor Pott, his master, until Christmas next—come twelve months. And that Doctor Pott is to deliver up his indentures and make him free, and give him one suit of aparell from head to foot and the barrels of corn" (V. M. 25, p. 231).

Randall Holt, founder of the Holt family of Surry came in William

---

[2] V. M. 24, p. 144.
[3] V. M. 21, p. 56.
[4] V. M. 51, p. 327.

Ewen's ship, *The George,* 1620, and was living with Dr. Pott at the Main 1624-25. He founded the fortune of the family by marrying Mary, daughter and sole heiress of John Bailey and acquired with her a large and valuable tract of land on Hog Island (See Holt family). At his time it was customary to call all persons who served another in any capacity "servants" and this did not necessarily mean menial or domestic servants. Noblemen, serving the King as his ministers, were called "servants" of the King.

Thomas Bunn, (Surgeon), sworn before the Court on the 27th of March, 1626, stated that William Atkins, "being sick and weak at his house" he asked him "how he meant to dispose of his estate." Mr. Atkins replied that he would leave all he had here in Virginia to the disposing of his Cozen Mr. Luke Boyse, to pay his debts in Virginia and send the remainder to his wife and children in England.

Luke Boyse was the son of Thomas Boys of Eythorne in Kent, and was baptized at Eythorne May 29, 1579. He was aged 44, January 1624/25, at the time of the taking of the census, which would make his above birth date about right *(Berry's Kent).*

Some cruel but not unusual punishments were inflicted in those days. The Court on May 10th, 1624, among whom sitting as Justices were Mr. George Sandys, Captain Roger Smith and Captain Ralph Hamor, well-known Surry planters, heretofore mentioned, ordered that "Edward Sharpless being sworn as Clerk to the Council of State hath betrayed our intentions in giving copies of our writings and letters to the King's Lords of the Privy Council out of the promise of reward.' * * * he shall be set upon the pillory in the market place in James City, *there to loose both ears* and there to have his ears nailed to it."[5]

Some early Surry settlers appeared before the court 13 August, 1626, when Ishmel Hill swore that he heard Martin Turner say before he died that Rice Watkins should have all of his estate in Virginia. Martin Turner came in the *George* in 1621 and was one of George Sandys' men. Rice Watkins, aged 30, 1624/5, came in the *Francis Bonaventure* and is listed as one of Mr. Blaney's men, "over the water" in Surry. (See Census, Ante.)

George Boucher also swore that about a month ago he was at Mr. Menefies' forge and heard Will Carter tell Martin Turner that Mr. Hamor was there and would have Martin Turner's bed. To which

Martin Turner replied to William Carter "Let not Mr. Hamor or any man else have my bed out of my house for when I work they shall find me lodgings but if I die I do give it to thee."[6]

Will Carter was the founder of the Carter family of Surry. George Boucher, on July 3rd, 1635, patented 200 acres in James City (Surry) between Hog Island and Lawnes Creek, due for his own personal adventure, that of his wife Anne, and their two children, John Jefferson, his wife's son, and James Butcher. There were two John Jeffersons in the Colony but it is not known which one had a wife, Anne. The Boucher family appears in the early Surry records but seems to have moved to York where a Jefferson family long flourished.

7th May 1626, the Court "ordered that Sarah Maycock for four servants brought over in the *Abigail* 1622 upon the account of Samuel Maycock, shall have 200 acres of land."[7] Sarah Maycock was then aged 3 years old. For in the Census of 1624-25 she was aged 2 years and was living in the family of Capt. Roger Smith in Jamestown. On May 20, 1617, the Governor of Virginia in a letter to the London Company, had asked "orders for Mr. Maycock, a Cambridge scholar, on acct. of the lack of ministers." He was a member of the Council in the First General Assembly in 1619 and was killed in the Indian Massacre of 1622. His daughter Sarah married George Pace, son of Richard Pace who warned the Jamestown settlers.

A CASE OF WITCHCRAFT IN SURRY

Before a Court held the 11th of September 1626 appeared Lt. Giles Allington, a member of the London Company of Virginia and a substantial citizen of the Colony. By his testimony he accused "good wife" Joan Wright, of witchcraft. She was the wife of Robert Wright, aged 44 in 1624-25, who came in the *Swan* in 1608. In 1625 he and his wife and two children both born in Virginia, were living in Elizabeth City at Kicoughtan but at the time of this trial had moved to Mr. Perry's plantation in Surry.

Giles Allington "sworne and examined sayeth that he had spoken to good wife Wright for to bring his wife to bed but that the said good wife being left-handed his wife desired him to get Mrs. Gray which he did and said that the next day after his wife was delivered the said

[6] V. M. 26, p. 3.
[7] V. M. 25, p. 342.

good wife Wright went away from his house very much discontented in regard the other midwife had brought his wife to bed. Shortly after this his wife's breast grew dangerously sore and it was a month or five weeks before she recovered at which time this deponent himself fell sick and continued so far the space of three weeks. Further that his child after it was born fell sick and so continued for the space of a month, and afterwards fell into extreme pain for a space of five weeks and so departed.

Rebecca Gray sworn and examined "sayeth that good wife Wright did tell her, this deponent, that by a token that this deponent had in her forehead she should bury her husband and further sayeth the good wife Wright did tell this deponent she told Mr. Felgate he would bury his wife, which came to pass, and further this deponent sayeth that good wife Wright did tell this deponent that she told Thomas Harris he should bury his first wife being then betrothed unto him which came to pass, and further this deponent sayeth good wife Wright did tell her that a woman said to her. 'I have a cross man for a husband', to whom good wife Wright replied, 'be content for those shall shortlie bury hime.' (which came to pass)."

Thomas Jones (of whom we shall hear hereafter) was sworn and said that Sargeant Booth told him he had words with goodwife Wright and after the said Sargeant Booth went forth with his peice to shoot and came to good game and very fair to shoot at but for a long time after he could never kill anything.

Robert Wright sworn and examined said he had been married to his wife sixteen years but knew nothing touching up "the crime she is accused of."

Mrs. Isabella Perry * * * "sayeth that upon the losing of a log of light wood out of the fort, goodwife railed upon a girl of goodwife Yates for stealing of the same, whereupon goodwife Yates charged goodwife Wright with witchcraft and said she had done many bad things at Kickotan, whereupon this examinant chided goodwife Wright. * * * and said why do thou not complain and clear thyself of same. Goodwife Wright replied 'God forgive them' and made light of it but that goodwife Wright threatened goodwife Yates girl and told her if she did not bring the light woods again she would make her dance stark naked and the next morning the lightwood was found in the fort. * * *

Alice Baylie sworn * * * said she asked goodwife Wright whether

her husband should bury her, or she bury him, to which goodwife
Wright answered, I can tell you if I would but I am exclaimed against
for such things and I'll tell no more."

Goodwife Wright was found guilty by the Court but was fined only
100 lbs. of tobacco.

An accusation of "witchcraft" was, nevertheless, considered a fearful
and dreadful charge. In 1641, Mrs. Jane Rookins, the mother of Major
William Rookings, famed in Bacon's Rebellion, had a quarrel with
George Boucher's wife, and in a culmination of abuse, called her a
witch. Mrs. Boucher, who was in fear that it might bring down
ostracism and a wave of popular rage against her, complained to the
General Court of such a frightful charge. Mrs. Rookins stated in court
that she had no recollection of using the word, but if she did, apolo-
gized as a body should, for having used it. The apology was accepted,
but the Justices ordered George Boucher to pay the costs of court.

An early Surry settler, one Thomas Harvey, who resided at Captain
Roger Smith plantation in February 1624-25 (See ante) acquired a
wife free of any expense. From the record of the case in the General
Court October 7th, 1826, it appears that this arose from a mistaken or
misplaced generosity on the part of one Thomas Edwards. Edwards
brought suit against Harvey for his wife's passage money to Virginia
and "upon the testimony of Captain Roger Smith and Mr. Francis
Bolton, minister, it appeareth that Mr. Thomas Edwards did freely
give to his maid Mary, now the wife of Thomas Harvey, her passage
into the country, that the said Thomas Edwards did freely deliver her
to the said Thomas Harvey to be his wife because he went to Mr.
Bolton and requested him to ask their banns in the church. Whereupon
it is ordered that Mr. Thomas Harvey shall not be liable to pay Mr.
Edwards for his wife's passage.[8]

Among the settlers shown at Captain Roger Smith's plantation,
February 4, 1624-25, were Stephen Webb, aged 25; John Butterfield,
aged 23; and Thomas Molton, aged 25. Also since the Census was
taken Thomas Gray and Rebecca his wife had acquired land near there.
Near them were Thomas Jones and Margaret his wife who at the time
of the Census of 1624-25 were living at Pashbehays on north side of the
river, but had evidently removed to the Surry side. Margaret Jones was
one of those stalwart viragos who oftentimes appear in the early court

[8] V. M. 26, p. 118.

records. Thomas Jones will be remembered as a witness against good-wife Wright for witchcraft.

All of these persons appeared before the General Court, 12th day of Oct. 1626. Two of the members composing the court were Captain Roger Smith and Colonel William Claiborne. You may be amazed at the sentence.

Steven Webb was first sworn and said that about a month ago "John Butterfield came to this deponent's wife all belabored over his face and said that Goodwife Jones had beat him and further the next day as he remembered being Sunday in the morning, the said Butterfield went into her own plot of pease to gather some. Whereupon the wife of Thomas Jones followed him and would not suffer him to gather any. Then this deponent came hither and found them skuffling together, she striving to take away his bag. Then the deponent asked Butterfield if he were a man. Whereupon Butterfield gave him leave to gather some pease and he stooping and gathering some the said Margaret Jones flew upon this deponent and struck him with a tobacco stalk, then there came Goodman Wright (the witches' husband) and quailed her * * * Thomas Gray and Thomas Moulton being sworne and examined sayeth and affirmith as much in all points as the aforesaid Stephen Webb had done."

The court "ordered that for ye severall offences of the said Margaret Jones, she shall be towed or dragged from a boats stern in the River from the shore unto the *Margaret and John* and thence unto the shore again."[9]

Some of the above mentioned persons lived to be prominent citizens of Surry. Steven Webb was Burgess 1643-44 and his name appears often in the early records after 1652. (See Index.) Thomas Gray was founder of the Gray family of Surry where some of his descendants yet reside.

Edward Grendon, who owned "Grendall's Hill" in Surry and was a Burgess for the south side in 1623-24, on October 26, 1626 presented a power of attorney from Richard Bailye (evidently in England) guardian to Mary only daughter and heir to John Bailye late Planter here in Virginia. The Court approved his lease of her lands on Hog Island to Sir George Yeardley for three years." She afterwards married Randall Holt.

At Court 13 Nov. 1626, "Upon request of Mr. Hugh Crowder, planter, that by reason of the barreness of the ground whereon he now liveth belonging to Captain John Hudleston, he desireth to remove and plant upon the ground of Captain Francis West at Chippokes Creek" which the Court gave him leave, "for him and his company living with him so to do."[10]

On 11th Jan. 1626-27 the Court gave Maximilian Stone leave to remove from Kecoughtan and plant at Hog Island. John Dodds, formerly a Surry planter (see ante) testified he was at the house of Luke Boyse, gent., who deceased about ten days ago "that Boyse said he had no need to make a will" that his estate should go to "his wife Alice and child."

Robert Edwards, who came on the *Marygold* in 1619, and was living at Mr. Sandys plantation in 1624-25, was given leave to remove from Warasquoke (Isle of Wight) to Elizabeth City. He afterwards reappears in Isle of Wight (See 17th Cent.).

At this court Mrs. Alice Boyse brought in an account of the cattle in controversy between Captain John Martin and Captain (John) Bargrave and desired to give them up as she was unable to give security for same." Whereupon Captain William Tucker in behalfe of Mrs. Bargrave, her kinswoman, the wife of Captain Bargrave, desired to give security." This Captain John Bargrave was from Patricksbourne in Kent[11] and his family was related to the Boyse family (See Boyse and Bargrave in *Berry's Kent*).

John Day, aged 24, came over on the *London Merchant* with his wife in 1620 and is shown as living at Hog Island in census of 1624-25. (See Ante.)

Defamation of the character of those living in high places brought swift and sharp punishment in those days. Richard Crocker, who is shown in the Census of 1623 as living at Hog Island (See Ante) proved to be a rash talker, for at this same court Thomas Ward said that John Day at Hog Island sold nails for a barrel of ears a thousand, but he will sell no more because Captain Hamor sells nails for a barrel of corn and £10 of tobacco a thousand," then Richard Crocker answered, "there are two of them that are not fit to sit at the Council table,

---

[10] V. M. 26, p. 246.
[11] V. M. 7, p. 146.

which is Captain Hamor and Mr. Peirsey, the merchant, for they deal upon nothing but extortion."[12]

The Court, after hearing further testimony, ordered that Richard Crocker (then of Martins Hundred) for his offence of taxing Captain Hamor, deceased, and Mr. Peirsey, unjustly of extortion, saying that they were unfit to sit in Council, shall suffer one month's imprisonment, and shall in the end thereof set in the pillory and have his ears nailed, and shall further pay a fine of 300 pounds of tbco.[13]

An order was entered on the 26th of November 1626 by the Council distributing the Tenants of the London Company, many of whom will be recognized as living in Surry, as follows: (In part)

To Capt. West	Capt. Smyth	Capt. Mathew	Mr. Piersey
Rolfe Ashborne	Frances Fowler	Christ Redhead	John Tios
Wm. Hampton	Christ Lawson	John Butterfield	Ishmore Hill
John Jefferson	Steven Webb	Richard Alford	Wm Pilkenton

On the 7th of May 1627, Ensign John Utie complained before the court that Richard Bickley (one of his servants at Hog Island) had resisted and opposed him in his command in denying to take arms and discharge his public duty (which was confirmed by the Oaths of John Day and Francis Burke) whereupon the court ordered "that he shall be laid neck and heels for 12 hours and by way of a fine shall pay 200 lbs of tobacco."[14]

On the 4th of July 1627, the Court decided "to draw out parties from all our plantations and go upon the Indians and cut down their corn. The day set for these expeditions was August 1st. Captain Francis West, brother of Lord Delaware, former Governor, was to command the detachment against the Tappahannas in Surry and Edward Grendon was to be second in command.

Benefit of Clergy Claimed

In March 1628, in Virginia, a person found guilty of manslaughter escaped death because he could read and write. The persons concerned in the case are not Surry people but it is thought this incident may be of general interest.

One William Bentley, who patented land in Elizabeth City in 1624

---

[12] V. M. 27, p. 145.
[13] V. M. 27, p. 147.
[14] V. M. 28, p. 96.

(C. P., 50) was brought before the General Court on a charge of man-slaughter. The first witness was Richard Rich, aged 25, who testified "that on the 8th day of February last, Thomas Godby, the deceased, was at the house of William Parker at Merry Point, and that he, the deponent, and divers others, drank between them five pints of burnt claret wine, that Thomas Godby consumed about four cups of the same. At which time William Bentley, who had just come ashore in a boat, came into the house and asked if it were not their orders when they heard men call to come and help them out of a boat. Whereupon Godby answered 'do you think we have nothing to do but to fetch you out of the water.' * * * Bentley replied 'hold your peace' and Godby called Bentley a rascal and a rogue and Bentley did the like to him. Thereupon the said Bentley, sitting upon the bench on the left side of Godby, struck him from the bench and presently rose up and gave him a kick as he lay upon the ground. * * * Godby could not sit up but tumbled down crying out, 'Oh Bentley, thou has killed me', and also said of him 'I am cruelly foxed.' * * * And in the morning Godby was found dead in the said house."

William Bentley had pleaded "not guilty" and had asked for a jury trial (Put himself upon the Country). A jury of 12 men of whom one was Francis Fowler of Surry, "found the said Bentley guilty of manslaughter and he being asked what he had to say for himself that he ought not to die demanded his clergy whereupon he was discharged to the Ordinary."[15]

Before the ordinary in a church court Bentley would be required to plead not guilty and to produce witnesses who would state that they believed the defendant's oath. Nothing as to the fate of Bentley is shown but he probably escaped further punishment as no witnesses were heard against a prisoner in a church court and he was usually purged of the charge and set free.

Thus it seems the English doctrine of the Benefit of Clergy became part of the Virginia laws.

In England, when a prisoner claimed benefit of clergy, the text usually selected by the Court for him to read was the first verse of the 51st Psalm beginning "Miserere mei deus", "Lord have pity on me". This was commonly called his "neck verse".

---

[15] V. M. 31, p. 152.

The "neck verse" became a joke in literature. In the *History of King Lear* (pre-Shakespeare) it appears thus:

> "Madam, I hope your grace will stand
> Between me and my neck-verse if I be
> Called into question for opening the King's letter"

The British Apollo of 1710 has this:

> "If the clerk had been taken
> For stealing of bacon
> For burglary, murder or rape,
> If he could but rehearse
> (Well prompt) his neck-verse
> He never could fail to escape."

Chapter X

CUSTOMS AND MANNERS OF THE SEVENTEENTH CENTURY

THE records of Surry do not begin until 1652 and the records of James City County prior to that time are destroyed. Extracts from the records after 1652 show something of the customs, manners, religious beliefs and general conduct of the early settlers who came to this country to obtain a fuller measure of liberty. We can thus determine how far we have progressed. Then as now the harshness of the laws on one generation are modified in another. Sometimes re-enacted they were enforced by other leaders and governors with great vigor. Even in our own times, from 1920 to 1932, no one was free to buy a drink of anything stronger than near beer. So we need not consider as very queer and harsh some of the customs and laws of those early times. "Eternal Vigilance is the price of Liberty." Today we not only have a multiplicity of laws but often a "duplicity" of them. The fewer the laws and regulations the more freedom of individual liberty. Nuisance laws are usually brought about by minority pressure groups contrary to the will of the majority.

The first General Assembly of Virginia passed a law requiring every citizen to attend divine services on Sunday. If one was delinquent the penalty was a fine of three shillings. This fine was reduced to one shilling in 1652. In 1675 the grand jury of Surry presented twenty-nine persons for violating the Sabbath by not attending their parish churches. They were Thomas Clarke, presenting himself; Nathaniel Knight, Henry Briggs, William Rookins, Barthalmew Owen, William Nance, Richard Parker, George Middleton, John Moss, Richard Tias, Thomas Senior, Edmond Howell, John Orchard, Old Mrs. Symonds, John Barker, Jr., William Short, William Harvey, William Draper, Edward Greene, Long John Phillips, John Hunnicutt, James Watkins, Adam Heath, John Miniard, Thomas Busby, Richard Royer, Thomas Bird, Daniel Williams, John Skinner. (Bk. 2, p. 83.)

On December 30, 1678, Thomas Sowerby, Samuel Judkins, John Watkins and John King, members of the Grand Jury, presented to the Court, Thomas Hunt and Robert Lee for not attending church. Also Thomas Senior, Edward Davis, John Rawliston, Nicholas Johnson, Robert Evans, Walter Vaughan, Richard Tyas, Sr. were presented by Thomas Crews.

Martin Thorne, Nicholas Wilson, Matthew Swann, Robert Kae, of the Grand Jury of the Lower Parish presented for not attending church: John Bynum, John Shepheard, Daniel Wade—not settled and not attending church. (Bk. 2, p. 194.)

Many of the above persons refused to pay tithes or attend church because they were Quakers.

Nowadays golf games on Sunday morning seem to prevent some persons from attending church, but in those days people lingered in taverns. Samuel Thompson, the son of William Thompson, a former minister of Southwark Parish, and a Burgess and prominent citizen, like many of the prominent citizens of those days kept an "Ordinary" or Inn. In 1681 he gave a bond of a thousand pounds of tobacco that he would suffer no person, except his servants, to linger in his tavern on Sundays during the hours of Divine service in the parish church. (1671-84, p. 52.)

Gifts of ornaments, costly cups and plates to churches during the seventeenth century were frequent. In 1674 Christopher Lewis bequeathed to the church warden of Southwark parish "a silver flagon of two quarts measure", to William Thompson minister "1500 lbs. of tobacco" and "desires to be buried in ye chancel of ye church and to have a tombstone over me and a funeral sermon" preached for which his executors are to pay. (1671-8, p. 34. Book 2, p. 36.)

Captain George Watkins, who died in 1673 "Desires to be buried in the chancel of the church at Lawnes Creek Parish as his predecessors have been in the chancel of the parish churches where they dwelt" and bequeaths a thousand pounds of tobacco to the church for the purchase of a piece of silver plate. (Bk. 2, p. 36.)

George Jordan who died in 1678 provided in his will that "on the 15th day of every October a sermon of mortality be had at my house, the day my daughter Fortune Hunt died. If the day came on Sunday, Holy Communion to be given. Whoever shall enjoy the land, be it one thousand generations, who so possesses the land shall perform both Sermon and Prayer." Also he bequeathed to the church a baptismal basin of silver valued at three pounds sterling. In accordance with a wish often expressed in the wills of those times he "desired to be buried by wife and children in Major Browne's orchard. (Book 2, p. 191.)

In 1662 two worthy citizens of Surry were required to "stroke the corpse" of a deceased maid servant to see if her death had been brought about by a blow or a bruise. It was an ancient superstition that if the corpse of a person who had died by violence was "touched" by a guilty person there would be some indication of returning life. The master and mistress in the presence of a coroner's jury composed of such leading citizens as George Watkins, Augustine Hunnicutt, Charles Barham, Arthur Long, George Carter, Richard Drew, Richard Jarrett, Wm. Tuke and John Mason, were required to run their hands over the inaminate facé and form of the deceased. The jury brought in a verdict of natural death. (Vol. 1645-47, p. 265.)

An education in Surry, or rather in Virginia, appears to have been difficult to obtain in the seventeenth century. The physical conditions prevailing in Virginia, owing to the plantation system, were not as favorable as the conditions prevailing in New England under the town system. (See *Seventeenth Century Isle of Wight,* Chapter X.) Dr. Bruce in his *Economic History of Virginia in Seventeenth Century* (Vol. I, p. 528) says the average area of the plantations acquired by patent after the middle of the century was about six hundred and twenty-eight acres. For the ten years between 1657 and 1666 the average land grant in Isle of Wight County was 959 acres. (*Seventeenth Century,* p. 105.) In New England the concentrating of inhabitants in towns made it possible to have a school for each community. In Virginia, with such large plantations and no towns, comparatively few children could congregate in a school. Consequently, in Surry we often find provisions in wills for the education of a testator's children.

Richard Jarrett of Surry who died in 1672 provided in his will that his only son Charles be placed in a teacher's care to learn to read, write and cast accounts. Edmund Howell who was deceased in 1679 also left an only son William and he made a provision in his will similar to Richard Jarrett's.

Major William Rookings who died in jail a captive of Berkeley's during Bacon's Rebellion, gave instructions in his will that all of his slaves should continue at his plantation and engage in raising tobacco sufficient to pay all of his debts and provide "clothing and schooling" for his children. (1671-84, p. 329.)

In Surry County between 1679-84, a period of five years, about fifty guardians gave bonds which bound them to educate their orphan wards. (1671-84, p. 558-584.)

Masters were often required by articles of indentures to educate servants. In 1666, Dorothy Thorne was indentured to serve her master Charles Barham, 6 years, and one of the requirements of her indenture was that she be taught to read.

In 1671 John Carey "being by God's mission bound for England and there to continue with my wife and children as far as yet I do not know and whereas I am guardian to Walter Flood, orphan, and brother unto my wife, who being intended to go to England with me * * * to enter school" places young Flood's entire fortune in the hands of a trustee who "are to see after him in his school in England." (1645-72, p. 420.)

John Carey's daughter Mary married, first, a Mr. Young and secondly, Nathaniel Harrison (1677-1727).

Henry Hartwell, a former member of the Council and an eminent lawyer, died in England while there on affairs pertaining to Virginia. His will provided that his executors bring over his nephew, Henry, and see that he obtained the best education that English institutions of that day afforded. This young man returned to Surry and died without issue. (See Hartwell family.) (Waters' *Gleanings*, p. 314.)

When Governor Berkeley in 1671, "thanked God there were no free schools in Virginia," he was only speaking "politically" for the Benjamin Simes free school in Elizabeth City had been in existence since 1636,[1] and several other free schools had been established by 1671.[2]

An early plantation called the College Plantation "existed in Surry until 1667 when all the buildings were destroyed by a "Great Gust". This "Gust" was one of the severest in early annals. A description of the buildings is given in the records. The name still exists in the small creek or run called "College Run".

---

[1] See *Seventeenth Century Isle of Wight*, page 90.
[2] Bruce, *Institutional History*, page 353.

Chapter XI

BURGESSES AND PROMINENT MEN OF SURRY BEFORE BACON'S REBELLION

AS stated before Surry was a part of James City County and James City's records were totally destroyed in the Richmond fire of 1865. Surry is first mentioned as a county, November 25, 1652. (Hening I, p. 373.)

A short account of some of Surry's earliest settlers has been given from contemporary sources before 1652, but nothing is known of the daily lives and transactions of Surry people within the county prior to that date.

The "Surry Side" of James City, however, was often represented in the House of Burgesses by able men. In fact, one of James City's representatives in the First General Assembly of Virginia in 1619 was Captain William Powell heretofore mentioned as an early Surry land owner. Edward Blaney was one of James City's Burgesses in 1623. He evidently held a large plantation in Surry for in the Muster of February 3, 1624-25, there were fifteen men at his place there. He lived in Jamestown where he was factor and agent of the London Company and keeper of the "Colony Magazine".

On March 4, 1626, he was a member of the Council and then married to the widow of Captain William Powell. He then disappears from the records. In 1628, his home in Jamestown was in the tenure of Dr. John Potts, another member of the Council.

Other Surry land owners resided in Jamestown and tilled their land across the water. From the description given in their grants of land within the "Precincts of James City", they were very often near neighbors.

In order to encourage building in Jamestown, it seems that in 1623 Richard Stephens received the first recorded patent to land in that place. It was for only "three score rods" issued "for his better convenience and that others may be more encouraged by his example to build and enclose some ground about their houses for gardening, * * *, situate and being about a convenient dwelling house which he has lately builded and erected in James City, on land which lies south upon the way along the great river, east upon land of Captain Ralph Hamor, west on land of John Jackson." (C. P. 2.)

This Richard Stephens is the person of that name heretofore mentioned, who wounded Lieutenant George Harrison, an early Surry settler, in a duel at Jamestown in 1624 from which Harrison died fourteen days later.

On August 14, 1624, Captain Ralph Hamor received one and one-half acres for the "greater commodity of his house by him erected and builded in the New Towne within the precincts of James City, adjacent Richard Stephens, John Chew and George Menefie." (C. P. 2.)

Ralph Hamor was a son of Ralph Hamor, the elder, merchant tailor of London, who resided in the Parish of St. Nicholas Acorn, London. The family is shown in the visitations of London, 1634. Ralph, the elder, married Susan, daughter of Robert Owen, wealthy gun founder of London, whose family was related by marriage to the influential Farrar family of the Virginia Company.

Both Hamors were members of the Virginia Company in 1609, the elder paying £133.68. The elder Ralph was also an incorporator and director of the East India Company. He died in 1615, leaving two sons, Ralph and Thomas, who both came to Virginia. (Will P. C. C. 78 Rudd.)

Ralph, the younger, later of Surry in Virginia, came over in 1609 and remained until June 18, 1614 when he returned to England on board the *Treasurer* with Captain Argall. While in England he wrote a pamphlet about Virginia entitled "A True Discourse of the Present State of Virginia."

He was a great friend of John Rolfe and in his "True Discourse" said of him "During the time of his abode there, which draweth nigh upon six years, no man hath labored more to his power by good example there and worthy encouragement unto England by his letters than he has done."

Captain Hamor returned on the *Sea Flower* to Virginia with his brother, Thomas, in 1622, and was at "Bennett's Plantation" in Isle of Wight at the time of the Massacre. (See 17th Cent., p. 35.) By the time the Muster of 1624-25 was taken he had married Mrs. Elizabeth Clements (See Clement's family) and was living at Jamestown, but owned a plantation on Hog Island, tilled by seven servants. He was a member of the Governor's Council in 1625-26 and died in 1626 while in that office.

John Chew, merchant, had a grant in Jamestown of "1 rod, 9 poles,

August 7, 1624, south upon Richard Stephens, east upon Captain Hamor" (C. P. 3). He is said to have come from Somerset, England, with the Bennetts on the *Sea Flower* in 1622, but the muster of 1624-25 shows that he came on the *Charity* and was then residing at Hog Island with his wife, Sarah, who came on the *Sea Flower.* He was Burgess for Hog Island with Captain John Utie in 1623-24 and 1627-28, but later moved to York County which he also represented in the House of Burgesses 1642-43.

John Chew followed the Puritans to Maryland when they were driven out by Governor Berkeley and became the ancestor of many distinguished people of that state and Pennsylvania.

William Spencer, member of the General Assembly, 1624, also resided in Jamestown, "near Goose Hill", where he patented 12 acres. (See "Ancient Planters".)

Captain Roger Smith, another valiant Surry planter, held a parcel of ground in 1624 in Jamestown, "northward upon ground of Sir George Yeardly * * * divided into two pieces by the highway which parteth it, the said highway being about 3 poles broad." (C. P. 2.)

Some other plantation owners of Surry, heretofore mentioned, who also lived in Jamestown, were, Captain William Pierce, Captain John Utie, Edward Grendon, William Perry and John Smith. These planters represented their respective Surry plantations in the General Assembly at different times between 1619 and 1632.

After the massacre of 1622, the main purpose of the settlers was to secure themselves against further Indian attacks. This is revealed by the acts of the General Assembly during the years above mentioned (See 17th Cent., pp. 84-87). The second General Assembly of Virginia which met in March of 1624, enacted "That every dwelling house shall be pallisaded for defense against Indians. That inhabitants go not aboard ships or in such numbers as thereby to weaken and endanger the plantations. That beginning next July the inhabitants of every corporation shall fall upon the savages as we did last year."

In 1627, the Assembly ordered that the midsummer wars against the Indians were to continue. On October 1629, the General Assembly resolved that "It was the opinion of the whole body of the Assembly that we shall go three several marches upon the Indians at three several times in the year, the 1st in November, the 2nd in March and the 3rd. in Juily, and to effect these the colony is divided into four divisions."

In 1629, Richard Tree represented Hog Island, and he and Richard Richards represented that Island in 1631-32. Richard Tree also resided in Jamestown as shown by a patent granted him for 50 acres, August 24, 1624, as "Carpenter of James City, who came to this country with Master Abraham Percye, Cape Merchant, in the George as a free man, adjacent to Edward Grendon and Richard Craven * * * near unto the highway leading to Black Point." (C. P. 4.) In the census of 1624-25, he is shown as coming over in 1619, and had a son John aged 13.

Richard Richards came on the *London Merchant* in 1620, and was at "Burrow's Hill" in Surry in 1624. He and Captain William Perry were Burgesses for "Captain Perry's downward to Hog Island" in February and September 1632 and for James City (Surry side) in 1641. He had moved to the north side of the river by 1648, for on November 12th of that year, he patented 350 acres at Archer's Hope. (C. P. 178.)

In 1633, "Smith's Mount, the other side of the Water, and Hog Island," was represented by Thomas Grendon, son of Edward Grendon, heretofore mentioned as an "Ancient Planter", and owner of "Grindall's Hill".

Colonel Thomas Grendon was a London merchant who resided frequently in Virginia. He married Elizabeth Stegge, widow of Colonel Thomas Stegge, Puritan Commissioner to Virginia who was lost at sea in 1651. (17th Cent., p. 62.) Elizabeth Stegge was the mother of Grace Stegge who married John Byrd, goldsmith of London, father of the first Colonel William Byrd of Westover.

Colonel Thomas Grendon's will was probated in London, December 15, 1678. He described himself as "of St. James Duke Place, London, citizen and draper", gave his son Thomas Grendon, "now in Virginia", lands in Sheriton, County Stafford, and to his daughter Hannah Duke, "now in Virginia" certain property there. (Sherwood, *American Colonists*, p. 53.)

Thomas Grendon, Jr., died at sea, dsp. in 1685. Hannah Grendon was married four times. Her husband was Thomas Jennings of London, merchant, by whom she had a son Thomas, also a London merchant, living there in 1685. She married, secondly, William Bird of Martin's Brandon in Charles City, on the south side of the James, now Prince George. William Bird had succeeded Captain Charles Sparrow as Virginia representative of the London merchants, John Sadler and Thomas Quiney. One of Thomas Quiney's brothers had

married Shakespeare's daughter, Judith. William Bird was associated
with and may have been related to John Byrd of London, for in 1658-
59, he gave a note to "John Bird, citizen and draper, of London." In
1661, he was a Justice in Charles City along with Robert Wynne.
(V. M. 42, pp. 41, 247.)

On July 4, 1671, he purchased from Thomas Busby "a grist mill
and appurtenances at head of Chippokes Creek" in Surry, also 150
acres adjoining, and another tract of 300 acres adjacent to William
Shorte. (Bk. 1, p. 386-7.) By September 29, 1672, William Bird was
deceased and his widow had remarried. His son and heir, Thomas
Bird, was in possession of the mill (OB. 1, p. 18.) March 5, 1674-75,
William Duke, who had married the widow, was ordered to pay a debt
due by William Bird's estate to Anthony Wyatt. (Mins. Gen. Court.)
Duke died in 1678 and on November 28, 1681, William Archer was
granted 600 acres of land due his predecessor, William Duke. (Bk. 2,
p. 38.)

Thomas Bird, son of William, in 1680, bought more land from
Thomas Busby, and added to his mill property. He was deceased before
January 5, 1688, for by that time his relict, Mary, had married George
Nicholson. (B. 4, p. 113.) He left three daughters as shown by a
deed made March 4, 1728, by Elizabeth Lanier, wife of John Lanier of
Southwark Parish, who conveyed to Richard Jones and Tabitha, his
wife, "daughter of Thomas Bird, who by his will dated January 21,
1680, devised land to his three daughters, Mary now deceased, and
Elizabeth and Tabitha, 300 acres on the South Branch of Upper
Chippokes Creek."

The mill remained in possession of the Lanier's for several years.

Contemporary with Thomas Grendon in the House of Burgesses in
1633, was John Corker, Burgess for Pashbehay, Chickahominy and
James City in that year and also in 1645. He was Clerk of the House
1645-53. On March 20, 1657, he patented 1,150 acres in Surry "on
south side of James River and on south side of the head of Graye's
Creek, called the 'Ware Neck' * * * opposite the mill and over the
swamp to Mr. Rolfe's line, 500 acres purchased of John Kempe 24
October 1639, and 650 acres by patent to said Corker. December 2,
1640." (C. P. 374.)

John Corker lived in Jamestown for February 10, 1637, he patented
"6 acres in James Island, near Goose Hill * * * next to land of those
ancient Surry planters, William Spencer and Richard Tree." (C. P. 81.)

William Corker, his son, was Burgess for James City, 1655-56, and Captain of Militia. He married the widow of Captain John White, Burgess for James City, 1641. He made his will in Surry, September 4, 1677, naming children: Susanna, wife of George Branch of Surry; Judith, wife of William Clay; and Lucy, wife of Thomas Jordan.

The following persons shown below were appointed "Viewers of Tobacco" in 1639. These persons were required to view the tobacco fields and see whether or not the laws governing the planting and growing of tobacco were being observed.

The penalty for planting tobacco out of the prescribed season (after July first) was a heavy fine. All tobacco leaves on the ground were to be burned. Any hidden tobacco was to be confiscated. A person finding same or informing about same was to receive one-half of the tobacco, the other half was to be burned. The object of such strict regulations was to prevent an over-production and the raising of an inferior quality. It was hoped by these means to maintain a high price for tobacco. (V. M. 5, p. 120, 274, 277.)

VIEWERS OF TOBACCO 1639

Charles City County

South Side

From Maycock's downward to Mr. Hayes,
Mr. John Hudd, John Glipps, George Pace

James City County

South Side

For the Easterly Side of Chippoakes Creek to Mr. Hudd's,
Mr. Benjamin Harrison, William Gapin, Edward Minter
For Mr. Hudd's plantation to Mr. Graye's,
Captain Henry Browne, John Carey, Henry Carmen
From Smith's Fort to Grindall's Hill,
Mr. Thomas Swan, John Bishop, William Mills.
From Grindall's Hill and both sides of Lower Chippoakes Creek,
Mr. Thomas Stampe, Stephen Webb, Erasmus Carter
From Lawne's Creek and Hog's Island,
William Spencer, Robert Larchett, John Dunston

Isle of Wight County

From Lawne's Creek to Castle Creek,
Mr. William Barnett, Richard Jackson, William Lawson

Thomas Fawcett represented Upper Chippokes or Smith's Fort, Lower Chippokes, Lawnes Creek and Hog Island in the General Assembly of 1639-40. He also represented other settlements north of the James and evidently was not a Surry land owner. In those days, a person did not have to reside in a settlement in order to represent it in the House of Burgesses. This custom is still followed in England in connection with elections to Parliament.

In 1641, Richard Richards, heretofore mentioned as a Burgess in 1631-32, together with Jeremiah Clements (See Clements family) and William Butler, residents of the Surry side, represented James City in the Assembly.

William Butler also appears in the House in 1642. He represented Surry in 1653, also in 1657-58, and also was a Captain and Major of Surry Militia. On August 29, 1643, he patented 700 acres "upon the south side of James River at head of Lawnes Creek adjacent Captain William Pierce." Among persons brought over by him were, himself, John, Mary and Elizabeth Butler. He was a great friend of Captain William Pierce and is mentioned with him in Anthony Barham's will as "my gossip William Butler" (17 Cent., p. 291).

William Butler died in 1664, leaving wife, Mary, and son, William, Jr. William, the son, patented 590 acres in 1672, "on north side of old field where Major William Butler formerly lived." William died in 1678, and wife, Joyce, administered upon his estate.

Three of the Burgess shown for James City in 1644, were from the Surry side. They were Stephen Webb, Thomas Warren and George Jordan. Of these three Stephen Webb was the only "old timer". The Ancient Planters and early settlers shown in the Census as living in Virginia at the time of the Massacre were now dying out. The other two Burgesses were newcomers. Thomas Warren, had arrived only four years before and George Jordan had come over in 1635.

A full account of Thomas Warren has been given in the chapter entitled "The Warren House" and he will not be further mentioned here.

Stephen Webb, aged 25, was living at Captain Roger Smith Plantation in Surry in 1624-25. On June 30, 1635, he patented 300 acres "near mouth of Chippoakes Creek, extending eastward towards Lawne's Creek." (C. P. 23.) He represented the Surry side in the Assemblies of March 1643 and October 1644. He had two sons who died single.

The birth of these sons, Robert, November 16, 1636, and William, February 15, 1645, are recorded in the Surry records. (B. 1, p. 75.)

Stephen Webb died before July 24, 1659, for on that day in Surry was recorded a certificate from the minister and church wardens of the Parish of Bushly in Worcester showing that his surviving brother was William Webb, born May 10, 1601, then living in the parish and that Steven was born September 5, 1598. (B. 1, p. 139.)

Colonel George Jordan was one of Surry's most prominent citizens. He was in the House of Burgesses at intervals for nearly thirty years, serving in the Sessions of 1646-47, 1658-59, 1674-76. He was a Justice in Surry in 1652 and afterwards, and was Attorney General for Virginia from 1676 to his death in 1678.

In 1673 the Surry Court granted him a certificate showing his right to have land in Surry for the transportation of 38 persons, among whom was Fortune Flood, his sister, who married Colonel John Flood; Arthur Jordan, his brother; and Charles and William Jordan.

Colonel Jordan lived near Four Mile Tree. At this plantation is one of the oldest tombstones in Virginia with a legible inscription. It was erected to the memory of his wife and reads:

> "Here lyeth the Body of Alyce Myles
> daughter of John Myles of Branton
> near Herreford Gent. and late wife
> of Mr. George Jordan in Virginia who
> departed this life the 7th of January 1650
> > Reader, her dust is here inclosed who was of
> > Witt and grace composed
> > Her life was Vertuous during health But
> > Highly Glorious in her death."

Colonel Jordan desired to be buried in Major Browne's orchard near his wife and children. One of his children was his daughter, Fortune, who married Thomas Hunt. As heretofore related he provided in his will that "on the 15th day of every October a Sermon of Mortality be had at my house, the day my daughter, Fortune Hunt, died. If the day come on Sunday, Holy Communion to be given. Whoever shall enjoy the land, be it one thousand generations, who possesses the land shall perform both Sermon and Prayer." (B. 2, p. 191.)

One wonders how long this admonition was observed and let him who owns the land today beware.

A great Indian Massacre occurred in 1644, instigated by old Opecanough of former massacre fame, who though still alive was so feeble he could not lift his eyelids. When it was necessary for him to see, an attendant raised them. Notwithstanding his feebleness he still cherished his implacable hatred of the English.

Governor Berkeley, alarmed by the spreading civil war in England, had ordered that Good Friday, April 18, 1644, be kept as a special day of fasting and prayer for the King.

However, upon Opecanough's orders, on Holy Thursday, the Indians fell upon the outlying settlements and from 300 to 500 persons perished under their tomahawks.

The Assembly in 1644 provided that the county of Surry and other counties shall prosecute the enemy and defend those parts from "Upper Chipoake downward" by constant marches upon the enemy.

An Act was passed defraying the charges of the Pamunkey and Chickahominy march against the enemy. Captain Shepard and Mr. Swan were to raise 50 men, in Surry. In all 300 men were to be raised for the march to Pamunkey.

For better measure of defense against the Indians, the Assembly in March 1645-46, enacted "that 45 soldiers be raised to garrison Fort Henry on the Appomattox, and that 45 soldiers be raised from the inhabitants of Basse's Choice upwards including the said Basse' Choice (In Isle of Wight). All of which soldiers shall be raised by the Lieutenants and deputy Lieutenants within the said limits either by impressment or otherwise, Surry to furnish 15 men."

The Burgesses in 1644-45 were John Corker, heretofore mentioned, and George Stephens. Stephens represented the Surry side in the Assemblies of February 1644-45, November 1645 and 1652. On December 12, 1668, Edward Collier sold Richard Rogers 300 acres on Chippokes Creek called "Cabin Point" formerly patented by Mr. George Stephens and bought from him by John and Richard Taylor who sold to Collier.

George Stephens had a son James who was deceased before May 7, 1667, for on that day Colonel Joseph Bridger of Isle of Wight, made over to Mary Pitt, daughter of Colonel Robert Pitt of Nansemond all land property, etc. of James Stephens, stating that "she was the heir because she was the daughter of Elizabeth Pitt, sister of Mr. George Stephens, deceased, father of the aforesaid James Stephens. (B. 1, p. 282.)

Mary Pitt afterwards married John Brasseur of Nansemond. (17th Cent., p. 510.)

Colonel Thomas Swan and Colonel John Flood also appeared in the Assembly of November 1645, from James City. They were both residing then on the Surry side.

Colonel Swan was also Burgess from James City in 1649 and from Surry, 1657-58. In 1659, he was appointed a member of the Council which place he held until his death in 1680.

Lt. Colonel John Flood was an Ancient Planter. He came to Virginia in 1610, and represented Flowerdew Hundred in 1930 and Westover, Flowerdew and Weqanoke in 1632, before removing to Surry. He not only represented James City in 1645 but also in 1650 and the session of 1655-56. (See "Ancient Planters and Flood family.)

Captain Robert Shepard was the new representative appearing for the Surry side of James City in 1646. He came over in the "Hopewell" at the age of 20 and was living at Mr. Edward Blaney's plantation over the Water in the Muster of 1624. He was respectively Lieutenant, Captain, and Major in the Surry Militia, Justice of Surry, Burgess also in 1647 and 1648. (Dr. Holtzclaw 47 V. M., p. 367.)

On July 19, 1635, he patented 300 acres near the head of Chippokes Creek toward Sunken Marsh, also 650 acres in the same locality in 1638 and on October 8, 1650, he was granted 1,000 acres on the Main Blackwater. This last patent was regranted to Robert Hart, his grandson.

Captain Shepard's first grant was for the personal adventure of himself and his wife, Priscilla Shepard. (C. P. 28.) In the grant of 1638, he brought over Henry Meddows (C. P. 94), and was designated as a "Lieutenant". In the last grant his title was "Captain". He then brought over Priscilla, Dorothy and Mary Shepard. (C. P. 204.)

"Major Robert Shepard" is the way he was designated in a deed of gift he made to Henry Meddows August 14, 1653. (B. 1, p. 59.) Major Shepard was dead by July 5, 1654, when his second wife, Elizabeth, then a widow, wrote a note to Captain William Cockerham called Captain Cockerham "dear brother" signed same "your loving sister" and asked him to represent her in court. (B. 1, p. 53.)

Captain Cockerham had married a daughter of William Spencer, Burgess, 1624, and it appears that Elizabeth Shepard was another daughter of the redoubtable William Spencer. (Dr. Holtzclaw, V. M. 47, p. 368.)

Mrs. Elizabeth Shepard married, secondly, Mr. Thomas Warren as heretofore related (See Warren House). Of Major Shepard's six children mentioned in the marriage settlement between Mrs. Elizabeth Shepard and Thomas Warren, only one, Anne Shepard, survived. Anne married first, Thomas Hart, who died in 1669, and then she married William Newsom.

The descendants of Major Robert Shepard, Burgess of Surry, are represented only in the two lines of Hart and Newsom.

Among the Burgess in 1649 from James City was John Dunston who lived on the Surry side. On June 1, 1636, he patented 250 acres "in Hog Island Main, east upon Robert Shepard, and S.W. upon Chippakes Creeks * * * for transportation of his wife, Cicely, etc." (C. P. 40.)

John Dunston was among the 31 persons living on Hog Island in 1623. He also patented 850 acres of land in 1639 in Chippokes Creek. (C. P. 48, 109, 111.) He was dead by January 24, 1659-60, as his sons, John and Peleg Dunston, "make over to our brother Ralph Dunston, all our rights to land left us by will of our father, John Dunston, late of Lower Chippokes Creek." (B. 1, p. 143.) Ralph Dunston likewise releases his right to them for their lands. This family may have moved out of the country very early as it seems to disappear from the Surry records.

In 1652 that portion of James City County lying south of the James River was separated from James City, and a new county called "Surry" was organized. As before stated Surry is first mentioned as a separate county in the Journals of the House of Burgesses on November 25, 1652. (Hening 1, p. 373.)

As the list of Burgesses from Surry was increasing from year to year and the same ones served so often, to repeat the lists each time would be only a mere repetition of names. From here on only the names and history of new Burgesses will be given. A complete list of all the Burgesses from Surry is shown hereafter.

William Thomas and William Edwards represented Surry in the

House in 1652. William Thomas died in 1656, leaving no heirs, his property escheated.

William Edwards, after serving a term in the House of Burgesses, became Clerk of Surry in 1653. He served in that office until his death in 1673, and was succeeded by his son, William, who held that office until his death in 1698. Albert Sterling Edwards II, (1848-1922) his descendant, was Clerk from 1871 to 1822.

In 1654 the Burgesses from Surry were William Batt and James Mason.

Mr. William Batt, on April 11, 1649, patented 128 acres "upon Lower Chippokes Creek", called by the natives the "Indian Pacotacke" adjacent land of George Powell (C. P. 179). On July 1, 1656, William Batt purchased 800 acres of William Powell, who was the administrator of his nephew. As "William Batt of Lower Chippoakes", he sold "Rich Neck", later the ancient home of the Ruffins, to Ralph Jones in 1658. The deed recites that said 275 acres was "formerly patented by William Newsum, March 3, 1636, and was commonly called "Rich Neck". (B. 1, p. 127.) In 1658 he represented Elizabeth City in the House.

William Batte was the son of Elizabeth (Parry) and the Reverend Robert Batte of Okewell County of York, England. The Reverend Robert Batte was a fellow and Vicar Master of University College, Oxford.

William Batte of Surry was a brother of Captain John Batte of Virginia. Also he had another brother in Virginia, one Henry Batte. He and his brother Henry assigned 300 acres of land in James City, on Chickahominy River, to Thomas Symons, June 8, 1639.

In 1666, William Batte witnessed a deed in Surry from Nathan Stanton to Captain Thomas Swann (B. 1, p. 281). In 1668 his name was in the list of Southwark Tithables which seems to be his last appearance in the records.

A full account of James Mason, Surry's other Burgess in 1654 is given in an account of the Mason family hereafter.

In the session of 1657-8 for the House, the only new Burgess was Captain William Caufield. In 1652, Major Robert Shepard sold "Lieutenant" William Caufield 1,100 acres of land. This was afterwards confirmed to him in a patent dated March 4, 1656 in which he was called "Captain" William Caufield (C. P. 342). The land was located on Lawne's Creek and had been originally patented by William Spencer. In his next patent, for 550 acres, dated January 24, 1662, he is designated as "Major" William Caufield.

Major Caufield also represented Surry in the House in 1659 and 1660. He died intestate, left one son, Robert, and a daughter, Elizabeth, who married William Seward. Robert Caufield was Burgess for Surry in 1676. He married Elizabeth, sister of Arthur Allen, 2nd, and died in 1691. She married, secondly, Joseph John Jackman, sometime Sheriff of Surry.

Robert Caufield, in his will dated January 2, 1691, leaves many legacies as he had no children. He gave his "niece Elizabeth, wife of William Holt", land bought of William Gray; "niece Mary, wife to James Bruton", land purchased of John Rogers; "nephew John Seward, land left me by my father on Hog Island." (B. 4, p. 240.) These two "nieces" and one "nephew" were respectively daughters and son of William Seward who made his will March 16, 1702-03, same probated May 4, 1703. He names his daughters, Mary Bruton and Elizabeth Holt. (B. 5, p. 275.) His son, John Seward, had predeceased him in 1699. (B. 5, p. 186.)

From 1661 to 1676 Governor Berkeley ordered no new elections for Burgesses. The General Assembly which served during this time was known as the "Long Parliament". It was not until Bacon's Rebellion had begun to spread that Berkeley yielded to popular calmor and issued writs for an election of Burgesses. He said in a proclamation that although he must testify to the ability and services of the present burgesses yet "Finding by too frequent complaints that the so long continuance of the present Assembly is looked upon as a grievance, he most regretfully did dissolve them."

The only new Burgesses who appeared for Surry in the House during this long time were Captain William Cockerham who served in 1663; Captain Lawrence Baker who served from 1666 to 1676; and William Browne who served in 1673. Accounts of Captain William Cockerham and William Browne are shown in the history of their families. (Post.)

Captain Lawrence Baker, who served ten years in the House, apparently had no sons, and only one daughter, Catherine, who married Arthur Allen II of Surry. Captain Baker was a Justice from 1652 to his death in 1681. He gave his wife one-third of his estate and his daughter the other two-thirds.

Chapter XII

AMERICA'S FIRST TAX STRIKE

THE BIRTHPLACE OF INDEPENDENCE

SEVERAL communities in the United States have claimed that their particular place was the "Birthplace of Freedom" because early in colonial times its citizens made protests against the payment of unjust and burdensome taxes.

We wish to advance the claim of Lawne's Creek Parish Church in Surry County as the "Birthplace of Freedom" in America for some of its parishioners met there on December 12, 1673 "to declare they would not pay their public taxes."

There was no freedom of assembly in those days and this unusual and unauthorized meeting alarmed the authorities. Two Justices of the County Court, by virtue of an English statute nearly 300 years old which empowered Justices to inquire into such "Riots", ordered the sheriff to arrest these "seditious" people and bring them before the court for trial.

This was only a prelude to Bacon's Rebellion in 1676. Governor Berkeley was America's first modern dictator. It will be noted in the following chapter on the Rebellion, that his methods of obtaining absolute rule was somewhat like that of Huey Long's and governors of other states to whom subservient legislatures gave autocratic powers.

America's freedom was not won by a single stroke. It was of slow growth, as typified by this and other like protests made from time to time, until it finally burst forth in a greater rebellion than Bacon's, the American Revolution.

But let us get along with the story. On January 3, 1673-74, following the gathering at Lawne's Creek Church, Lawrence Baker and Robert Spencer, Justices of the County Court issued the following writ which was recorded January 13, 1673: (Bk. 2, p. 40.) "Of how dangerous consequence unlawful assemblies and meetings have been is evident by the choronicles of our native country which are occasioned by a giddy headed multitude, and unless restrained may prove the ruin of a country, and therefore we, LAWRENCE BAKER and ROBERT SPENCER, two of ye justices of this county, being informed that on about the 12th of December last past, a company of seditious and rude people to the

number of 14 did unlawfully assemble at the Parish Church of Lawne's
Creek, with intent to declare they would not pay their public taxes, and
they expected divers others to meet them, who failing they did not put
their wicked design in execution, and for the good law made against
Rogues and Riots and particularly the Statute of 13 Henry IV, chapter
7, and injoining Justices to inquire of such meetings, we therefore sent
our warrant to the Sheriff of this county to Cause,

Matthew Swan	John Barnes	William Hancock
William Tooke	Robert Lacy	John Gregory
Thomas Clay	Michael Upchurch	John Sheppard
George Peters	William Little	John Greene
James Chessett		

to appear before us, yet the said persons not being satisfied with this
former unlawful meeting, did this day, the greatest part of them meet
together in ye old field called 'Devil's Old Field', and as we justly
suspect did confederate not to discover who were the first instigators or
moved them to their unlawful assembling as afore and we upon their
examination to find they have unanimously agreed to justify their meetings, persisting in the same as appears by the open declaring of Roger
Delke that if one suffers they would all burn, and we find their con-
temptuous behavior and carriage not respecting authority; have therefore committed ye persons aforesaid to the custody of the Sheriff, until
they find security for their appearance at the next County Court and
also for keeping the peace which we conceive consonant to the law in
such cases, and ye mutinous persons aforesaid being so many in number.
We have by Virtue of the Statute of ye 2d of Henry 5th command ye
aide and assistance of several of the neighborhood for their security.
Given under our hands the day and year aforesaid." (Book 2, p. 40.)

Many of the above fourteen men were respectable landowners.
Matthew Swan was perhaps related to Col. Thomas Swann, one of the
most prominent men in the county at the time and a member of the
Council. William Tooke was the son of James Tooke of Isle of Wight
County, who had served in the House of Burgesses. Thomas Clay was
connected with the family of John and William Corker, burgesses and
prominent in the early history of the county. John Barnes was a Quaker
and a fairly prosperous man, who later married Mr. Tooke's widow.
William Hancock married Elizabeth, daughter of Nicholas Spencer, and
a relative of the same Capt. Robert Spencer who caused his arrest.

Roger Delke was the son of Roger Delke, Sr., who had been Burgess for Stanley Hundred in the session of 1632-33. John Gregory was the step-father of Roger Delke, Jr., as he had married Alice Delke his mother.

The depositions of all fourteen of the above men are recorded immediately after the above warrant from Capts. Spencer and Baker (id., pp. 40-41). That of James Chessett was the first: "James Chessett being this day at ye house of Capt. Law. Baker & coming with Thirteen psons who were summoned to appeare there to give an acct. of theire Rioutous or unlawful Assemblying att ye Church of Lawnes Creeke on ye 12th Xbr. Last, & for yt ye sd Chessett was not summoned, but comeing with ye Rest, he was brought before us ye subscribed, & being asked who gave him notice to come with ye Rest, he said he came of his own Simple head; he was also asked If he was of them yt mett at ye Church, he Answered 'yes', he being (asked?) why he invited Geo. Peetrs to yt meeting, he said it was to see his neighbors, soe yt he seemes premptorily to give an acct. of ye first pmoter or Instigator of that meeting."

He was followed by Roger Delke who "being this day brought before us the subscribed, and complaint being made to us by William Sherwood, sub sheriff of this county, the said Delke did this day say that 'we will burne all before one shall suffer.' Ye said Delke acknowledged he said ye same words, and being asked why they met at the church he said by reason their taxes were so unjust and they would not pay it. He was demanded who was the person that invited him to meet, he peremptorily denied; but ye said Delke on his own behalf and on the behalf of the others then met did declare their meeting was to be relieved from payment of Drams and Cyder which they never had. All the rest assented to what he said save only Michael Upchurch."

Robert Lacy then deposed that William Hancock took him to the meeting at the Devil's Field, though he was warned to the contrary, and that John Barnes, Michael Upchurch, John Greene and John Sheppard were also there. He also said that he was at the meeting at the church, about which John Sheppard told him. Thomas Clay deposed that William Hancock told him of the meeting and was the first to tell him that the levies were unreasonable. William Hancock denied who told him of the meeting. "very obstinately persisting."

George Peters testified that James Chessett asked him to go to the church. Then Michael Upchurch denied who told him of the meeting or that he knew of the business they met about.

Matthew Swan's testimony was as follows: "Matthew Swan being this day brought before us the subscribed and being asked why he and others met at the Church, the 12th Xber, last, he said it was to agree about a redress from their taxes which were heavy. He was asked how he knew their taxes were unreasonably laid, he said Mr. Mason (Francis Mason, one of the justices) told him and also Mr. Goring said the same, and that there were some extraordinary taxes, he being demanded what discourse he and Mr. Goring had about the meeting, he said Mr. Goring said he would be there if he did not go from home, and the said Swan have also very obstinately persisted in the Lawlessness of the meeting, and said that all or most of the Country were of his mind."

John Greene in his deposition denied who instigated him to go meeting. William Little said that he went with John Barnes, but denied who instigated him to go. John Sheppard agreed with the others to meet at the church "to be redressed from their Levys"; he said that he heard from Samuel Cornell that the levies were unjust, and that Cornll said Mr. Holt (*i.e.*, Randall Holt) told him so.

John Barnes then being called denied who said first that the levies were unreasonable and said that he heard it from everybody. William Tooke also denied knowing who said first that the levies were unreasonable.

The examination was concluded by the deposition of Francis Taylor, a person not involved. "The deposition of Francis Taylor being called before Capt. Law. Baker, Mr. Robert Caufield, and Capt. Robert Spencer to swear his true knowledge concerning a meeting of some of the Parish on Friday 12 Xbr., 1673, at Lawne's Creek Parish Church is as follows: 'That being at my lodging—looking out I espyed John Gregory going through the Field, and called him to desire him to make me a waistcoate, which he told me he would, but he asked me if I would not be at the Church for there was to be a great part of the Parish meeting there this morning concerning ye Levys. I told him I knew nothing of it, neither was I concerned in it, as being no house-keeper, but I did not much care if I went with him to see what was done. He told me he was going to Mr. Caufield's to take measure of one of his men, to make his freedom clothes and he would holler for me as he came back, which accordingly he did and we went together. When we came there we found about halfe a score men sitting there, and asking them how they did, and what they met for they said they did expect some more to come intending civilly to treate concerning the Levy for they did understand that there was several officers to be paid tobacco out of the Levy, which they knew no reason for, by reason they were put to as much trouble and expense as they were. Colonel Swan was to have 5000 lbs. tbco. for the officers and the Colonel was to be levied on this parish only. Their company not meeting yet they stayed there about an hour, and so resolved to speake about it on the next Sabbath being sermon day. In the Interior on Saturday, I being at Mr. Sherwood's (the sub-sheriff) requested him to see the list of the Levy which he did show me and there I saw the charge was levied on the whole county. Which I spoke of at the Church, they hearing said no more, and further saith not." (Book 2, pp. 42-3.)

This simple meeting of citizens to complain about their taxes seems to be a "tempest in a tea pot" from a 20th century standpoint. However, it appears to have been regarded as an extremely serious matter in 17th century Virginia under Berkeley's autocratic rule.

The case was speedily disposed of as follows at a court held for Surry County January 6, 1673/4 (O. B. 1671-90, p. 42): "for that they were sorry for their offence & were no projectors of ye same, John Gregory, Robert Lacy, James Chessett, Thos. Clay, Michll Uuchurch, Wm. Tooke, Wm. Little and John Greene be ordered committed until they give bond for their future good behaviour and pay costs and be dismist." (George Peters seems to have been unintentionally omitted from the above list.) John Barnes, John Sheppard, and William Hancock were ordered to "be committed untill they give ye like bond and pay each of them one Thousand pounds tobo. fine, to ye use of his Majesty, and pay costs." Roger Delke "altho he were noe Ring Leader in ye faction, yet for saying after much fair admonicon yt if one of them suffered they would burne all, he shall stand Comitted untell he give ye Like bond and pay ye Like fine of 1000 pds. of tobo. wth costs." ... "& for ye sd Mathew Swan was a Chief projector of ye design & being asked if he were Convinced & said yt ye Cort had unjustly proceeded in ye sd Levy & Charged ye Cort therewth at ye Barr, it is therefore order'd that he stand Comitted untell he give bond for his good abearing wth security for his appearance at ye 3'd day of ye next Genrall Cort before ye Right Honourable ye Governour & Councell for his Dangerous Contempt & Unlawful project & his wicked Prsisting in ye same; & being called again one by one & strictly

Examined how & by whome ye sd unlawfull Assembly was projected & sett on foot; it appearing yt ye sd Mathew Swan, Jno. Barnes, Jno. Sheppard and Wm. Hancock at ye house of ye sd Jno. Barnes did first resolve & conclude upon ye meeting & yt ye rest (with a great many more whome they intended to prsuade were only drawne on from ye beginning)."

The case of Matthew Swan was finally brought before the Council and General Court of Virginia on the afternoon of April 6, 1674 and settled as follows: "It is ordered that the order of Surry Court Against the mutinuss Psons he Confirmed and that Mathew Swan the ringleader of them, who was bound over to the Court be Fined Two Thousand pounds of tobacco and Caske and that all fines of the Psons goe towards the ffort at James Citty And that they pay all Just Costs and Charges." (Minutes of Council and General Court, p. 367.)

This, however, did not end the matter, for there is always a court of public opinion to which even dictators sometimes bow. This action caused so much resentment among the colonists that Governor Berkeley found it advisable to remit the fines which he finally did on September 23, 1674. (W. M. 23, p. 122.)

It is significant that these events occurred a full two years before the outbreak of the Rebellion, and the case indicates the discontent of the people and their sullen attitude toward their rulers. Only Lawnes Creek Parish men were involved in the above. When the actual rebellion broke out, most of those involved with Bacon—in fact, a very large majority—were inhabitants of Southwark, the other parish in Surry. Perhaps the spirit of the Lawnes Creek men had been broken by the condemnation of Matthew Swan and his colleagues.

Matthew Swan, the ringleader of this protest against high taxes, has many descendants in Virginia and the South. In 1675 he married Mrs. Mary Spiltimber, widow of Anthony Spiltimber and daughter of Robert Harris. His will was dated December 14, 1702 and probated Jan. 5, 1702/. He mentioned daughter, Elizabeth, wife of John Drew, daughter, Sarah; Elizabeth, daughter of John Drew; son-in-law, John Drew; daughter, Mary, wife of William Phillips; and grandson, John Phillips. Executors were John Drew and Sarah Swann. Witnesses were Arthur Allen, William Chambers, John Allen, and Robert Ruffin.

Children:

I. Elizabeth, m. (1) John Drew, d. 1703. (See Drew.) (2) John Sugars. (No children.)

II. Mary, m. William Phillips of Surry County, Va., who in his will dated Feb. 14, 1720/21, probated April 19, 1721, mentioned wife, Mary; sons, John, William, Swann, and Mathew Phillips (the three last named under 16 years of age); and daughters, Anne, Mary, and Elizabeth Phillips. Executors were wife, Mary, and sons, William and Swann Phillips. Witnesses: Joseph Wattell, William Newsum, Carter Crafford.

III. Sarah, m. Carter Crafford (1682 ?-1743). (See Crafford.)

Chapter XIII

SURRY COUNTY IN BACON'S REBELLION

BY B. C. HOLTZCLAW

THE story of Bacon's Rebellion in the colony of Virginia in 1676 has been told elsewhere. One of the best accounts is the almost contemporary one entitled the "True Narrative of the Rise, Progress and Cessation of the Late Rebellion in Virginia" by the Commissioners sent over from England by Charles II to settle affairs in Virginia. This is published in Volume IV of the *Virginia Magazine of History and Biography*. Mrs. Mary Newton Stanard's *The Story of Bacon's Rebellion* is a good modern account, and a recent interesting work on the rebellion is Wertenbaker's *Torch-bearer of the Revolution*. Our purpose here is to tell the story of Surry County's rôle in this early struggle. We shall, therefore, not attempt to enter too fully into the events of the rebellion elsewhere, although it will be necessary to give some account of the causes and history of the whole movement in order to understand the part played by Surry.

The deepest rooted causes of the rebellion were the long-standing economic, social and political grievances of the common people of Virginia. The English Navigation Acts of 1651 and 1660, restricting colonial trade to English vessels, had for many years forced the planters of Virginia to sell their products to home monopolists at the latter's own prices. This had depressed the price of tobacco, Virginia's chief export, till in the 1670's, according to one writer, it had become almost worthless. With this lowering of income there was a steady increase in taxation, which was assessed upon the common people without their advice or consent. Government had become more and more a close oligarchy in Virginia, concentrated in the hands of Sir William Berkeley, the royal governor, for the benefit of himself, his favorites, and the small ruling cliques in the various counties. The governor had kept the Assembly of 1662, which was strongly royalist, in office for many years by adjourning the meetings from year to year and preventing new elections. The justices of the counties were appointed by the Governor; the vestrymen of the parishes were self-perpetuating bodies continuing from year to year; and these two bodies assessed the county and parish levies arbitrarily without the people having a voice in the matter. The government at James City was expensive, and corruption and favoritism were strongly suspected. The Assembly of 1670 had abolished manhood suffrage and had substituted a property qualification for voting. Added to all these grievances there were complaints against overbearing tax-collectors, excessive fees demanded by sheriffs and county clerks, and money wasted and embezzled in public works which the people had to pay for through taxation. These were the underlying causes of the rebellion and they manifested themselves even before the outbreak of that movement. In 1667 the small planters were reported to be on the point of rebelling, and in 1673 there were movements in various counties to protest against the taxes.

Due to the disturbances of 1676, no list of tithables for Surry County is recorded for that year. The list of 1675 (Book 2, pp. 92-4), however, gives us some idea of the state of the county at the time of the outbreak of the rebellion. 434 tithables are shown, 194 of these being in Lawnes Creek Parish, and 240 in the larger parish of Southwark. No white women were tithable and no white males under 16 years of age. The majority of the heads of families appear to have been small planters, mostly owning their own land. Probably half of them had establishments large enough to have one or more servants or helpers. One is surprised at the large number of white servants or hired laborers, but we must remember that negro slavery was far from the flourishing institution that it became in the 18th century, and there were still hundreds of people coming over annually from Great Britain and taking their place in Virginia as indentured servants in order to pay their passage money. Only 30 negro slaves appear among the tithables of 1675 in the whole county, although there may have been a few more, as Mr. Benjamin Harrison's list for part of Southwark Parish does not specify the character of the tithables, and the same is true for a few other households in other sections of the county. As far as the list of 1675 shows, negroes were owned only by Col. Thomas Swann, Major William Browne, John Pulistone, Francis Mason and Nicholas Meriwether in Southwark Parish; and by Peter Dale, Capt. Lawrence Baker, Robert Ruffin, William Newsum, Arthur Allen, Robert Caufield and John Goring in Lawnes Creek Parish. Several of the above owned only one negro, though most of them had additional white servants. The largest number of negroes was owned by Francis Mason, who had 7 at his plantation in Southwark, and 2 more at another plantation in Lawnes Creek, though some of these may have been owned by his stepson, Thomas Binns. Judging from the tithables, as well as other records, the wealthiest men in Southwark Parish appear to have been Lieut.-Col. George Jordan, Attorney-General of Virginia, with 7 tithable servants; Rev. William Thompson, the minister, with 6 white servants; Col. Thomas Swann, Member of the Council, with 3 white servants and 2 negro slaves; and Francis Mason, with 6 white servants and 7 negroes in Southwark, and 2 negroes in Lawnes Creek. Capt. Robert Spencer had 4 white tithable servants, and Nicholas Meriwether had four also, one white and 3 negroes. Other rather prosperous people appear to have been Christopher Foster (nephew of Col. Jordan), Drs. Nathaniel Knight and George Lee, Lt. Thomas Busby, William Rookings (later to meet a tragic fate in the Rebellion), Benjamin Harrison and his mother Mrs. Mary Sidway, William Simmons and his mother Mary Simmons (he also being later involved in the Rebellion), William Edwards (who held the lucrative position of Clerk of the County Court since the death of Capt. George Watkins in 1673), Major William Browne with 3 negro slaves, John Pulistone (also involved in the Rebellion), and John Solway, who owned the Warren or "Rolfe" House. In Lawnes Creek Parish, the wealthiest men seem to have been Capt. Lawrence Baker with 4 white tithable servants and 2 negroes, Arthur Allen with 4 white servants and 4 negroes, Robert Caufield with 5 white servants and 1 negro, and John Goring with 3 white servants and 1 negro. Others fairly well-to-do were: Richard Drew, Richard Harris, Peter Dale, Joseph Rogers (a tanner, later involved in Bacon's Rebellion), Capt. Samuel Swann (son of Col. Thomas Swann), Walter Bartlett, Charles Amry, John Barnes (connected with the unfortunate tax-gathering in 1673), Robert Ruffin (who had married the wealthy widow of Capt. George Watkins), William Newsum, William Chambers, David Williams, Randall Holt, and Capt. Charles Barham.

On the whole, there appears to have been no vast wealth in the county in 1676, though the above figures for tithables in the various households must be augmented by fairly numerous female servants in the wealthier families, as well as white servant boys under 16. Some of the families were certainly in extremely comfortable circumstances and owned a large amount of costly furniture and household goods. The inventory of Capt. George Watkins in 1673 shows a surprising wealth in furniture and goods; and Arthur Allen is stated to have been plundered of personal property amounting to 1,000 pounds sterling during the time that the Baconians held his house during the Rebellion (*Va. Mag.* V, 67). On the other hand, many of the people were poor, either owning no land or working their own plantations without the assistance of indentured servants or slaves. At least 135 of the heads of households in 1675, out of a total of 238 families, had no tithable white servants nor negro slaves. Many, also, were indentured servants and hired laborers. It was the class of small planters on whom the burden of taxation rested most heavily and in whom the seeds of rebellion found a most fertile planting ground.

The real rulers of the county in 1676 were practically identical with the wealthier men. The two most prominent persons were Col. Thomas Swann, Member of the Governor's Council, and Lieutenant Colonel George Jordan, Attorney-General of Virginia. Both were elderly men, Col. Swann being 60 years of age. Col. Jordan and Capt. Lawrence Baker had been members of Governor Berkeley's "long" Assembly since 1674. It had been Berkeley's policy since 1662 not to have new elections, but to keep the same Burgesses by adjourning the same Assembly from year to year. However, there had been several changes in the Surry Burgesses because of death. Thomas Warren and William Cockerham were the burgesses in 1660/61; by 1666 William Cockerham had been replaced by Lawrence Baker, and William Browne appears with Baker in 1673, being succeeded by Col. Jordan in 1674 (*Journals of the House of Burgesses,* 1659/60-1693, p. viii). The justices, in the order of their appointment to the Commission, were as follows: Lieutenant-Colonel George Jordan, Capt. Lawrence Baker, Major William Browne, Capt. Charles Barham, Mr. Robert Caufield, Capt. Robert Spencer, Mr. Benjamin Harrison, Mr. Nicholas Meriwether, Capt. Samuel Swann, Mr. Arthur Allen, and Mr. Francis Mason. They and their families had long been powers in the county. Major Browne had been a Burgess, and was the son-in-law of Col. Henry Browne, a Member of the Council in earlier days; Robert Caufield was the son of William Caufield, who had served as a Burgess, and Benjamin Harrison's father had also been a Burgess during his lifetime. Capt. Samuel Swann was the son of Col. Thomas Swann. Arthur Allen was the son-in-law of Capt. Baker. Francis Mason's father, James Mason of "Merry Mount", had been a Burgess. It appears that during the critical last days of the Rebellion they all remained faithful to Governor Berkeley (with the possible doubtful exception of the two Swanns), as the Governor on March 31, 1677 reappointed them all to office, naming on the Quorum Col. Jordan, Capt. Baker and Major Browne (who were apparently already on it), and adding to the Quorum Robert Caufield in place of Capt. Swann, and Arthur Allen, now called Captain Allen (Book 2, p. 120). William Edwards was Clerk of the Court, he being the son of an earlier William Edwards who had served as a Burgess from Surry. Capt. Samuel Swann was High Sheriff in 1676, and John Solway, owner of the Warren House, was Sub-sheriff (O. B. 1671-90, p. 125). Rev. William Thompson was minister of Southwark Parish, and probably also of Lawnes Creek. Thomas Busby was a Lieutenant of the militia (*id.*, p. 119), and Roger Potter, who had been a Lieutenant in 1675, was now promoted to Captain. Whether the aged Thomas Pittman, Sr., who is mentioned in documents both as Lieutenant and Captain, was still an active militia officer, is doubtful. All three of the last named were from Southwark Parish and Pittman was one of Bacon's men in the Rebellion.

We have mentioned that the deep-seated cause of the movement known as Bacon's Rebellion was economic and political. The immediate cause of its outbreak in 1676 was a series of Indian raids on outlying settlements in 1675. Governor Berkeley had himself taken the field against the Indians in the wars thirty years before, and the colonists appealed to him now for aid. The Governor, however, had a profitable fur trade monopoly with the Indians which brought him a large income and which he did not wish to disturb. He was appealed to early in 1676, but refused to declare war, postponing any action till the meeting of an Assembly which he called in March, 1675/6. The Indian raids grew worse, and by March it is said that over 300 whites had been massacred by the savages, and indignation with the Governor ran high, particularly in the border counties of Stafford in the north, and Henrico and Charles City in the south and west. When the Assembly met in March, it remained subservient to the Governor, and limited its action to levying 500 men from the counties for military service and ordering the construction of nine forts for the protection of the colonists. They were to be erected on the Potomac in Stafford County, the Rappahannock in Gloucester County, the Mattapony in New Kent County, at Mahixon on the Pamunkey River in York County, on the James River in James City County, the Appomattox in Charles City County, the Black Water in Surry County, at Currawaugh probably in Nansemond County, and in Accomac County on the Eastern Shore. Most of these forts appear to have been perfectly useless for the purpose in hand, as there seems to have been no danger from the Indians in many of the locations. In this regard, the building of the Accomac fort seems especially ridiculous, and so were several of the others. Even in the border counties, the people claimed that the forts gave them no real protection, and later on it was claimed that in many cases the contractors, who were Berkeley's favorites, embezzled the money and even failed to build the forts, or left them unfinished. The people in the border counties needed a punitive evxpedition against the Indians to protect them, but Berkeley and the Assembly forbade any such attack on the enemy without the Governor's specific order, which he was not likely to give. As a climax, two million pounds of tobacco were added to the people's taxes for building these forts, which they felt to be useless.

Surry's Burgesses in this Assembly were the old ones, George Jordan and Lawrence Baker. For the fort in Surry County the order was for "fforty men in the county of Surry to be garrisoned at one ffort or defenceable place neare Richard Atkins upon the *black water* in the same county of Surry, of which ffort captain Roger Potter to be captain or cheife commander" (Hening *Statutes*, II, p. 318). 180 pounds of powder and 440 pounds of shot were ordered to the Black Water fort (*id.*, p. 329), and Col. Thomas Swan and Lt.-Col. George Jordan were ordered to make choice of the garrison and impress the men and provisions for the fort (*id.*, p. 330). One wonders as to the identity of these men, and whether any of them later followed Bacon. It is interesting to note that exactly forty men received the act of pardon in Surry County, February 6, 1676/7, and that they were nearly all from Southwark Parish, where the fort was located. It is probable that this was one of the useless forts. There were Indians to the far south in Surry, but we find no record that they were making trouble. This is indicated, also, by the fact that the appropriation for ammunition for the Black Water fort was the smallest of all the nine with the single exception of that on Currawaugh Swamp in Isle of Wight or Nansemond County. The trouble in Surry was not with the Indians, but was economic and political.

It was far different in the border countieso, where the people felt that the government had failed them in its primary duty, that of protection against external aggression. In the month of April, 1676, the people of Charles City County, who with the people of Henrico had

borne the brunt of the Indian raids, gathered together and sent deputies
to the Governor, John Lanier and John Woodlief, begging that he
would permit them to take the field against the Indians at their own
expense, but Berkeley refused this and other like petitions and forbade
the people to make any further requests of the sort. Indignation ran
high and 300 men gathered in Charles City County resolved to make a
punitive expedition against the Indians without the Governor's consent.
They only lacked a leader, when at this juncture they were visited by
Nathaniel Bacon, a young squire of Henrico County and a member of
Berkeley's Council, who rowed across the river with several other
Henrico gentlemen to the meeting. Bacon was acclaimed their leader,
accepted the place offered him by the enthusiastic band, and late in the
month of April, he and his army started out against the southern and
western Indians without the Governor's authority. Thus began the
rebellion in the proper sense of the word—a rebellion not against the
King nor the law, but against a tyrannical governor and an oppressive
government indifferent to the people's needs. I can find no record of
any Surry men who were in this first expedition. No doubt the people
of Surry, like a great many others over the colony, although not immediately affected by danger from the Indians, were thoroughly sympathetic with the rebels' action against the hated savages. And they
already had cause for indignation against the Governor and his clique.

Berkeley immediately started raising a force to stop Bacon, but
arrived in Charles City too late, as the expedition had already started.
On May 10, however, he issued a proclamation declaring Bacon a rebel
and a traitor. But the people of the colony were now thoroughly roused,
and it looked as though rebellion were about to break out behind him
in other counties because of both the Indian troubles and the long-
standing grievances against the government. The Governor, therefore,
on May 18, reluctantly ordered an election for a new House of Burgesses, the first in fourteen years, as a sop to the popular discontent.
Late in the month Bacon and his troops returned, having gone far to
the southwest, to the Roanoke River, and won a decisive victory over
the Indians there. He and his men were enthusiastically greeted, and
he was almost immediately elected to the new Assembly as one of the
Burgesses from Henrico County, in spite of the fact that he was
technically a rebel. Surry County for this new Assembly of June, 1676,
which was later to be known as Bacon's Assembly, elected two new
men, younger members of the Commission of Justices, namely, Robert

Caufield and Francis Mason (*Journal of the House of Burgesses,* 1659/
60-1693, p. viii).

The months of June and July, 1676 offer the brightest spots in the
gloomy history of the Rebellion, for during a large part of that time
Bacon and Berkeley were, at least outwardly, reconciled and coöperat-
ing. The story of Bacon's taking his seat in the Assembly, of his reconciliation with Berkeley, of Berkeley's plot to seize him, of Bacon's escape
and return at the head of armed forces, of a second reconciliation, and
of Berkeley's final reluctant grant of a commission to Bacon as Commander-in-Chief and General for the prosecution of the Indian war,
makes interesting reading, but we shall not deal with it here. Our main
interest is the Assembly, which took its seat on June 5th and adjourned
probably on June 25th, when news of an Indian massacre in New Kent
County not forty miles from James City, caused Bacon to depart to
prosecute the Indian war, after filling out thirty blank commissions
handed him, signed, by Berkeley, for officers in his army.

The first act of the new Assembly, which was dominated by Bacon
and the reform party, was to make adequate provisions "for carrying
on warre against the barbarous Indians" (Hening, *Statutes,* II, pp. 341-
349). An army of 1,000 men was ordered to be raised by levy (if
Bacon could not find sufficient volunteers) to be maintained and paid
by their respective counties, the men to have liberty to nominate their
own officers. We note that Surry County was to raise thirty-two men
for this levy. The second Act of the Assembly was one prohibiting
trade with the Indians, an obvious attack on Berkeley's fur monopoly
(*id.,* p. 350). More interesting to us are the Acts instituting govern-
mental reforms. County sheriffs and under-sheriffs were not to hold
office more than one year in succession, and the sheriff's place was to
devolve on the justices in rotation. No person was to hold the offices of
sheriff, clerk, surveyor or escheator at the same time. A heavy fine was
enacted for clerks and other officials who exacted more than their legal
fees. County courts were to appoint and dismiss their clerks at pleasure
(a privilege apparently not hitherto granted them). Vestrymen in the
parishes, instead of being self-perpetuating bodies, were to be elected
once every three years; and the Act of 1670 forbidding freemen to vote
for burgesses was repealed, and all freemen to vote as formerly together with freeholders and householders. Representatives of the
people, equal in number to the county justices and elected by parishes,
were to sit with the Justices when the taxes were assessed and were to

have equal votes with the Justices. No member of the Governor's Council was to be allowed to sit in the County Courts, and the families of Councillors and ministers of the Established Church were to pay levies like other people, and no longer to be exempted from taxation. It was thus that the new Assembly adjusted the grievances of Mathew Swan and the "mutinous persons" of 1673. Virginia would have been a happier place in the following years had these laws been allowed to stay on the statute books. They were all repealed, however, in Berkeley's reactionary Assembly of Feb., 1676/7. A curious prohibition law was also enacted by Bacon's Assembly. All ordinaries and ale-houses were to be suppressed throughout the colony except three, one at James City and one on each side the York River at the ferries. These latter were to sell only beer and cider, and no other strong drink. Any seller of strong drink after Sept. 10, 1676 was to be fined 1,000 pounds of tobacco. Just what was the reason for this law, it is hard to determine, though we are reminded of Roger Delke's testimony in Surry County in Jan., 1673/4, that the meeting at Lawnes Creek Church was "to be relieved from payment of Drams and Cyder which they never had." The Assembly of June, 1676 finally closed with an act of general pardon and oblivion for treason, murders, etc. committed between Mar. 1st and June 25th, 1676; and a final act, disabling Edward Hill and John Stith of Charles City County from holding any office. It is interesting that Berkeley had ardent partisans in the counties on both sides of Surry. Col. Hill and Mr. Stith are here singled out as violent anti-Baconians in Charles City. Later on, Col. Joseph Bridger of Isle of Wight County was mentioned especially as one of Berkeley's "wicked and pernicious councellors" in a "Declaration of the People against Berkeley" made later on in the summer by the Baconians (*Calendar of Transcripts, Va. Dept. of Archives, Eggleston Manuscripts*, pp. 21-24). Col. Bridger, also, appears to have accompanied Berkeley on his first flight to the Eastern Shore in the latter part of July, and complaint of him is made by name in the "Grievances of Isle of Wight Co.", made in 1677. The only man connected with Surry who is mentioned as a "wicked councellor" in the "Declaration" was William Sherwood, who had lived for several years in Surry and had been sub-sheriff in 1674; but he was living at James City in 1676, and someone apparently scratched out his name in the final draft of the declaration. Although several of the wealthier men in Surry went away when Berkeley fled the second time from Bacon in September, if anything, it appears, as

we shall see later, that all Surry was pro-Baconian, at least until the
burning of Jamestown on September 19.

The month of July was spent by Bacon in gathering his army for the
Indian War under the commission reluctantly granted him by the
Governor. We have no record of Surry County during this period. In
fact except for two significant entries in August, 1676, the Order Book
of the County Court has no entries from May, 1676 till February 17,
1676/7. Doubtless this was due to the turbulent conditions and the
prevalence of the military authority in the colony over the civil. Probably during these days the Baconian forces in Surry were organized,
and Bacon's commissions granted to the Surry leaders, Major William
Rookings, Capt. Arthur Long, Lieutenant Robert Burgess and Ensign
William Simmons. All the above were from Southwark Parish except
Arthur Long. It will be noted that all this military organization was
perfectly legal, being in accordance with the orders of the Assembly of
June 1676, and under Berkeley's commission. At the end of the month,
however, the Governor plunged the colony into real civil war by again
proclaiming Bacon a rebel and traitor, trying unsuccessfully to organize
a force against the Baconians in Gloucester County, and finally fleeing
to the Eastern Shore, where the inhabitants were not threatened by the
Indians and were more docile to their Berkeleian masters. At just this
time, Bacon had finally completed his preparations and with his army
was on the point of starting a new expedition against the western
Indians. He and his troops turned back from the Falls of the James,
however, to oppose the Governor in Gloucester; but the latter's flight
left Bacon in sole control of all Virginia except the Eastern Shore,
where at the home of Col. John Custis, Berkeley and his henchmen
were collecting troops and organizing war against him. This left the
major part of Virginia in a cruel condition of divided allegiance. On
the one hand, Berkeley had the authority of the King in the colony;
on the other, Bacon was backed by the Governor's own commission and
by the legal authority of the June Assembly. And now these two were
at open war. Many of the chief men of the Western Shore fled with
Berkeley, but none from Surry County.

Now that there was open war declared, Bacon had two tasks before
him. From the military side, he now had the task, not only of defeating
the Indians, but of crushing the Governor as well. On the political side,
he had the problem of consolidating the country, including the leading
men, behind him. The month of August marked advance toward both

goals. On August 1, realizing the importance of naval action in the war, Bacon, having captured two ships lying off Jamestown, despatched them with an armed contingent to wage war against Berkeley on the Eastern Shore. An Indian massacre occurred in New Kent County, and most of the latter part of the month and the early days of September was taken up with an expedition against the Indians in that neighborhood, which finally resulted in the crushing of the Pamunkey Indians, the Governor's protegees. From the standpoint of Surry County, Bacon's political action is most interesting. On August 3, 1676 he assembled at the house of Major Otho Thorpe in York County as many of the prominent men of the colony as he could gather, and after exerting some pressure on them, secured the signatures of sixty-nine of them to the following document (*Eggleston Manuscripts*, pp. 36-38, *Calendar of Transcripts, Va. Dept. of Archives*):

Declaration of the people of Virginia concerning the adherence with Bacon.

"Whereas the Country hath raised an Army against our common Enemies the Indians and putt the same under the Command of Nathaniel Bacon Esqr Generall, being upon the point to march forth against the said common Enemy, hath been diverted, and necessitated to move, to the suppresssing of forces, by evill disposed psons raised ag^t the said Gener^{ll} Bacon, purposely to foment and stirr up civill warre amongst us, to the ruine of his Maj^{ties} Country: and whereas it is notoriously manifest, that Sr Wm Berkeley kn^t Govern^r of ye Country assisted, councelled, and abetted by those evill disposed psons aforesaid, hath actually commanded, fomented and stirred up the people to the said civill warre, and failing of success herein, hath with drawn himself to the great astonishment of the people, and unsettlement of the Country: and whereas the said Army raised by the Countrie for the causes aforesaid are drawn downe, and remain full of dissatisfaction in the middle of the Country, expecting attempts from the designes of the said Governour, and his evill Councillours aforesaid: and noe proper means found out for the settlement of the distractions within and preventing the horrible outrages, and murders daily committed in many pts of the Country by the barbarous Enemy.

It hath been thought fitt by the said Generall, to call unto him all such sober and discreete Gentlemen: as the short exigence of ye distracted condition of the Country would admitt to the middle plantation, to consult and advice the settling of the peace of that Country, and the Gentleman of this 3ᵈ day of August 1676 accordingly have mett, and in order to the said settlement doe advice, resolve, and declare, and conclude, and for ourselves doe swear in manner following.

First that we will at all times joine wᵗʰ the sᵈ Nathaneel Bacon his Army, against the Common Enemy in all points whatsoever.

Whereas certain psons have lately contrived and designed the raising of forces agᵗ the said Generall, and the Army under his Command, thereby to begett a civill warre. We will endeavour the discovery and apprehending of all, & every those evill disposed psons, and then for to secure them, till farther order from the said Generall.

And whereas it is credibly reported, that the Governʳ hath informed the King's Maᵗʸ yᵗ yᵉ said Generall and the people of the Country in Armes under his command, their aiders and abettors are rebelling and removed from their Allegiance, and this and such information, hee the said Governʳ hath advised and petitioned the King, to send forces to reduce them; Wee doe farther declare beleive in our consciences, that it consists with the wellfare of his Maᵗⁱᵉˢ Countree, and yᵗ it is consistent wᵗʰ our Allegiance to his most sacred Maᵗʸ for us and every one of us the Inhabitants of Virginia to oppose, and suppresse all force whatsoever of that nature, untill such time as the king and his Councell be fully enformed of the States of the Case, by such pson or psons shall be sent from the said Nathaneel Bacon Genˡˡ, in the behalfe of the people; and the determination thereof to be remitted hither. And we doe swear yᵗ we will him the said Generall and the Army under his command, aid, and assist accordingly."

The first two signatures affixed to the above declaration are those of Thomas Swan and George Jordan. It is uncertain whether there were any other representatives of Surry County among these sixty-nine men, among whom were included Councillors and Burgesses, as well as Bacon's chief political advisers. The names of Thomas Clark, John Grey and John Butherford appear in the list, and it is possible that the first two are identical with Thomas Clark (later a Justice) and John Grey of Southwark Parish; while the name Butherford seems obviously a miscopy for John Rutherford of Southwark Parish, who was later indicted as a prominent Baconian.

Col. Jordan and the other possible Surry representatives to this meeting seem to have gone home by the following day, August 4. However, Col. Swann remained, and his is again the first signature to the following somewhat more extreme declaration signed by only twenty-nine gentlemen on that date (*id.*, pp. 39-41):

"Whereas certain informations is now made, that the Ammunition at the fort of Tindalls point is commanded away and putt aboard a ketch, and y^t ye great quantity of arms are removed & carried away out of Glocest^r County, and from Mr. Secretaries house at Richneck, and that certain psons in contempt of the Authority of Nathaneel Bacon Esqr Gener^{ll} appointed over the forces for the Indian warre, are in open hostility in the County of Westmoreland and the fort on the head of Rappahanack River; not surrendred to the said Gener^{lls} Command, And whereas it is much doubted, that severall psons lately fled, and also such as they can stirr up and arms with the Ammunition aforesaid, will fall in amongst some of the Northern Counties, or other defensible places to the diverting the forces aforesaid, from the defence of the Country, and engaging the Country in a civill warre, which threatens the utter ruine of this Country, if the same be not timely prevented. And whereas the said Generall hath demanded the Councell, and advice of us the Subscribers, what is fitt in this Exigence to be done, to prevent the universall ruine impending the distracted Country. Wee doe advise and request the ^{s}aid Generall, that as soon as may bee an Assembly may be summoned by some precepts or oth^r warran^{ts} or writts directed to the Counties from Some Gentlemen of ye Councell. And that in the meantime the civill Administracon of Justice may remain constant, & run in the same course and Channell as formerly, and that the Subscription^s made yesterday by the Gentlemen then summoned and mett together, there at the middle plantation to consult ye settling of the present distracions of the Country, bee sent to all the Counties in the Country, and y^t ye said Generall authorize fitting psons in those Counties, to take the said Subscriptions, and administer the said Oath. And lastly that the Generall and forces under him efectually prosecute as well the Indian warre, as by all meanes and waies oppose, suppresse, and wth open hostility prosecute all manner of psons whatsoever, their Confederates, Councellors, aidors, and abettors, that doe or hereafter shall combine, conspire, or attempt ag^t ye s^d Generall, or his the forces under his Command, or that shall disturb or raise tumults or otherwise impeach the domestick peace and Safety of the Country."

"Given at the middle Plantation aforesaid, this 4th of August 1676."

On August 11, 1676 Nathaniel Bacon, with the four members of the Governor's Council who had signed the "Declaration" of August 3, namely, Thomas Swann, Thomas Beale, Thomas Ballard and James Bray, sent a proclamation to the Sheriff of Westmoreland County, stating that since Governor Berkeley had absented himself from the government, he was under their authority to proceed to call an election of two representatives from Westmoreland to sit in a new assembly of the House of Burgesses, to meet at James City on September 4th, 1676. (*Sainsbury Abstracts,* Vol. XVI, p. 29.)

During the month of August, both the authorities and the common people of Surry County appear to have been thoroughly Baconian. Due probably to the prestige of Cols. Swann and Jordan, the following entries appear in the Order Book (1671-90) on pages 131 and 132:

"   Aug. 10, 1676

Present   Lt. Coll. Jordan

Majr. Browne)	Mr. Harrison)	
Capt. Barham	Mr. Meriwether	
Mr. Caufield	Mr. Mason	Coms.
Capt. Spencer	Mr. Allen	

At a meeting of ye Cort at Southwarke this day to Setle ye Com. in peace, according to ye Comand of ye Honoble Genll & having reced a Comand from him this day to pvide bread for our pporcion of three hundred men for a month, for ye Countrys service In pformance of ye sd Comand of ye Honble Nath. Bacon Esqr Genll It is Ordrd ytt every mr. of a family doe forthwith provide ffoure pds of good sound bisquett for every tithable in his ffamaley, and yt ye Mill do lay all private Grinding aside untill this be done, & yt all ye housekeeprs. in ye lower pish doe Carry in yr. pporcion of bread to ye House of Capt. Arthur Long, & all those in ye uper Pish to Carry their pporcion to ye house of Mr Wm Thompson, they being desired to receive & serve ye same, & yt it be all brought in to ye sd places by Thursday next being ye 17th Instant & this ordr to be forthwth published through ye County.

Vera Recordtur   Test W E Cl Cur."

It is noteworthy that all the Justices were present on this occasion save only Capts. Baker and Swann. Col. Thomas Swann sat with a Commission composed of Lt.-Col. Jordan, Major Browne, Capt. Swann, Mr. Caufield, and Capt. Spencer, on August 24, 1676, to enact the following order (p. 132):

> "In Order and Obedience to the Genll Ordr, It is Ordered that Every Master of a family in this county doe forthwith provide five pounds & a halfe of good sufficient Biskett for Every tithable pson in his ffamily, (also for Every tithable two pds & a halfe of dryed beefe or bacon if they have it, but if they have it not the said beefe or bacon, then they are to pay for theire pporcon to those psons that shall provide it)—the said Bread & meate being for our pporcon of two months provisions for our Souldrs undr the Comand of the sd Genll According to Act of Assembly, It is also ordered all the tithables below Ware Neck carry their pvissions to the Houses of Capt. Charles Barham & Mr. Francis Mason, & all above Ware Neck to the houses of Major Wm Browne & Doctor Nathll Knight, who are requested to receive & serve the same."

Surry County so far seems to have been united. We now come to the turbulent days of mid-September, 1676, when Berkeley's and Bacon's forces clashed in open war, and Surry County, like many others was split between Berkeleians and Baconians. Early in September, when Bacon and his wearied troops returned from the expedition against the Pamunkey Indians in the swamps of what is now King and Queen County, he found that Berkeley had by a ruse captured the small fleet sent against him, and himself embarking with troops on a number of ships, had reentered and seized Jamestown on September 7th or 8th. Bacon hastened to the capital city and laid seige to it. Between September 15th and 18th (the exact chronology is difficult to follow), Berkeley's troops finally sallied out of town and attacked Bacon's forces, but were defeated and withdrew in confusion. The Governor, finding he could not rely on his troops, became disheartened, and sending word to a number of the ruling class on both sides the river that all was lost, secretly embarked in the night, and with a large number of the wealthier people, took refuge a second time on the Eastern Shore. On September 19th Bacon entered Jamestown, and feeling that it was not defensible against ships, burned it to the ground, that it might not again become a stronghold of the Governor and his fleet. At the same time his followers seized and occupied strategic buildings (usually the homes of wealthier planters) in the various counties, and took over the county governments. Thus Bacon and his men, now distinguished more prominently than ever as "the poor" in contradistinction to "the rich", became absolute masters of most of Virginia.

In Surry County we are told that "all the great ones" went away with Berkeley on this second flight, leaving the county to Bacon's men, with the exception of Col. Thomas Swann, who apparently remained calmly at his home at "Swann's Point." It is probable, also, that Col. Swann's son, Capt. Thomas Swann, remained in the county. We have mentioned that Col. Swann signed both "Declarations" in favor of Bacon early in August. His son, Capt. Swann, was the son-in-law of William Drummond, a Scottish gentleman who lived at Jamestown, who had once been Governor of North Carolina, who was one of Bacon's most ardent supporters and best advisers, and who was finally executed in a brutal manner and his family terribly persecuted by Governor Berkeley after his final victory. Col. Swann was certainly suspected by some of Baconian partisonship, as indicated by the following deposition of Alice Marriott, wife of Matthias Marriott and daughter of Thomas Warren, builder of the "Warren House" and former Burgess from Surry (Book 2, p. 149):

"Deposition of Alice Marriott, aged 32 years, or thereabouts, sworne saith:

"That about the middle of last Febry your deponent being at the house of William Foreman, in the company of William Foreman and his wife, Lawrence Meizle, Katherine Witherington and Thomas High; said Thomas High began a discourse about the late Rebellion and plundering, Katherine Witherington made answers that the great ones went all away and left the poor ones and they were forced to do what they did. No said Thomas High, 'the Great Toad tarried behind', and one of the company asked Thomas High who he meant by 'the Great Toad'. He replied he meant Coll. Swann, the old rebel and traitor, your deponent knows not which. Your deponent made answer she never heard Coll. Swann did meddle or make in the late troubles. 'No' said he, when Coll. Swann sent a note to Mr. Bishop by Christopher Foster to raise men and come down with them to stop the Governor's men, the horses, saddles and bridles of ours would have been taken had it not been for Colonel Swann.

"Katherine Witherington made answer again that he might hold his tongue for his saddle was saved by her sister, and further your deponent did hear Thomas High say that Swan did send for a boate load of apples from Mr. Masons, for that he thought Mr. Mason would never come again. That Thomas High said Coll. Swann did sit in the Council of War for burning the town and when the Governor went away from town he sent for Coll Swann but he would not come to him. As soon as Bacon came to towne he would take a boate and go over to him and he hoped Coll. Swann would be plucked bare.

"Sworne Nov. 15, 1677."

Much of the above is probably malicious slander by Thomas High, who had formerly been one of Bacon's men. It is true, however, that Col. Swann did stay in the county, and that he did not allow himself to be thrown into a panic by Berkeley. The county might have been better off had more of the prominent men stayed at home. As it is, we are not certain that literally all the Justices and officials left with Berkeley. The only ones of whom we are certain are Arthur Allen, Robert Caufield, John Solway, and Francis Mason, who later prosecuted a number of people for seizing their houses during the Rebellion and appropriating their property. Probably others went, too. Col. Swann did not suffer for his conduct later on. When the Royal Commissioners arrived in Virginia late in January 1676/7, to investigate the rebellion and make a report to the King, the Governor refused to entertain them at his home, "Green Spring", in James City County (Jamestown being destroyed), and Col. Swann offered them the hospitality of his home at Swann's Point across the river, which they made their headquarters during their stay in the colony. In the Minutes of the Council of Trade and Plantations, at a meeting held at Whitehall December 6, 1677 it was recommended that certain "rash and fiery men" be excluded from the Governor's Council of Virginia, but that Col. Swann be continued in office. It was also mentioned that the Governor refused to receive His Majesty's Commissioners into his home, and recommended that "Col. Swan be recommended to Col. Jeffreys (the new Governor) for some reward for his kindness and expense in doing so" (Calendar of Transcripts, Va. Dept. of Archives, Vol. XVII, Sainsbury Transcripts, pp. 99-100). One rather admires Col. Swann's calmness and level-headedness, which is also illustrated by the following testimony of

Christopher Foster, Col. Jordan's nephew, given November 15, 1677
when he was twenty-seven years of age (Book 2, p. 149):

> "That being at Coll Swanns house about ye same day ye late
> Governor Sr Wm Berkeley Sallied out of Towne, Coll. Swann thinking
> ye County being in some danger of ye upland men did desire yr.
> depont. to goe up to Mr. Busby's & to see whether there was any
> guard kept there or noe & withall to tell Mr. Busby he would speake
> with him, but when yr. depont. Came there he found noe body at
> Mr. Busby's home but Mrs. Busby a woman or two more, & Wm
> Pickerall a lame man, and further saith not."

One wonders from the above deposition what had happened to
Lieut. Busby and the guard at his house. The following depositions
also give tantalizing glimpses of the stirring events of late August and
mid-September in Surry County, though they do not allow us to piece
together a connected story (Book 2, p. 130):

> "John Price aged about 27 yse. of Age saith.
> That I being at the house of Mr. Long (Capt. Arthur Long, the
> Baconian) aboute the last of August saith that Roger Rawlings Come-
> ing into Mr. Longs, the said Long said O that is well you are come,
> for I was going to send to you for you must be ready to Carry men
> over to Towne (*i.e.* Jamestown) tomorrow morning for the Governor
> is Comeing up with severall Indyans and others to destroy us all &
> further saith not.   sign
>   Signed   John   P   Price
> Sworn in Surry County Court
>   July 4, 1677   Test W E Cl Cr
>   Vera recordtur   July 9th p. W E Cl Cr."

> "John Clarke aged aboute 25 yse of Age saith
> That three men that came from Nansimond prest me to show them
> the way to Roger Rawlings for Mr. Long had sent them to the sd.
> Rawlings to Carry them over the River. They said they had Capt.
> Long's warrant, and when wee came downe to the sd. Rawlings & his
> boate, he asked them who sent them, and Mr. Collins gave him a
> paper but what was in it, I doe not know, & further saith not.
> Sworn in Court July 3, 1677."

"William Kitto aged aboute 37 yrs of Age saith

That morneing before wee went over to Towne Mr. Long sent to my house to warn me to prepare my boate, soe I went downe to him at Chipooks, & I tould him my boate was but small, shee would not carry above 7 or 8 people, O said he that is noe matter, I have prest Roger Rawlings and his boate, then said I well shee is bigg Enough to carry all that is to goe, & when we weare at Towne Mr. Alsope tould us that they had all the Governor's Goods at Lawrences (*i.e.*, Richard Lawrence of Jamestown, one of Bacon's chief men), then said Rawlings a pock take it they have brought us to keepe theire Stolen goods, he wished himselfe at home, whereupon the Next day I went to Mr. Long & asked him if wee should not goe home, & he snaped me up & said noe you shall waite my Leisure, you shall not goe, & further saith not.

Sworn in Surry County Court

July 4, 1677."

"Jeremiah Ellis aged 34 yse or thereabouts saith

That Whereas yr Depont. comeing to the house of Henry Francis yr. Depont. did heare the sd. Francis say that Mr. Rookeings (*i.e.*, Maj. William Rookings, Bacon's commander-in-chief in Surry) had sent to him for a horse downe to the Guard by Robert Lee (son of Dr. George Lee), which horse did belong to Capt. Barham as yr. Depont. had heard before, wch. horse the sd. Lee had away with him & the sd. Francis did desire me yr. Depont. & Tho. Bentley to take notice that he did deliver the horse well & in good condition upon which words yr. Depont. did looke on the horse & he appeared to be very well & in good likeing to the best of yr. Depont.'s judgment, & the said Lee did say he will leave his own horse there whilst he rid the other to Mr. Busby's for he had rode his owne a great way & had need to favour him & further saith not.

Sworn in Surry Co. Ct. July 4, 1677."

The deposition of John Fenley, aged 24, on July 3, 1677, one of Arthur Allen's servants, shows that Mr. Allen was at Jamestown with Governor Berkeley, during the siege. Perhaps others of the Justices of Surry were also with the Governor already. The deposition is as follows (Book 2, p. 135):

"That on or neare about ye 15th of 7ber last yr depont being sent

by his Master Mr Arthur Allen from James City to Coll. Swann's &
from thence to goe home to his sd. masters house, was by Robt.
Burgess (Bacon's Lieutenant in Surry) on ye road neare Southwarke
Church comanded to stand, who after a short Examination permitted
him to proceede on his Journey, but before he had Rode halfe a mile
the said Burgess with another Horseman Armed Rode after the depont.
& forcably carried him back to ye place where he then kept his
Rendezvous & Emediately Comanding ye depont. to alight, seized &
tooke away his horse, Carbin, powdr. & shott & asking whether yt.
horse were good for anything or not, ye depont. made answr for
Very Little, to which Burgess replyed noe Matter he will serve me to
goe to Mill with, & within halfe an hower aftr. yr. depont. was
carried away prisonr. to Robert Jones (an old soldier in the army of
Charles I, living in Charles City Co., later condemned to death, but
finally pardoned) his house in flour-d-hundred & from thence to
Newitt Wheelers in Martin Brandon where he remained in that quality
the space of Eleven weeks, although he often & very Earnestly solicited
for his Liberty, & further saith not."

The above deposition shows that Bacon's men were already by
September 15th assuming the offensive against the men and their de-
pendents who were known to be on the Governor's side. On September
18th, 1676, the day before Bacon burned Jamestown, the Baconians in
Surry under their commanders, Major William Rookings, Capt. Arthur
Long, Lieut. Robert Burgess and Ensign William Simmons, to the
number of about seventy strong, seized Arthur Allen's brick house
(still standing and known as "Bacon's Castle") in Lawnes Creek
Parish and established their headquarters there, ruling the county till
they were finally driven out on December 28th or 29th. Others mentioned as prominent rebels were Joseph Rogers of Lawnes Creek Parish
("who was so eminent as sometimes to bear command," O. B. 1671-90,
p. 144), John Rutherford (who "as Comr. in chief led a party of men
to pltf's (Robert Caufield's) house and plundered it above £500
sterling," (id., p. 164), and John Clements who, Arthur Allen states,
"had often been captain of rebels at his house," (id., p. 167). All the
above leaders except Long and Rogers were from Southwark Parish.
Two other men who were so prominent in Bacon's forces that they
were summarily executed by Governor Berkeley in March, 1677, were
John Whitson and William Scarborough, both of Southwark Parish.

We can find no record of the exact part that they played, however. About the same time that the rebels seized Mr. Allen's house, they also seized and occupied (probably as sub-headquarters) the houses of Robert Caufield in Lawnes Creek Parish and of John Solway (the "Warren House") and Francis Mason in Southwark Parish. They thus had their troops well situated at strategic points in the county.

There was naturally a good deal of damage and destruction to the property of these men, as well as some looting and plundering during the Baconian supremacy in the county, for which Messrs. Allen, Caufield, Solway and Mason later brought suit against various individuals. The general attitude of the Baconians seems to have been that of Katherine Witherington, that "the great ones went away and left the poor ones and they were forced to do what they did." Or as Thomas Gibbons deposed on September 4, 1677 (Book 2, p. 144), when Owen Myrick and Richard Steel were packing up several things belonging to Francis Mason in two bed ticks and wanted Gibbons to keep them at his house, "deponent said he would have a share of them if Mr. Mason never returned" and the things were sent to his house. After order was restored, much of the plundered property was returned to the owners.

A number of interesting depositions were made in connection with these suits which throw light on the situation in the county during the Baconian rule. The deposition of John Price, aged about 27, on July 3, 1677 (Book 2, p. 133), states:

> "That aboute ye 23d of September last ye Depont. being a prisoner at the house of Mr. Arthur Allen, did heare Arthur Long (who then had the title of Capt.) ordr. & Command Tho. Gibbons to take his Gun & shoote some one of the sd. Mr. Allen's Cattle, & if he could not find any of the old Steeres to kill the first he could meete with, upon which the sd. Gibbons went out & killed a beast wheather Steere or Cow the Depont. knows not but that night (to ye best of yr. Deponts remembrance) the said Long with Capt. Pitman (another prominent Baconian) gave him Leave to goe home Conditionally that he should bring his dogs with him in the morning to Catch Mr. Allen's Cattle if any of them should be shott & not killed, but the depont. returning according to time (but wthout his dogs) mett the sd. Long in ye old field neare his owne house, who Commanded him Emediately to assist Gibbons in driveing up and killing one other of ye sd Mr. Allen's Cattle, & tould them if one was not Enough they should kill

two, but the Cattle being very shye they could not drive them to the house as they Intended wherefore Gibbons shott at a Steere of about 5 years old in ye open field & killed him, wch when they gave ye sd. Long an acct. of, he said yt would serve today & they must kill one or two more tomorrow, but wheather any more were killed on ye morrow or not yr. depont. cannot certainly tell, but some small time after ye said Long released yr. depont. out of prison to grinde some of Mr. Allen's wheate (at his hand Mill) which when he had ground the sd. Long carried the Meall home, & committed yr. depont. to prison againe, & further saith not."

Thomas Gibbons, aged about 30, confessed to the same on the same date (*id.*):

"That aboute ye 23d of 7 br. last yr. depont. being at ye house of Cap. Arthur Allen was commanded by Mr. Long (then called Capt.) to take my Gun & shoote some one of ye sd. Mr. Allen's Cattle & if he could not finde any of the old steeres to kill ye first he mett with, upon wch. yr. depont. did shoote and kill a steere of about 4 or 5 yeares of age & about 3 or 4 days afterwards he commanded yr. depont. with ye assistance of John Price to kill another of ye sd. Mr. Allen's cattle, & if one would not doe to kill more but there was but one killed & further yr. depont. further saith he was commanded as above, but he cannot certainly say by Long, but to ye best of his remembrance it was by Long & further saith not."

In the above depositions, it is rather curious that John Price, though a prisoner, was allowed to go and come on parole. The cattle were obviously killed to supply the troops, and may have been justified by military necessity. The following depositions on July 3, 1677, refer to the less military pilfering of Joseph Rogers and Robert Burgess (Book 2, pp. 134-5):

"Elizabeth Blesley, aged 29, deposed that Arthur Allen's house was seized by the rebels about the 18th of Sept. last; that Joseph Rogers and one man came armed to the house about 3/4 hours after it was entered by 'the rebel crew'; that several times afterwards Rogers inquired where Mr. Allen's plate was hidden; and that Rogers' man about June 7, 1677 brought back a large Dutch case with 6 or 7 pint bottles, which the deponent believed to be Mr. Allen's property, but

Mr. Allen told Rogers' man he would not receive it, because he had entered a suit against Rogers."

"Margaret Hodge, about 22 years old, deposed that 'very shortly after Mr. Arthur Allen was by ye late wicked Rebells forced from his house,' her deceased husband, John Cooper, found some saddles, etc. belonging to Mr. Allen which were put into a chest at her house, but that Joseph Rogers came to her home and forced her to give him the saddle, bridle, etc.

"Elizabeth Blesley again deposed that about the 18th of Sept. last Robert Burgess ('who afterwards I heard called commonly Sert.') with about 70 other men in arms entered Mr. Allen's house and seized his estate 'Ransacking & making what havoc they pleased within Dore & without'; she enumerates a surprising amount of household linen, etc. which she claims Robert Burgess took, and that he has not brought it all back."

Walter Taylor, aged about 33, deposed:

"That about ye 21st 7 ber last ye depont. Comeing to ye house of Mr. Arthur Allen, founde ye same possest & Engarrisoned by a Considerable Number of the Rebells undr. the Comand of Wm Rookeings, among whom were Robert Burgess, whome the depont. Ever heard Called Sert. wch. place or office he Exercised soe long as the Guard was kept by them being all waies accounted & Esteemed (next to Rookeings) ye Cheife Comander thereof, & Mr. Wm Simons who yr. depont. saw severall times Carry the Coulours, & had allwayes ye title of Ensigne & yr. depont. further declaireth yt. ye very night ye house was quitted by ye Rebell Crew, he saw ye sd. Burgess thrust severall things (which he supposed to be household Lining) into his Breeches Just upon their departure & likewise saw ye sd. Simons (assisted by John Rutherford, Putt up severall bookes into a pillow case & had tabel Lining, Canvis & other things in theire hands ready to putt up with ye sd. bookes (as yr. depont. supposeth) for he afterwards saw ye sd. Simons have ye same pillow case filled full with something, & Carried it away with him at ye same time & further saith not."

Depredations of Owen Myrick and others at the house of Mr. Francis Mason were cited in the depositions of Thomas Watson, aged 30, and Thomas Gibbons, aged 30, on September 4, 1677 (Book 2,

p. 144). Thomas Watson testified that some time in the preceding September at Mr. Mason's he saw Owen Myrick have a bed tick in which there were several things, that he saw Myrick take down a green valence with silk fringe and put it in the bed tick, and that he saw feathers which he believed were emptied out of the tick by "that Crew & Mirick." Thomas Gibbons deposed that in September last he was at Mr. Mason's with Owen Myrick and Richard Steele and several others; that Myrick and Steele were packing several things into two bed ticks; that deponent said he "would have a share of the things if Mr. Mason never returned" and that the things were accordingly sent to his house; that during Mr. Mason's absence Myrick commonly rode Mr. Mason's mare and abused her; and that the deponent has returned the things he had to Mr. Mason, except one pewter dish.

The recorded depositions regarding looting end on November 17, 1677, when Thomas Sowersby, aged 44, and Nicholas Witherington, aged 30, testified against John Rutherford and others at Mr. John Solway's house (Book 2, p. 154). Sowersby testified that on September 18, 1676 he was forced to go with Mr. John Rutherford and others to Ware Neck, "where were the sd. Rutherford, John Rogers, and Wm. Rookeings, their chief commander"; that Mr. Solway's house was locked, but was opened presently, and Mr. John Rutherford, John Rogers, and others were in the house drinking wine. Nicholas Witherington testified that on September 18, 1676 at the house of Mr. William Thompson, Mr. William Rookeings, their chief commander, and other persons "commanded me to go with them to Ware Neck", where he saw Mr. John Solway's house open and several persons there drinking wine, among them Mr. John Rutherford and John Rogers.

Bacon's forces were in absolute control of Surry County for over three months. After his victory over the Governor, Bacon himself planned to organize the colony and to go ahead with the Indian War. He drew up a new oath of allegiance to himself, and made plans to appoint three committees, one to take charge south of the James River and stop the plundering that he heard was going on there, one to accompany the army and prevent depredations, and one to supervise the management of the war. Late in September or early in October he went to Gloucester County, and tried to persuade the Gloucester men to take the new oath to him and his government. This they were loath to do, and he met some active opposition there. The truth of the matter seems to be that neither Berkeley nor Bacon could get the complete

support of the people, because of the problem of divided allegiance
mentioned before. Bacon had the popular sympathy, and the legal
authority of the June Assembly behind him. On the other hand, he
had been proclaimed a rebel and traitor by Berkeley, who with all his
unpopularity, had the royal authority behind him. Bacon was disappointed at his reception in Gloucester, and while trying to settle the
affairs of the county in his favor, he died there of dysentery October
26, 1676. With the death of the leader the popular movement rapidly
declined. Joseph Ingram became commander-in-chief after Bacon's
death, but the "rebel" forces were scattered in the various counties,
Berkeley's army was rapidly increasing, and one by one the rebel con-
tingents and strongholds were either captured or surrendered. Ingram
himself surrendered at West Point, and by December most of the colony
north of the James had been reconquered by Berkeley. Land forces
were used to subdue the rebels north of the James, but Berkeley used
the Royal Navy in conquering the southern counties. Here the sup-
pression of the rebellion was chiefly due to the sea-captains, Morris,
Couset, Grantham, Price and Gardner. Groves, the Baconian commander-in-chief south of the James, was slain by Capt. Couset, and his
forces routed. The subjugation of the Baconians in Surry was due to
Captain Robert Morris, Commander of the Governor's ship, *Young
Prince*. The journal of the *Young Prince* from September 9, 1676
to January 29, 1677 contains the following: "28th (Dec., 1676) our
men marched downwards to secure the lower parts; the guard at Allen's
brick house we hear is run away; letters from Rookins and from the
Surry gentlemen. 29th We carried the fort, and at night our forces
came up, being 120 foot and horse, not having been above 10 miles
down." (*Wm. and Mary Quarterly*, 1st Series, V, pp. 189-90, from
Calendar of State Papers, Colonial America and West Indies, 1675-6.)
We note that "the great ones" of Surry had returned by December 28.
It is doubtful whether there was a fight between Rookings' forces and
the contingent from the *Young Prince*. In any case, 70 or more
ill-equipped militiamen were hardly a match for 120 regulars. Thus
ended the rebellion in Surry County and the hopes of the people for a
more representative government. The aftermath dragged on for over
a year, however.

By January 11, 1676/7 Berkeley was once more in complete control
of the colony. On that date he began a series of court-martials, which
resulted in the death of a large number of chief rebels and caused

Charles II later on to exclaim that "the old fool had executed more men than he himself had caused to die for the death of his father, Charles I." One of the men executed during this period in a peculiarly brutal manner was William Drummond, father-in-law of Capt. Samuel Swann. After the execution, Drummond's wife and children were driven from their home and almost perished in the swamps of James City County. Another Surry man condemned to execution was Major William Rookings, Bacon's commander-in-chief in the county. He was tried by a military court-martial at Green Spring, the Governor's residence, January 24, 1676/7, as one "taken in open rebellion", and was adjudged to death, but before execution died in prison (Hening *Statutes,* II, pp. 370, 547). Major Rookings was the son of William and Jane Rookings, early settlers of Surry, and was a brother-in-law of Capt. Nicholas Wyatt, a Baconian of Charles City County. In his will, dated July 13, 1676 and probated July 1, 1679, he is called William Rookeings of Flying Point, Surry County, leaves his property to his three minor children, William, Elizabeth and Jane, leaves a legacy to his cousin Mary Short's children, Capt. Nicholas Wyatt, William Simmons, and John King to be overseers of his will and guardians of his children (Book 2, p. 213). Major Rookings' estate was first confiscated by martial law, but in April, 1677 we have recorded a petition of N. Wyat in behalf of William and Elizabeth Rookeings, orphans of William Rookeings of Surry County, that the estate condemned by martial law might be secured for the benefit of the children and creditors until the King's pleasure should be known *(Calendar of Transcripts, Va. Dept. of Archives,* Vol. XVI, *Sainsbury Abstracts,* p. 236). Apparently the petition was granted, as the will was finally probated. Major Rookings' son William was a Justice of Surry County in 1714 *(Va. Mag.* II, 12).

On January 29, 1676/7 Col. Herbert Jeffreys, Col. Francis Morrison, and Sir John Berry, Royal Commissioners, arrived in Virginia, being appointed to investigate grievances, suppress the rebellion, and summon Sir William Berkeley back to England, relieving him of the Governorship that he had exercised so long. Jeffreys later became Governor after Berkeley's departure, but the stubborn old Governor was temporarily still in power. He refused to have the Commissioners at his mansion at Green Spring, and as we have mentioned, Col. Swann offered them his hospitality at Swann's Point in Surry County. The Commissioners brought a pardon for the rebels from the King, but they could not halt

the Governor's thirst for revenge, and he carried on his series of trials
and executions, only substituting civil trials for military court-martials
on March 3d. During this period of executions, two Baconians from
Surry suffered the death penalty. On March 16, 1676/7 John Whitson
and William Scarborough of Southwark Parish were convicted of
"divers Rebellions Treasons and other misdemeanors", were sentenced
to death, and shortly executed, their estates also being confiscated
(*Minutes of the Council and Gen. Court*, p. 459-60, Hening *Statutes*,
II, p. 370). Whitson was the son-in-law of Capt. Robert Spencer, one
of the Justices of Surry, and left an only daughter, Martha Whitson.
Scarborough's widow married (2) Thomas Tyus (O. B. 1671-90, p.
194). He, also, left descendants in the county.

Another Surry man selected for special punishment by the colonial
government was Arthur Long of Lawnes Creek Parish, Bacon's captain.
Berkeley called an Assembly at Green Spring February 20, 1676/7,
and Long was among those who, as a "notorious actor" in the rebellion,
was selected for punishment not extending to his life (Hening *Statutes*,
II, p. 371). Later the Assembly enacted "that Arthur Long of Surry
county doe upon his bended knees, with a rope about his necke acknowledge his treasons and rebellion before the right honourable the
governour and councell, and begg pardon for his life, and that in like
manner he doe acknowledge his crimes in the county court of Surry, and
that he be committed to safe prison untill he shall give good security
for his future good behavior (*id.*, pp. 379-80). We do not know when
this sentence was carried out before the Governor and Council, but the
Surry records show that it was done July 4, 1677 in the Surry County
Court (Book 2, p. 133), as follows: "At a Court held for Surry County
July 4, 1677, Arthur Long appeared in Open Court and made the
following submission with a rope about his neck on bended knees.
'I, Arthur Long, that all bystanders may take notice of this my sincere
repentance of my Rebellion, do here most humbly upon my knees with
a roape about my neck implore pardon of God, My King, the Hon.
Governor, Council and Magistrates of this his Majesty's country and
humbly crave the benefit of his Majesty's most gracious Acts of Mercy
and Pardon for my treason and rebellion. And this my submission and
his Majesty's royall pardon to be granted me thereupon may be entered
on record to make the same available to me, in the pleading thereof if
occasion shall hereafter be. God Save the King, and Prosper the
Governor and Majistrates of the County, with all happiness and Good

success." Another man, Anthony Hartland, was condemned by the General Court to make the same confession and do the same penance as Arthur Long before both the Surry and the Charles City County Courts (Hening II, p. 378). In addition he was fined 5,000 lbs. of tobacco. He seems to have been a Charles City man, however, and not a resident of Surry.

The colonial government seems not to have prosecuted the other two officers of Bacon in Surry, namely, Robert Burgess, Lieutenant, and William Simmons, Ensign, though both were later sued for depredations. The depositions of Elizabeth Blesley and Walter Taylor, given before, state that Robert Burgess was commonly called "Sert.", by which I suppose "Sergeant" is meant; but Arthur Allen in his suit brought against Burgess July 3, 1677 specifically states that Burgess bore the title of Lieutenant, and was Commander-in-Chief next to William Rookings (O. B. 1671-90, p. 145). Burgess was fined 8,000 lbs. of tobacco, the largest fine placed on any of the rebels, and was finally forced to mortgage his plantation to pay this debt. On April 20, 1678 Robert Burgess, blacksmith, and his wife Ann deeded to John Moreing and George Proctor, Gents., their plantation on Upper Chipoaks Creek with brick house and other edifices, in return for Moreing and Proctor going on Burgess' bond for a debt of 6,315 lbs. of tobacco to Arthur Allen, for which he had been kept in prison many months (Book 2, p. 182). Burgess died in 1683 leaving no children, though he mentions children of his brother Thomas Burgess (*id.*, p. 332-3). William Simmons received a smaller fine and seems to have succeeded in paying it more easily. He was the son of Mary Simmons of Burcher Swamp, Surry County, whose will, dated April 16, 1677 and probated May 7, 1678, mentions her son William and granddaughter Mary, and leaves legacies to John Rutherford and Francis Gregory, both of whom were Bacon's men (Book 2, p. 172). William Simmons' son John and grandson Benjamin Simmons were Burgesses from Southampton County in the 18th century. Of the other Baconian leaders in the county, Joseph Rogers confessed some of his pillaging and was fined. He was a tanner, and appears to have left no descendants in the county. He may have moved to North Carolina some time after the Rebellion, as a Joseph Rogers appears there in the early 18th century. John Rutherford was another, like Burgess, whose sufferings were long drawn out. On March 5, 1677/8, being already in prison because of a judgment to Robert Caufield for depredations at the latter's house, the sheriff went

to arrest him again to answer charges made against him by John
Solway, but Rutherford refused to come to court, and was in his absence
condemned, and fined again (O. B. 1671-90, p. 195; Bk. 2, p. 162).
He must have submitted finally, however, and got out of prison, as in
1681 he signed the guardian's bond for Thomas Cockerham, orphan
of Capt. William Cockerham. Rutherford, also, is said to have left
descendants in the county. All the above men were from Southwark
Parish, except Long and Rogers.

The less prominent Baconians, to the number of 40, laid hold of
the King's pardon February 6, 1676/7, as indicated by the following
record (Book 2, p. 149):

> We whose names are hereunto subscribed having heard and read
> of his Majesty's gracious and most surpassing acts of Pardon and
> Mercy . . . do with all humility and earnestness implore and lay
> hold on his Majesty's most gracious act of pardon aforesaid . . . and
> in conformity to his Majesty's royal instructions (pray it) may be
> entered on record.

Surry County February 6th 1676

Walter (V) Vahan	Robert (X) Evans	Thomas Pittman, Sen.
Ja: Forbes	Thomas (X) Gibbons	John Hunnicutt
John (X) Skinner	Henry (H) Baker	John Clements
Thomas Senior	Robert Judkins	William (H) Heath
George Williams	William Pettway	John Pulestone
Mathew (M) Magnus	George (X) Harris	Edward Petteway
William Rugbye	Ni (X) Johnson	Samuel Pearce
Fra (X) Every	Stephen Lewis	William (W) Blunt
Edmund Howell	William (W) Newett	Alex (A) Spencer
Jonas (X) Bennett	George Proctor	Cor (X) Cardenpaine
William (X) Jones	John (X) Philips, Sr.	John Skelton
Richard True	Edward (X) Davis	Samuel (X) Judkins
Thomas (K) King	Stephen Allen	Thomas (H) High
John (X) Tarvett		

Recorded Xbr 1st 1677, W. E. Ct. Clk.
It was delivered to me to be recorded
by Captain Spencer 9 br 14, 1677
W E Cl Crt.

Of the above 40 men, it is again noteworthy that practically all
were from Southwark Parish. The 1675 list of tithables shows that 30

of them were positively Southwark men, 6 probably from Southwark judging by their surnames, 3 unidentifiable, and only one positively from Lawnes Creek Parish, namely, William Newitt. It looks as though Southwark was the stronghold of the Baconian movement, while Lawnes Creek tended to remain faithful to the Justices and the established government, though it can hardly be said that anyone in Surry County was an ardent partisan of Governor Berkeley. Most of the above men were small land-owners, several were freemen who worked on plantations belonging to others. Edward and William Petway were father and son. Robert and Samuel Judkins were brothers, and stepsons of the aged Thomas Pittman, Senior, who had been a Lieutenant in the county militia. George Proctor later became a Justice of the county, and had married the widow of Major William Marriott, a former Burgess. John Hunnicutt's wife was the daughter of Thomas Warren, prominent in the early history of the county.

Although the above forty men had submitted to Berkeley's government, and one of them, George Williams, served on a jury which later on condemned a number of his fellow Baconians, there was still rebellion in the hearts of many at the return to the old unjust state of affairs. On March 26, 1677 eight of the above men were put under bond to keep the peace, especially toward "ye Rt Honoble Sr Wm. Berkeley Knt Governor and Capt Genll of Virginia" (Book 2, p. 119). They were Thomas Pittman, John Clements, Edward Pettway, William Blunt, Thomas Gibbons, John Skelton, Matthew Magnus and Stephen Allen. John Clements, we have noted, was called a leader among the Baconians and was later sued for depredations. We have already noted Thomas High's criticism against Col. Thomas Swann in Feb., 1676/7, indicating a feeling that the Baconians had first been encouraged by the authorities, and then punished for their action. On Feb. 17, 1676/7 Elizabeth Regan, wife of Daniel Regan of Southwark Parish (whom we have not heard of previously as involved in the rebellion), was accused of having at several times and in several places "fomented many Malignant & rebellious Words tending to sedition"; and the Court ordered Samuel Judkins, the Constable (himself a Baconian), to carry her to the common whipping place and give her ten lashes well laid on, on her bare back (O. B. 1671-90, p. 133). On September 4, 1677 Mary, the wife of John Skinner (one of the forty men above), was ordered to be given twenty lashes for "speaking words tending to sedition or mutiny, & in favour of the late rebellion"; and on the same date, John Skinner, her husband, was ordered to be arrested for the same reason (*id.*, p. 154-5).

Besides the above forty men and their leaders, Rookings, Long, Burgess, Simmons, Rogers, Rutherford, Whitson and Scarborough, the later suits ,and additional documents show us others involved in the rebellion, Richard Atkins, John Rogers, Sr. (an old man, probably identical with a John Rogers who was Burgess from the county in 1644 and 1645), Owen Myrick, Richard Steele, John Ironmonger, Richard Browne, Thomas Hyard (possibly identical with Thomas High) all from Southwark Parish, and Henry Goard and Robert Kay from Lawnes Creek. We learn of the last two men's connection with the rebellion, not from the Surry records, but from those of the colony. Soon after regaining power, Governor Berkeley issued a warrant to seize the estate of Robert Kay and bring his sheep to Green Spring, and there is on record the certificate of Samuel Swann, sheriff, that he did seize and inventory the said estate January 30, 1676/7 (*Calendar of Transcripts, Va. Dept. of Archives, Sainsbury Abstracts,* Vol. XVI, p. 110). In April, 1677 there is on record the complaint of Henry Gord to the Commissioners of Virginia against Capt. Roger Potter (another Surry man), Gaoler of the prison at Green Spring, for not suffering him to leave, where he had been confined for one month by the Governor (*id.*, p. 239). Others who were at least sympathetic with the Baconians were Adam Heath, Edward Green and John Immers, who signed a document along with several old Baconians which was extremely obnoxious to the Assembly of October, 1677. Other more doubtful cases we have learned of from the depositions—young Robert Lee who on an errand for the Baconians, took Capt. Barham's horse; Henry Francis, who let him have the horse; William Kitto and Roger Rawlings, who ferried Bacon's men across to Jamestown at the siege; "Mr. Bishop", to whom Thomas High reported that Col. Swann sent a note; John Price, who was under a singularly lax imprisonment by Bacon's men at the Allen house; Walter Taylor who visited the rebels at "Bacon's Castle"; Thomas Watson who was present at Francis Mason's house when he claimed that Owen Myrick ,and Richard Steele were looting; Nicholas Witherington and Thomas Sowersby, who were present at the seizure of John Solway's house, the latter saying that he was "forced to go with the rebels"; possibly, also, Lieut. Thomas Busby, at whose house no guard was found in the critical days of mid-September and who agreed to pay Arthur Allen damages, along with a number of

Bacon's men, November 15, 1677 (O. B. 1671-90, p. 172), John Barker who agreed to pay Arthur Allen on the same date (*id.*, p. 173), and even John Goring of Lawnes Creek, who was ordered to pay Robert Caufield 2,702 lbs. of tobacco May 1, 1677 (*id.*, p. 137), although it is not stated that it was for damages done during the Rebellion. All these latter, however, are much more doubtful cases, and probably took no active part in the Rebellion.

Governor Berkeley's new Assembly met at Green Spring February 20, 1676/7, and Surry's representatives were William Browne and Benjamin Harrison, new Burgesses, but old Justices. The first act of the assembly was to pass an act of indemnity and pardon in accordance with the King's letters patent of October 10, 1676, but with twenty-five or thirty notable exceptions, among whom we have mentioned Rookings, Whitson, Scarborough and Long from Surry County. The next act was to abolish all the reform laws passed by "Bacon's Assembly" in June, 1676. However, some recognition of the need for reform was manifested (we suspect largely through the influence of the Royal Commissioners) by new laws making Members of the Council and ministers of the established Church pay levies; repealing the obnoxious amerciements, or taxes, on persons engaged in law-suits; and allowing six elected representatives of the people in each parish to sit with the vestrymen when parish levies were assessed. The Commissioners had brought orders from England, also, that the people of the various counties were to have the right freely to express their grievances and make formal petitions to the Assembly for remedial action. Thus we see that the influence of the Baconian movement was not entirely lost. Most of the counties availed themselves of this right at the new Assembly, though in a few (*e.g.*, Westmoreland), the counties were so thoroughly under the thumbs of the oligarchy that the petitions did not really express the grievances of the people, and were rather ridiculous. This was not the case with Surry County, which handed in a lengthy set of "Grievances" as follows (*Va. Mag.* II, p. 170-173):

> 1. That ye last assembly continued many yeares and by their ffrequent meeting being once every yeare hath been a continuall charge and burthen to the poor Inhabitants of this Collony; and that the burgesses of the sd Assembly had 150 lb tobacco per day for each member they usually continueing for three or 4 weekes together did arise to a great some, And that the said assembly did give to severall

gentlemen (for what service we know not) great somes of tobacco, all which with the publique nessessary charge did Raise the Levy to a very great & excessive heith.

2. That great quantities of tobacco was levyed upon ye poore Inhabitants of this Collony for the building of houses at James-City which were not habitable by reason yt were not finished.

3. That great quantityes of tobacco has been Raised for the building of fforts & yett no place of defence in ye Country sufficient to secure his Majesties poore subjects from the ffury of fforaine Invaders.

4. That notwithstanding the great quantities of ammunition by the shipps for ffort dutyes for the Countryes service & considerable somes of tobacco raised to maintain a magazine yett upon all occasions wee are forced to provide powder and shott at our owne perticuler charge or else fyned;

5. That upon any fforaine Invation wee his Majestyees poore subjects are called to James City a place of vast expence and extortion upon his Majestyes service and the defence of his Majestyes Collony, in which service if wee be maimed wee are utterly ruined as to or ffurther subsistence, we are forced not onely to pay or owne expences but ye expences of or Commannders and thene also for their service.

6. That the 2 s per hhd Imposed by ye 128th Act for the payment of his majestyes officers & other publique debts thereby to ease his majestyes poore subjects of their great taxes: we humbly desire that an account may be given thereof.

7. That severall persons estates are seized and part of them taken away before ye owner is convict of any crime notwithstanding they laid hold of the honnorable Governor his Acts of Indemnity and were admitted to take the oath of allegiance to his gratious Majesty & fydelity to his majestyes Honnorable Governor.

8. That by the assembly in June last wee were Injoyned (upon a great penality) to send armes & provisions to that laste rebell Nathaniel Bacon Junr (the Honnorable Governor not contradicting itt altho itt was some tyme after the sd Rebell has Rebelliously fforced his Commission) to or great losse and dammage: Wee humbly pray that as wee expect no redresse for or (obedience to the sd assembly) for or damage then reced, that that assembly may not Increase or sufferings by being chargeable to us.

9. That the erecting of fforts together with the slackness of prose-

cuting ye Indian warr as also the subtle Insinuations of Nathaniel Bacon, Junor, his pretences has been the cheefe cause of the late & unhappy warr.

10. That it has been the custome of County Courts att the laying of the Levy to withdraw into a private Roome by wch meanes the poore people not knowing for what they paid their levy did allways admire how their taxes could bee so high.

Wee most humbly pray that for the future that County Levy may be laid publickly in the Court house.

11. That wee have been under great exactions of sherifs and Clarks ffees for these severall yeares. The assembly having assertained but some fees and left the rest to the breast of the County Corts wee most humbly pray that for the future all clarkes and sherifes fees may be assertained and a great penalty laid upon such as shall exact.

12. That contrary to the lawes of England and this country high sheriffs have usually continued two yeares and undersheriffs 3 or 4 yeares together: wee humbly pray that for the future that no person may continue sheriffe above one year.

13. That severall small debts bring in great proffitts to the Clarks & sheriffs by reason men are forced to sue for very small debts to the some of 200 lb tobacco to the great expence of all poore debtr and creditor. Wee humbly desire that a Justice of peace of the quorum or who else may be thought fitt may have power to grant order for any some under 450 lb tobacco & caske and like wise execution without further troble to the Court.

14. That we have not had liberty to choose vestrymen wee humbly desire that the wholle parish may have a free election.

15. That since his most Gratious Majesty hath been most mercifully pleased to pardon or late disloallty wee most earnestly and humbly pray that this present grand assembly would make an Act of Oblivion that no person may be Injured by the provoking names of Rebell Traitor & Rogue.

16. That the assembly did levy 60 lb tobacco per pole for two years together wee know not for what advantage to us did so heithen the levy that the poore people did sink under their burdens not being able to pay their great taxes & utterly despairing of any release from their Greeivous taxes and burthens for the future have beene for a long tyme much discontented and greeved, but being Informed by the honnorable ffrancis Morrison Esqr one of his majestyes commissioners

that his most gratious majesty has been most gratiously pleased to
return us or money againe by the honnorable Mr. Secretary Ludwell,
our greeved harts are exceedingly rejoyced & Inlivened and wee yield
his most gratious and sacred majesty all possible and humble and harty
thanks ffor his Royall mercyes Humbly praying the honnorable Mr.
Secretary may give a just account to the assembly of what money is
due to the country in his hands.

17. That the reson of the late and unhappy warr the Inhabitants of
this County may not been able to ffollow their callings do humblely
desire that they may not be sued to the Cort nor laid under execution
but be forborne their present debts till the next Cropp.

18. That severall men are likely to loose sevall somes of tobacco
wch are just debts out of sevrall condemned persons & other seazed
estates.

Wee humbly pray that all just debts may be payd out of the said
estates so seazed.

19. That ye Indians taken in ye late warr may be made slaves.

Wee ye subscribed being chosen to present yr Greevances of Surry
County do testifye that ye perticulers afforewritten are the Greevances
of the said County.

(signed)   Tho: Busby, George Proctor.

Sainsbury Abstracts (Calendar of Transcripts, Va. Dept. of Archives,
Vol. XVI, p. 163) adds the name of John Moring as signer of the
above grievances. All three were from Southwark Parish and Proctor
had been one of Bacon's men. It will be noted that they stated that
they were chosen to make this petition, implying that there had been
meetings to discuss the above proposals. This apparently more demo-
cratic procedure in Surry may be contrasted with that in some other
counties. The Westmoreland "Grievances" are apparently the work of
the Justices and in no way express the grievances of the people. In Isle
of Wight, it is hinted that the "Grievances" were the work of only a
few individuals, not popularly chosen to the task. Surry County continued to send in such "Grievances" to the Assembly from year to year,
even as late as the 1690's.

The answer of the Assembly of February, 1676/7 to the Surry
petition was as follows *(Journal of the House of Burgesses, 1659/60-
1693*, p. 89):

To the proposall in Surry County Grievances Complaining against
the taxes laid by the Grand Assembly

Answeared All people ought to acquiesse wth that lawes yt are
made by the Grand Assembly And whoever shall oppose them in
histile manner to bee deemed Rebells and psecuted accordingly

To the proposall about the seizing of severall mens Estates

Answeared That psons yt finde themselves agrieved may come and
petition to the Grand Assembly for redresse during this Session and
afterwards to the Governr and Councell

This rather summary answer was no doubt due to the influence of
Governor Berkeley, who dominated this Assembly. We have noted,
however, that it passed a few new laws tending to correct abuses. A
slight variant of the above petition is given in the above Journal (pp.
111-113), stating somewhat more specifically grievances against Clerks,
Sheriffs, ordinary keepers, and officials of the colony. Payment was
ordered to several Surry County men by this Assembly, indicating the
non-Baconian element in the county, to-wit, Capt. Robert Spencer, John
Goring, Mr. Benjamin Harrison, Capt. Roger Potter, Roger Rawlings,
Randolph Holt, and Col. George Jordan (*id.*, pp. 81-86). In particu-
lar, Col. Jordan was paid 12,309 lbs. of tobacco for the charges of the
Surry Fort, which had been ordered by the Assembly of March, 1675/6.
One wonders what happened to the fort and its garrison during the
Rebellion.

Trials for depredations made by the Baconians began in the Surry
Court in May, 1677. On May 1, Joseph Rogers was ordered to pay
Robert Caufield 1,304 lbs. of Tobacco (O. B. 1671-90, p. 139). On
July 3, Capt. Charles Barham was granted judgment against Henry
Francis for the horse loaned to the Baconians; and Arthur Allen sued
William Simmons, Robert Burgess, Joseph Rogers, and Arthur Long
for damage to his estate above 500 lbs. sterling in value, and for
plundering (*id.*, pp. 144-46). All were found guilty and fined heavily,
and all appealed their cases, though Simmons and Rogers later withdrew their appeals (Book 2, pp. 138, 169). The jury that convicted
them was composed of John Moreing, foreman, Arthur Jordan, William Newsum, William Gray, George Williams, Richard Jordan, Sion
Hill, Joseph Ford, Robert Lancaster, Edward Tanner, Thomas Sowersby, and Christopher Foster. Moring, the two Jordans, Williams,
Sowersby and Foster were from Southwark Parish, Newsum, Gray, Hill,

Ford, Lancaster and Tanner from Lawnes Creek. Foster and the two Jordans were relatives of Col. George Jordan, and Sowersby a close neighbor. George Williams is the only one of the group who had been one of Bacon's men. At the same court, Arthur Long made his submission, August 4, 1677.

The September Court brought new trials. On September 4, Roger Rawlings obtained judgment against Arthur Long for "pressing his boat several times during the late Rebellion", Mary Skinner was sentenced to twenty lashes for mutinous words, and her husband, John Skinner, arrested for the same reason (*id.*, pp. 154-5). On the next day, September 5, John Solway sued Richard Atkins for abusing his horse, breaking open his house, plundering, and drinking his wine during the Rebellion, and he was convicted and fined by a jury composed of John Moring, Joseph Ford, Walter Taylor, Richard Drew, William Newsum, John Watkins, William Gray, John Dunfield, Charles Amry, Samuel Cornell, Sion Hill, and Edward Tanner (*id.*, p. 162). This time there were only two men from Southwark Parish on the jury, namely, John Moring and John Watkins, the rest all being from Lawnes Creek. On September 6, Robert Caufield sued John Rutherford, Richard Atkins, John Rogers, Robert Burgess, and John Clements, and Arthur Allen sued John Clements, John Rogers, Sr., John Ironmonger and Richard Browne for plundering, etc. All were found guilty and fined by the same jury (*id.*, pp. 164-5, 167-8). On the same date Joseph Rogers confessed that he had seven hides belonging to Mr. Allen (p. 168).

The men convicted by these juries in July and September obviously felt that they had been unjustly treated, in view of the Act of Pardon and Oblivion, and they presented a new set of "Grievances" to the Assembly which met in October, 1677, Surry's Burgesses at this Assembly being William Browne and Samuel Swann. The aggrieved Baconians only found that they had got into more trouble by their petition, as indicated by the following notice from the House of Burgesses (*Journals, 1659/60-93*, p. 114):

> Oct. 10, 1677. A Petition being presented to this Assembly intituled the Grievances of Surry County, in behalfe of themselves and divers others, and subscribed by severall persons some of the cheife of them appearing personally, and the matter at large enquired into, the paper or peticion is adjudged to be highly Scandalous and notoriously

injurious to the Justices of Surry County and the Jurie therein meant, It is therefore Ordered That each subscriber thereof vizt Richard Atkins, Robert Burges, Richard Browne, John Arnemonger, John Rogers, William Symmons, Addam Heath, Edward Green, John Clemons, & John Immers be fined four hundred pounds of tobacco and Caske to the use of the Countie, and acknowledge their fault before two severall Courts holden for Surry County, and give security for their future good behaviour and whensoever the writer of the sd paper shall be discovered and made knowne he shall be fined four hundred pounds of tobacco and Casque to the use of the Countie afforesd, and make such acknowledgment, and give such securitie as is enjoined the Signers thereof, All which sd fines in Tobacco is Suspended from being levied untill the next yeare.

In the November Court, 1677 there are recorded in the Order Book agreements on November 15th of Arthur Allen with Lt. Thomas Busby, Owen Myrick and John Barker; of Robert Caufield with Owen Myrick; of Francis Mason with Owen Myrick and Richard Atkins; and of John Solway with Thomas Hyard, Robert Burgess and Owen Myrick; whereby all the latter were to pay the former for damage done (*id.*, pp. 172-5). On November 17 Arthur Long was ordered to give security for 100 lbs. of powder and 80 lbs. of shot commanded from Capt. Barham during the late Rebellion, and for 57 lbs. of powder and 100 lbs. of shot commanded from Lt.-Col. Jordan, Long to return the same by November 1, 1678 or pay 2,110 lbs. of tobacco (*id.*, p. 178). Thus the Court rescinded its acts of August, 1676 in favor of Bacon, and required poor Capt. Long to pay for the ammunition out of his own pocket; though it is possible that this ammunition was used after September 18, 1676, at which time the Justices began regarding the Baconians as real rebels. We have already mentioned the last traces of the prosecution of Bacon's men—John Solway's suit against John Rutherford March 5, 1677/8, the latter's refusal to come from prison and his condemnation in absence; and Robert Burgess' mortgage of his plantation to pay his debt to Arthur Allen on April 20, 1678.

We may close our account of Surry County in the Rebellion by summarizing an interesting account of the county funds for 1677, recorded by William Edwards, Clerk of the Court, November 19, 1677 (Order Bk. 1671-90, pp. 181-2). This account shows 453 tithables assessed 110 lbs. of tobacco per poll for the public levies, and 460 tithables assessed at 93 lbs. of tobacco per poll for the county levy, making a total of 203 lbs. of tobacco per poll, a high tax which had been complained of among the "Grievances." Out of the public levy, 4,570 lbs. of tobacco was paid in salary (to the Clerk?); 3,800 to Dr. George Lee; 1,800 to Capt. Robert Spencer; 224 to Richard Greene; 3,900 to Mr. John Goring; 540 to Mr. Benjamin Harrison; 5,000 to Capt. Roger Potter (mentioned before as Berkeley's Jailer at Green Spring, though a Surry man); 1,400 to Roger Rawlings; 360 to Mr. Randall Holt; 11,396 lbs. of tobacco to Col. Jordan "for souldrs & other Necessarys to ye forte"; 1,250 to Nicholas Meriwether and 8,300 to Col. Swann, both for various purposes only vaguely hinted at; 2,200 to Capt. Samuel Swann; 180 to James Forbes and 250 to Alexander Spencer (both these being old Baconians); and 5,000 "to Burgesses for boards." There is also an account of arms sold by Capt. Charles Barham and Lieut. Thomas Busby, with deduction for salary to them. Capt. Barham's account shows a pair of pistols, holsters and a sword sold to George Proctor and to himself; pistols and holsters sold to Sion Hill; and swords sold to Messrs. Robert Ruffin, William Edwards, William Newsum, John White and John Price. Lt. Busby's account shows pistols, holsters and sword for himself, and pistols and holsters secured by George Lee from Col. Jordan, and by John Rutherford from Lt. Potter (id., p. 81). We should like to know what was the purpose of the above sale of arms. Perhaps it was to keep order in the latter days of the rebellion or just after it. At any rate, it gives us a clue to the anti-Baconians in Surry, like the list of jurymen who tried the cases at the July and September Courts. George Proctor and John Rutherford, however, were among Bacon's men.

On the next page (p. 182) we have a list of payments from the county levy. The Surry Burgesses, Col. Jordan and Capt. Baker (session of March, 1675/6), Messrs. Caufield and Mason (June, 1676), Maj. Browne and Mr. Harrison (February 1676/7), and Maj. Browne and Capt. Swann (October, 1677), were paid amounts varying from 3,250 to 6,550 lbs. of tobacco. Robert Ruffin was paid "to Cary County Cort: to Assembly & his trouble alsoe for pressing hoate for Capt. Swann & for George Proctors, mending the Prison." John White was paid for powder, George Proctor for repairing the prison and "for Entertainemt Prisoners" (200 lbs. tobacco for the last). Col. Swann, Lt.-Col. Jordan, Capt. Baker, Maj. Browne, Messrs. Caufield and Allen, Capts. Swann and Spencer, Messrs. Harrison, Meriwether and Mason, were each paid 300 lbs. of tobacco for 160 lbs. of Biscuit. Capt. Spencer was paid "pr 5 Inquisitions"; Richard Hogwood for 35 lbs. of bacon; John Moring for 45 lbs. of bacon; Lt.-Col. Jordan "for Canvis for ye Biskett sent to Bacon by Act"; Robert Caufield was paid "for Charge on a wounded man at Towne", indicating that he was present in Jamestown with Berkeley during the siege; William Edwards was paid "for County service", Mr. Meriwether for 43 lbs. of bacon, William Foreman for a pair of hinges, Lt. Col. Jordan for 29 lbs. of bacon, and Capt. Barham for 45 lbs. of pork. Mention is also made of £22 1s 6d "due from ye Publique for amunition assign'd Major Browne." Much of the above must be payment for services by non-Baconians in the stirring days of 1676, while Bacon's men (like Arthur Long) had to pay finally for even the ammunition they used. Thus ends the story of Surry County in Bacon's Rebellion, with the victory of the old order. Surry men had to wait another hundred years before they secured a truly liberal and representative government.

Chapter XIV

PARISHES AND MINISTERS

THE parishes most often met with in the Surry records are Lawne's Creek Parish, Southwark Parish, and Albermarle Parish. When Surry was part of James City County it was also part of James City Parish which extended both north and south of the James River.

Lawne's Creek Parish was the first parish created within the present limits of colonial Surry County. This parish was cut off in January 1639/40 by the House of Burgesses, from James City Parish. It was originally of small extent and included only the territory between Lower Chippoke's and Lawne's Creek from their respective sources down to the James River and the creek that separates Hog Island from the mainland. (Wm. IV (2), p. 158). Hog Island remained a part of James City Parish until March 1642/3 when it and part of the territory between Lower Chippokes and Sunken Marsh Creeks were made into an independent parish called "Chippoaks", by reason of its remoteness from James City. (Hen. I, 277.) This new parish seems to have soon become absorbed into the Lawne's Creek Parish.

In November 1647 new settlers on the south side of the James petitioned for a new church. A new parish called "Southwark", named for a parish in London on the south side of the Thames, was established. This parish extended from College Run to Upper Chippokes Creek. (Hen. I, p. 347.)

However, this new parish was required to pay to the James City Parish all customary tithes and dues and all past taxes toward the cost of Jamestown's Church on which its members were in arrears. (Hen. I, p. 347.)

This agreement was rescinded in 1649 by Governor Berkeley as follows:

> "These are to certify that the agreement between the South Side of James River and this Parish is that the said South Side shall pay unto ye Parish of James City for the year, sixteen hundred and fifteen pounds of tobacco and 1 bushel of corne per head, and are for ever hereafter to remain a particular parish by Themselves without any

further payment at all to this parish. Witness my hand ye 3rd January 1649.

William Berkeley

"Recorded at the request and charge of Major Marriott 18th October 1670." (W.M. 3, p. 125.)

These two parishes were very extensive in length. The Rev. John Cargill, minister of Southwark Parish from 1708 until 1732, wrote the Bishop of London in 1724, "my Parish is twenty miles in width and one hundred in length, being a frontier Parish. It has 394 families. The school for Indians is on the borders of my parish. There are one church and two chapels and seventy or eighty communicants."

Lawne's Creek parish was one hundred and twenty miles in length. (Perry, Va. *Church History,* 306.) These two parishes, by reason of their length, extended into what is now Brunswick County. When that county was formed a new parish called St. Andrew's was cut off from the Surry parishes. On January 1, 1738-39, by act of the House of Burgesses, another new parish called Albermarle was erected out of that portion of Surry which lies below the Blackwater River. (Hen. V, 75.) By this act also that portion of Surry lying north of the Blackwater was placed in the parish of Southwark. This thereby brought to a close the existence of ancient Lawne's Creek Parish.

The first minister of Albermarle Parish was the noted Reverend William Willie who began the invaluable parish register so often quoted in the volume to follow. On February 1, 1753/4 the new county of Sussex was formed out of Albermale Parish.

The first church erected within the present bounds of Surry County is probably the one mentioned in the "Minutes of the Council and General Court" under date of October 1628 (p. 175) when John Day was sworn and examined before the court. He said "that he heard that Richard Tree did work upon the Church at Hogg Island a week or fortnight, as he verily thinketh, after Mr. Uty came home from the General Assembly. Andrew Roe, sworn and examined, saith that about the beginning of August last he saw certain several parcells of dub'd boards lying at the Church at Hogg Island and that since that time he hath seen the said Tree and his servants fetch boards from thence. For as much as it appears to the Court that Rich: Tree hath neglected the building of the Church at Hogg Island contrary to his covenant, whereby he should forfeit one thousand pounds of tobacco. It is ordered that the said Tree shall, before the 20th of December next, finish the said Church and the inhabitants are to bring the timber necessary for the finishing of the work to the place where the Church is to be built by the last of this present October, and shall find him nails sufficient for the said work. And if the said Tree shall neglect to finish same according to this order he shall forfeit the sum of 1000 lbs. of tobacco, and the work to be done by the said Tree without any to be paid him therefore in regard to his neglect."

The site of this church and a larger succeeding church is "On a high point between two ravines leading down into James River, just west of the main road to Hog Island and a half mile southeast of Hog Island Creek." (Mason, W. & M. 20 (2), p. 290.) From this location Jamestown Island is in plain sight on the opposite shore of the river.

The Reverend William Thompson, a wealthy man, was minister of both Southwark and Lawne's Creek Parishes from 1662 to 1675 when he became minister of Washington Parish, Westmoreland County, where he died. It is very probable he came here from New England for on July 1, 1664, "Wm. Norton of New England of New London, gent., sold to Wm. Thompson of Surry, minister of God's word, a neck of land situated in New London disjoyning upon ye great river." (Book 1, p. 52.) This property had been purchased by Norton from a former minister of the New London Parish. Was it possible that the Reverend Thompson was once a Puritan? In the assessment 1675, he was the owner of eight tithables, the second largest in the county.

In 1675, the Reverend Robert Parke, on arriving from England, became the guest of Randall Holt of Hog Island. While there he preached at the Lawne's Creek Church in the absence of the Reverend William Thompson, the regular pastor, and made a favorable impression. The congregation was so pleased with his sermon that they desired him to officiate at Lawne's Creek when the Reverend Thompson was holding services in the upper parish church. The vestry arranged that a meeting of citizens should be held on an appointed day and that Mr. Parke be requested to deliver a sermon with a view to his becoming Mr. Thompson's assistant. Much to the congregation's surprise the sheriff was there ahead of Mr. Parke and when Mr. Parke appeared he was forbidden the pulpit. The Reverend Thompson had complained to the Governor and Council and had obtained an order prohibiting Parke's appointment as his curate. (See Bruce, Vol. 1, p. 190.)

While the congregation was much disappointed and had to be dispersed by the sheriff, it seems nevertheless that the Reverend William Thompson, who served them many years was much esteemed for he is described in the records in 1674 as "a faithful and painstaking minister" who led a "quiet sober and exemplary life." (1671-81, p. 124.)

This short sketch of the parishes and ministers is given mainly to describe the location and bounds of the parishes mentioned in the records of Surry and Sussex. Anyone wishing more information should read the excellent account of *The Colonial Churches of Surry and Sussex Counties, Virginia,* by George Carrington Mason in *William and Mary Quarterly,* Vol. 20 (2), page 285.

A list of the ministers of Surry shown in Goodwin's *Colonial Churches* is as follows:

SOUTHWARK PARISH 1647	LAWNE'S CREEK PARISH 1640-1738
William Thompson 1662-75	William Thompson 1662-75
John Clough 1680 Minister of Jamestown 1676 Condemned to death by Bacon but released. Died and buried in Jamestown 1684.	John Wayne 1680 John or Thomas Burnet 1702 James Warden 1717-25. From Scotland, dismissed for immoderation.

Alexander Walker 1702

John Cargill 1708-23

Henry Elebeck 1747 *circa* to 1751 when he died.

Mr. Hotchkiss prior to 1754.

Peter Davis 1754-58.

Christopher McRae 1766-72. Moved to Cumberland County.

Benjamin Blagrave 1774-76. Son of John Blagrave of Oxford. Minister New Kent 1789.

Henry J. Burges 1785. Born in Virginia Nov. 28, 1744, died 1797. Member of Committee of Safety of Isle of Wight, son of Thomas Burges or Burgess, born in Stafford, England, Sept. 6, 1712; K.B. Nor. Car. Oct. 2, 1741; Minister Edgecombe Parish, Halifax, 1759-79.

Chapter XV

COUNTY GOVERNMENT—1652-1776

THE County Court appears to have been the heart of Virginia's county government. County courts were first established in 1634 when Virginia was divided into eight shires. Surry's county court was not formed until 1652 when Surry was made an independent county. These courts were presided over by justices selected by the governor from the most prominent and able citizens of the counties.

The members of the court were first called "commissioners." This was changed in March 1642-43, when the general assembly ordered that the commissioners be stiled "Commissioners of the County Court." When Richard Bennett served as governor during Cromwell's time it seems that the general assembly adopted the prerogative of appointing "commissioners," for on July 10, 1653, the general assembly ordered that "Mr. William Edwards be added to the Commissioners of Surry county." (Bk. 1, p. 11.) Also in Governor Bennett's time the "Gentlemen Justices," as they were later called, assumed the privilege of recommending certain persons to the governor from among whom he should choose the county officers. These nominations were not only for the office of Sheriff and other minor offices, but also consisted of persons suggested for membership in the county court. In this way the "gentlemen justices" perpetuated themselves in office and often served for life.

From the records of the Surry Court it seems that three or four persons were usually nominated for the governor's consideration as shown by the following orders of court.

"At a court held at Southwark, March 19, 1707, Present His Majesty's Justices: Capt. William Browne, Mr. Joseph John Jackman and Mr. Ethelred Taylor are severally recommended for the office of Sheriff of their county, for the ensuing year." (Cal. State Papers 1, p. 12.)

"Sept. 19, 1737, William Short, William Rookings, Thomas Cocke and Parks Nicholson were recommended by the Court as fit and able persons to execute the office of Inspector at Cabin Point warehouse; and William Clinch, Thos. Holt, William Seward and William Edwards were recommended for the same office at Gray's Creek." (Cal. State Papers 1, p. 233.)

The county court usually consisted of ten members but in 1694 the general assembly ordered that the "County Court is to consist of eight judicious persons to be appointed by the Governor. Four of whom being of the Quorum to make a court and they are impowered by this act to do all the things which the Justices of England may do." (V. M. 9, p. 378.)

Some duties could be performed by a single justice, others required two or more justices, but the majority of offenses could only be heard by the justices sitting as a body. The full court was required to meet four times a year and this resulted in such meetings being called "quarter sessions."

All of the justices were expected to attend these sessions but if some were absent causes could be heard provided a member of the Quorum was present. Those persons appointed to be "of the Quorum" were presumably persons of superior ability or learning but probably they were often friendly to the Governor.

It would appear that the Surry court early abandoned the habit of meeting "quarterly," for the general assembly, on October 1710, ordered that the Surry court meet on the third Wednesday of every month. (3 H. 506.) In October 1748, this meeting day was changed to the third Tuesday in every month.

As stated before a single justice could hear small causes. In 1662 it was ordered by the general assembly that "the court shall not take recognizance of any cause under the value of 200 lbs. of tobacco or 20 shillings sterling which a Justice may and is hereby authorized and impowered to determine." (2 H. 72.) Also in that same session it was provided that "whenever a jury is sent out, an officer sworn to that purpose shall keep them from meat and drink until they have agreed on their verdict." (2 H. 74.) This order probably brought about some speedy decisions.

The Governor seems to have retained the right to suspend "gentlemen justices" who displeased him, for on May 8, 1678, Governor Herbert Jeffries, in a letter to the Surry County Court, states that Capt. Arthur Allen and Mr. Robert Caufield, as members of the Court, held at Southwarke, had opposed his order that Capt. Swann should be High Sheriff of the County and had "filled the ears of the Peoplle in a full court with amazement and doubt, and drew the rest of the Commissioners to comply with them which was a bad example." He suspended "Robert Caufield and Capt. Arthur Allen from sitting in the

Commission or any other magisterial authority." (Bk. 2—Mar. 1671-July 5, 1684), p. 178.)

The power of the county court seems to be well illustrated by the following order taken from the records:

"Surry Court 4th Sept. 1672

Present, Col. Thos. Swan, Lt. Col. George Jordan, Capt. Lau. Baker, Major Wm. Broune, Mr. Robert Caufield, Capt. Robt. Spencer, Mr. Benj. Harrison, Justices."

Matthias Marriott was found in contempt of the court. This was based upon an Act of the Assembly restraining servants from walking abroad on Sundays. Also it was found that he gave his negro a note "to go abroad on Sunday," he having no business, also he rendered scurrilous language to the Court both yesterday and to-day." He was fined 200 lbs. of tobacco with costs.

"Whereas information hath been given to this court that too careless and inconsiderate liberty is given to negroes, not only in being permitted to meet together on Saturdays and Sundays, whereby they win opportunity to consult of unlawful projects and combinations to the danger of the neighbors as well as to their masters. Also that the apparel commonly worn by negroes does highten their foolish pride and induce them to steal fine linen and other ornaments, where if it is ordered from henceforth that no negro shall be allowed to wear any white linen but shall wear blue shirts so that it may be discovered if they steal or wear other linens."

Before considering other county officers it might be well to state that the Governor, who has been mentioned heretofore, was all powerful. Berkeley was virtually a dictator. In some cases the duly appointed Governor never came to Virginia and a Lieutenant-Governor acted for him. Besides having jurisdiction over all county officers, the Governor could convene, dismiss or prorogue the General Assembly and veto its acts. Also he presided over the General Court which was the highest in Virginia.

Next to the Governor in importance was the Council of State usually twelve in number. They were selected by the King from names submitted by the Governor. Oftentimes the King named the councillors of his own selection directly from England. The Councillors were chosen from men of the greatest wealth and social position in Virginia. Men who sometimes desired appointment to the council were turned down because their wealth was not sufficient to support the dignity of the office.

Next in importance to the Council were the members of the House of Burgesses, the law making body of the Colony. "The word 'burgess' denotes a freedman of a borough or municipality and recalls the fact that prior to 1619 Virginia was divided into four boroughs." (Mrs. W. P. Hiden, V. M. 54, p. 7.)

The Coroner and the County Surveyor were also nominated by the justice of the county court. The Coroner presided over the inquest of certain deceased persons, who died suddenly or violently, in order to determine in what manner they came to their deaths. The office was very ancient in England and existed as early as 1194.

It was the duty of the County Surveyor to lay out the bounds of patented lands so that patents or deeds to same could be obtained.

Constables were appointed directly by the county court and their principal duties were the serving of writs and summons.

The Clerk of the county court was appointed by the secretary of the colony. The clerk's office was one of great responsibility. (H. I. 305.) This often led to the office being perpetuated in families. Witness how long the Edwards family held this office in Surry, even after the office became elective.

The County-Lieutenant bore the title of Colonel or Lieut.-Colonel and was commander of the militia. The full colonels were nearly always members of the Council and were also judges of the general court. This system of holding several high places at one time gave rise to the power and prestige of about sixteen families who became rulers of Virginia by the formation of a virtual oligarchy during the first half of the eighteenth century.

The following families appear to have had the greatest length of service in that body—Beverley, Burwell, Byrd, Carter, Corbin, Digges, Grymes, Harrison, Lee, Ludwell, Nelson, Page, Randolph, Robinson, Taylor and Wormeley.

The Harrisons were the only members of this Oligarchy who resided in Surry. It will be noted from the records that they continually held office. Their rise in power and influence continued after Colonial days had passed, and enabled them to furnish two presidents to the United States.

From a report made by Governor Hugh Drysdale covering the "present state of Virginia" in 1726, something can be shown concerning the condition of the county in that year.

"Surry County 1726

Acres of Land: 228,770. Tithables: 2049

Sheriff: Benj. Edwards.

Coroners: Wm. Gray, Robt. Wynne.

Justices of the peace: Wm. Brown, Hen. Harrison, Jno. Simmons, Wm. Gray, Tho. Collier, Stith Bolling, Robt Wynne, Arthur Allen (Quorum) Tho. Cocke, Howell Edmunds, Wm. Edwards, Benj. Edwards, Wm. Brown, jun., John Mason.

Burgesses: Wm. Gray, Henry Harrison.

Clerk of County Court: John Allen.

Land Surveyor: John Allen.

Parishes: Southwark, Lawne's Creek. Minister: Mr. Cargill.

No. Militia: Horse 214; Foot 410.

County Lieutenants: Nath. Harrison.

Sort of Tobacco: Arronoco." (V. M. 48, p. 151.)

Since the functions of the Council, the House of Burgesses and the County Court have been discussed it might be well to relate some of their acts and orders pertaining to Surry County.

The King of the Weyanokes, on July 2, 1659, sold to Elizabeth Short, of Surry, a boy named "Weetoffen" for the full term of his life for a young horse foal aged one year.

This deed was set aside by the House of Burgesses because the King had no power to sell him as he was a Powhatan and not a Weyanoke Indian. Also because he spoke the English tongue perfectly and was desirous of baptism. (H. I., p. 155.)

A fort was established early on the Blackwater for defense against the Indians, for on March 1675-6, the House provided that "the Fort on the Blackwater River in Surry shall have 729 pounds of shot and 180 pounds of powder furnished it." (2 H., 329.)

In 1691 a post for the collection of custom dues for Surry county was established at "the mouth of Gray's Creek on the lower side thereof." (3 H. 61.)

In August 1702 the House enacted that the rate for ferrying across the James River should be as follows:

"At the mouth of Chipokes Creek over to the Row, or Martins Brandon, the price for a man 6 pence; for a man and a horse 2 shillings 6 pence.

"From Hog Island Maine to Archers Hope, the price for a man, two "ryals"; for a man and horse 2 sh. 6 d.

"From Swan's Point to Jamestown. the price of a man. a royall; for a man and horse, 2 royalls. (3 H. 219.)

By October 1705 the prices had fallen for it was enacted that "At the mouth of Upper Chipoake's Creek, over to the Row, or Martin Brandon, the price of a man 6 pence; for a man and a horse, one shilling." (3 H. 470.)

The county was well settled up to the Blackwater River by 1700, and some patents had been taken up on the south side of the Blackwater although that part of Surry was not legally opened for settlement until 1710.

The county extended to the Carolina line but its boundaries on the south and west were uncertain. In October 1705 the House passed a measure which provided that "on account of the inconvenience of the inhabitants of Prince George, Surry, Isle of Wight and Nansemond by reason of the uncertainty of the bounds of the said counties on the South side of the Blackwater Swamp, it ordered that the surveyors of the counties, before Dec. 25, 1706, shall survey and lay out the Blackwater Swamp and that the line agreed upon shall afterwards be the dividing line of each county backwards as far as this Government extends." (3 H. 480.)

Prior to December 8, 1710, persons were prohibited from entering or taking up land between the Nottoway and Meherrin River "within the bounds of the controversy between this government and Carolina." At that time this country was thrown open for settlement. (4 H. 546.) This resulted in a great rush for lands. (See "Land grants 1710-40," post.)

As mentioned above, part of this county and also the county of Isle of Wight were annexed to Brunswick in 1732. In May 1732 the Assembly provided that "After the first day of January next those parts of the said counties of Surry and Isle of Wight which lie between and are included in the bounds hereafter mentioned, and the bounds of the

County of Brunswick, as it now stands (that is to say) a straight line
to be run from the mouth of a branch of the Nottoway River, called
Chetacrie, between Colonel Harrison's Quarter and Matthew Parham
in the said county of Surry, to Meherrin River, to the line dividing the
said counties of Surry and Isle of Wight, and from thence down that
river to the line dividing this county and North Carolina to be annexed
to the county of Brunswick." (4 H. 455.)

The county below the Blackwater seems to have become well settled
by 1727, for petitions presented to the Council in that year indicate
that the settlers desired to have the court house located nearer the center
of the fast growing county. The order of the Council was as follows:

"March 6, 1727.

On hearing of the several petitions of the inhabitants of Surry County
with the allegations of the several partys touching the most convenient
place for holding the Court, it is ordered that for a more equal determination of the dispute between the said parties that the Surveyor of
the County is hereby required to place before this Board a map describing the place where the Court house now stands and a place prepared
for erecting a new Court House together with the distance of each from
the outward bounds of the county." (Council Journals, V. M. 32,
p. 381.)

The Council decided to move the Court House to a place near what
is now the town of Littleton in present Sussex County according to an
order entered June 13, 1728, as follows:

"It being represented to this Board that the place lately appropriated for
erecting a new court house in the County of Surry will be attended
with some inconveniencies to the inhabitants resorting thereto, and that
about a half mile from thence on the South Side of Blackwater there is
a convenient place near a good spring where the Court House may be
more properly fixed, it is ordered that the Court House be erected on
the land of Mr. Edmunds near the great wood which leads from the
bridge through his plantation, and as near as conveniently may be to
the spring. That place appearing to this Board to be most suited to the
general convenience of the inhabitants." (V. M. 33, p. 19.)

When the county south of the Blackwater was cut off to form Sussex
County, it was ordered on Feb. 17, 1756, that the Surry Court House

and prison be fixed on the land of William Clinch called "Troopers." This place which is now known as the "Old Court House" is about two and a half miles from the present Court House. The Court House was moved from Troopers to its present location in 1796. Robert Mc Intosh who kept a tavern at site then known as "McIntosh's Cross Roads" presented the land to the county. The first court was held here on April 25, 1797. The old McIntosh tavern was destroyed by fire June 16, 1925.

The court house of 1796 lasted one hundred years as it was not replaced until 1896 by a larger building. This building burned December 6, 1906. A new court house erected the next year was destroyed by fire January 17, 1922. The present building was completed in 1923.

Governor Spotswood made several visits into the southern part of the county. On October 6, 1711 he made a journey into Surry, and with some of the Surry militia, went on a week's journey to the Nottoway Indian towns. He went into Surry, Prince George and Henrico in 1713 and endeavored to raise two hundred volunteers to go with him against the Indians who infested the frontiers. (W. M. 3, p. 41.)

In 1716, Governor Spotswood journeyed to Fort Christiana, situated on the Meherrin River in what is now Brunswick. On his way he stopped at Hicks' Ford, now Emporia, where Captain Robert Hicks lived. The Captain's place, where his 1,000-acre grant was located, was on the extreme frontier. The land fell into Brunswick in 1732 and later, in 1782, became part of the newly formed County of Greensville.

A small insurrection of slaves occurred in 1709 and "Pursuant to an order of the Council on Mar. 24, 1709, Thos. Holt, Nathaniel Harrison, Wm. Edwards, Wm. Cocke and Ethelred Taylor were appointed to examine several Negro and Indian slaves 'Concerning a late Dangerous Conspiracy carried out by great numbers of said Negro & Indian Slaves for making their escape and for destroying and cutting off such of her Majestys Subjects as should oppose their design. They punished and discharged all except Mr. William Edwards' Scipio, Mr. Joseph John Jackman's Salvadore and Mr. Samuel Thompson's Tom Shaw, who they determined were the principal contrivers and they were ordered to be held in the county jail until further orders.' " (Cal. State Papers I, p. 129.)

From the records of a court held in Isle of Wight the same date it appears that Scipio turned "states evidence," for Manuell a negro be-

longing to Mr. John George of Isle of Wight was ordered to receive
forty lashes upon his bare back implicated by the confession of Scipio
a negro of Mr. William Edwards of Surry.

In 1736 a bridge was ordered built over the Nottoway River where
it divided the counties of Surry and Brunswick at a place called
"Swedes," on the land of Col. Benjamin Harrison, because it would
be beneficial and convenient to the inhabitants of both counties. (4 H.
530.)

A tobacco warehouse was burned at Gray's Creek in 1736 and the
House provided for a measure of relief for those who lost by the fire.
They ordered that inasmuch as there was "lately burnt, eighty hhgds.
of tobacco, 21284 lbs. for which transfer notes had been given, and
5561 lbs. of uninspected tobacco was lost in said fire, it is ordered that
the sume of £ 786, 9 sh. 8 d. out of public money arising upon duties
on liquor and slaves be divided among the sufferers according to their
losses." (4 H. 533.)

A tobacco warehouse also existed at Cabin Point at the same time.
On May 1732 the inspector at Cabin Point received a salary of £50 and
the one at Gray's Creek £30 per annum. (4 H. 335.)

The Parish was another unit of county government. As stated in the
former chapter, the county, on January 1, 1738-39, was divided into
two parishes, Southwark and Albemarle.

One of the activities of the parish that was civil was that of "pro-
cessing." This custom was at first religious. In Gaul in the fifth century, on the three days preceding Ascension Day, the priest led his
people around the parish with psalms and prayers for an abundant
harvest. Thus the knowledge of the bounds of the parish and of the
individual land owners became valuable and was introduced into English custom. (Mrs. Hiden, V. M. 54, p. 6.)

In Virginia, this perambulation or processioning was a yearly func-
tion of the vestry. There were two processioners appointed for each
district. In their journey over the parish lands they were usually accompanied by the interested land owners who were thus enabled to know
the exact extent and location of their lands.

An early vestry book of Albemarle Parish showing the bounds of the
parishioner's holdings is still in existence.

The Vestry also fixed the amount of tithes, generally in tobacco, that should be paid by each person in the parish. This was called the parish levy. It was expended in caring for the sick and poor and also for paying ministers' salaries. The Quakers objected to this payment and were often thrown in jail for not paying their parish dues. The parish levy was in addition to the county levy, or regular taxes, assessed by the justices of the county.

On November 1762, the House, in fixing the salary of its members, decreed that "over and above his daily allowance every Burgess from Surry shall be paid 15 shillings per day for attending upon and returning from the General Assembly. (7 H. 527.)

The House created the "town of Cobham" in February 1772. It was provided that "fifty acres on the lower side of Gray's Creek shall be laid off into lots and shall be called or known by the name of Cobham." (8 H. 617.) In 1781, on July the 4th, the British Army under Lord Cornwallis crossed over the James River from Cobham to Jamestown on their way to Yorktown. They were marching up from the south where they had recently fought the Battle of Guilford C. H.

The Committee of Safety for Surry, on Feb. 5, 1776, just prior to the signing of the Declaration of Independence, consisted of the following members: William Hart, Allen Cocke, William Brown, William Clinch, N. Faulcon Jr., Ethelred Gray, Charles Judkins, John Cocke, Jr., John Watkins, Jr., John H. Cocke, William Simmons, Benj. Putney, James Kea, John Cocke, John Watkins, Willis Wilson, William Hamlin, Henry Howard, William Nelson, Lemuel Cocke, Rev. Benj. Blagrave, John Wesson, Clerk. (W. & M. 5, p. 249.)

The Committee for Sussex May 8, 1775, was as follows:

Michael Blow, chairman; David Mason, John Cargill, William Blunt, John Peters, James Jones, Richard Parker, Augustine Claiborne, Henry Gee, William Nicholson, Robert Jones, John Mason, Jr., George Rives, George Booth. (Do.)

Not long before the battle of Yorktown, Colonel Benjamin Blunt of Southampton was in command of the militia ordered to assemble at Surry Old Court House. While there, on September 9, 1781, he wrote a letter to Colonel Davies about the condition of his troops, as follows (extract): "He has been ordered by Gen. Mühlenberg to take command of the militia and to assemble at this place. Only about 250 men arrived chiefly from Southampton, but the men from Greensville and

Brunswick are daily expected. These are in great want of lead, flints, salt and camp kettles. Indeed their guns are not fit for action. He urged the importance of attention to these wants." (Cal. State Papers, Vol. 2, p. 407.)

On September 11, 1781, Colonel Blunt wrote to General Mühlenberg that "He had collected the Militia of Southampton, Sussex, Dinwiddie, Greensville, and Amelia, in all amounting to 510 infantry and 39 horse. The Brunswick Militia under Col. Eliot are just coming in, 230 infantry and 32 horse but with only 20 guns. The horsemen are well mounted but in want of swords." (Do., p. 413.)

Colonel Blunt wrote on September 24, 1781, to Governor Nelson informing him "he had sent horsemen to several adjoining counties including Nansemond, to collect horses and in a few days should have a considerable number. His troops are reduced from about 400 to 200 with 11 officers, by severe sickness. A raging fever in Southampton has carried off a number of people. In consequence many men have been furloughed who may soon return. Requests to be informed if he is to march with his whole force or proportion of them." They probably marched to Yorktown.

After the Revolution migration from Surry, southward and westward, was very extensive. On February 8, 1787, James Allen Bradby advertised for sale in the *Virginia Gazette,* "his beautiful seat on the James River two miles below Cobham."

Surry was also invaded in the War of 1812. Colonel William Allen was then in charge of the county militia and he wrote the Governor on July 1, 1813, as follows: "The day I wrote you from Cabin Point by mail, June 29th, I ordered my regiment to convene at Surry Ct. House the next day. Have at this time all the men that have arms on duty, to prevent, if possible the British from committing depredations on the shores. Today I went down to Four Mile Tree, where I understood the British had landed from some of their Barges; unfortunately they had returned about half an hour before I got there with two companies of Infantry. They are destroying all the stock of sheep and cattle they can find and the furniture in the houses. They took from Four Mile Tree and Mount Pleasant this morning 26 Head of Sheep and the fowls, destroyed the furniture at Four Mile Tree and Mount Pleasant. They were also at Mr. J. D. Edwards but have not heard what damage he sustained. * * * Major Langley C. Wills, whom I have stationed between Cobham and Lower Chipoaks informed me that one of the Barges came ashore with a flag, informed he was sorry to hear the Barges were plundering up the river; that it was contrary to orders." (Cal. State Pap. 10, p. 239.)

BURGESS FROM PLANTATIONS

1623-24 From Incorporation of James City

Jamestown

William Pierce Clement Dilke
Richard Stephens Edward Blayney

Hog Island

John Utie John Chew

1625 Members of Convention

Council

George Sandys Roger Smith Ralph Hamor

1627-28   Burgess

John Chew Edward Grendon John Smyth
John Utie William Perry

BURGESS FROM SURRY PLANTATIONS

1629   Pace's Paine

William Perry John Smith

Hog Island

John Chew Richard Tree

1629-30   Pace's Paine and Smyth's Mount

William Perry

Hog Island

John Utie

1631-32 Captain Perry's downward to Hog Island

Captain William Perry Richard Richards

1632   Smyth's Mount and Perry's Point

John Smyth

Over the water against James City
Richard Richards

Hog Island
Richard Tree

1632-33 Smyth's Mount, the other side of the water and Hog Island
Thomas Grendon

1639-40 Chickahominy Parish and the Upper Chippoakes or Smith's Fort
Lower Chippoakes, Lawne's Creek and Hog Island
Thomas Fawcett

BURGESS FROM JAMES CITY

(Persons shown in capitals were from the Surry side.)

1619   CAPTAIN WILLIAM POWELL, Ensign William Spence
1623-24 Richard Kingsmill, EDWARD BLANEY
1629   George Menefie, Richard Kingsmill, Richard Brewster
1629-30 John Southerne, Robert Barrington, Richard Brewster
1631-32 John Southerne, Thomas Crump
1632-33 JOHN CORKER, Thomas Crump
1641   Captain Robert Hutchinson, Francis Fowler, John White, THOMAS
        HILL, RICHARD RICHARDS, Ferdinand Franklin, JEREMIE CLEMENT,
        Thomas Folles, WILLIAM BUTLER.
1642   Ferdinand Franklin, WILLIAM BUTLER, Francis Fowler, George
        Worleigh.
1644   Captain Robert Hutchinson, STEPHEN WEBB, Edward Travis,
        Thomas Loveing, GEORGE JORDAN, JOHN SHEPARD, THOMAS
        WARREN.
1644-45 Captain Robert Hutchinson, Ambrose Harmer, William Barrett,
        JOHN CORKER, Peter Ridley, GEORGE STEPHENS, JOHN ROGERS.
1645   JOHN FLOOD, Walter Chiles, THOMAS SWANN, Robert Wetherall,
        Ambrose Harmer, THOMAS WARREN, Peter Ridley, GEORGE
        STEPHENS.
1646   Ambrose Harmer, Walter Chiles, CAPTAIN ROBERT SHEPERD,
        GEORGE JORDAN, Thomas Loving, William Barrett.
1647   Captain Robert Hutchinson, Captain Bridges Freeman, CAPTAIN
        ROBERT SHEPERD, GEORGE JORDAN, William Davis, Peter Ridley.

1649   Walter Chiles, THOMAS SWANN, William Barrett, George Read, William Whittaker, JOHN DUNSTON.

1652   Robert Wetherall, LT. COL. JOHN FLUDD, Henry Soane, David Mansell, GEORGE STEPHENS, William Whittaker.

BURGESS FROM SURRY

1652   WILLIAM THOMAS, WILLIAM EDWARDS, GEORGE STEPHENS.

1653   CAPTAIN WILLIAM BUTLERS, WILLIAM EDWARDS

1654   WILLIAM BATT, JAMES MASON

1657-58 LT. COL. THOMAS SWAN, WILLIAM EDWARDS, MAJOR WILLIAM BUTLER, CAPTAIN WILLIAM CAUFIELD.

1658-59 CAPTAIN GEORGE JORDAN, THOMAS WARREN, CAPTAIN WILLIAM CAUFIELD.

1663   THOMAS WARREN, CAPTAIN WILLIAM COCKERAM

1666   LAWRENCE BAKER, THOMAS WARREN

1672   CAPTAIN LAWRENCE BAKER

1673   CAPTAIN LAWRENCE BAKER, WILLIAM BROWNE

1674-76 CAPTAIN LAWRENCE BAKER, GEORGE JORDAN

1676   ROBERT CAUFIELD, FRANCIS MASON

1676-77 WILLIAM BROWNE, BENJAMIN HARRISON

1677   WILLIAM BROWNE, SAMUEL SWAN

1679   WILLIAM BROWNE, THOMAS SWANN

1680-82 SAMUEL SWAN, BENJAMIN HARRISON

1682   WILLIAM BROWNE, ARTHUR ALLEN

1685-88 MAJOR SAMUEL SWANN, MAJOR ARTHUR ALLEN

1691-92 FRANCIS MASON, BENJAMIN HARRISON

1693   MAJOR SAMUEL SWANN, CAPTAIN FRANCIS CLEMENTS, THOMAS SWAN, JOHN THOMPSON

1695-96 MAJOR SAMUEL SWANN, JOHN THOMPSON

1697   BENJAMIN HARRISON, JOHN THOMPSON

1698   BENJAMIN HARRISON, THOMAS SWAN

1699   NATHANIEL HARRISON, THOMAS HOLT

1700-01 NATHANIEL HARRISON, SAMUEL THOMPSON

1702-06 NATHANIEL HARRISON, WILLIAM EDWARDS

1710-13 WILLIAM GRAY, JOHN SIMMONS

1715-18 WILLIAM GRAY, JOHN SIMMONS, HENRY HARRISON, SAMUEL THOMPSON.

1720-22 HENRY HARRISON, JOHN SIMMONS

1720-26 HENRY HARRISON, WILLIAM GRAY
1736-40 THOMAS EDMUNDS
1738-42 CAPTAIN JOHN RUFFIN, JOHN CARGILL
1744-47 CAPTAIN JOHN RUFFIN, RICHARD COCKE
1748-56 ROBERT JONES, AUGUSTINE CLAIBORNE
1756   BENJAMIN HARRISON, JR., WILLIAM CLINCH
1757   BENJAMIN HARRISON, JR., BENJAMIN COCKE
1759   HARTWELL COCKE, WILLIAM ALLEN
1761   HARTWELL COCKE, HENRY BROWNE
1763   HARTWELL COCKE, WILLIAM BAILEY
1766   HARTWELL COCKE, THOMAS BAILEY
1773   ALLEN COCKE, NICHOLAS FAULCON, JR.

BURGESS FROM JAMES CITY AND JAMESTOWN

1652, November 25th Robert Wetherall, William Wittaker, Abraham Watson, Henry Soane.

1653   Colonel Walter Chiles, William Whittaker, Henry Soane, Abraham Watson.

1654   Thomas Depwall, Abraham Watson, William Whittaker, Henry Soane.

1655-56 Lt. Colonel William Whittaker, Theophilius Hone, COLONEL JOHN FLOOD, Robert Holt, Robert Ellyson.

1657-58 Henry Soane, Major Richard Webster, Thomas Loving, WILLIAM CORKER.

1658-59 Walter Chiles, Captain William Whittaker, Captain Thomas Foulke, Captain Matthew Edloe.

1659-60 Henry Soane, Captain Robert Ellison, Richard Ford, William Morley.

1663   Captain Robert Ellyson, Walter Chiles, Captain Ramsey.

1666   Thomas Ballard, Captain Edward Ramsey, Major Theopilius Hone.

1676   Richard Lawrence

1683   Thomas Clayton

1684   Henry Hartwell

1685-86 Colonel Thomas Ballard.

1688   Phillip Ludwell, James Bray, William Sherwood

1692-93 Captain Miles Cary
1696   Phillip Ludwell, Jr., William Sherwood (dec.), Henry Drake, Miles Sherman
1698   Lewis Burwell
1702   James Bray, George Marable, Robert Beverley
1705-06
1710-12
1714   George Marable, Henry Soane, Jr., Edward Jacquelin
1718   William Brodnax, George Marable, Archibald Blair
1720-22 William Broadnax, John Clayton, Archibald Blair
1723-26 William Broadnax, John Clayton, Archibald Blair
1727-34 William Broadnax, John Clayton, Archibald Blair
1736-40 W. Marable, J. Eaton, Lewis Burwell
1742-44 Colonel Lewis Burwell, Carter Burwell, Phillip Ludwell
1744-47 Benjamin Waller, Carter Burwell, Phillip Ludwell
1748-49 Benjamin Waller, Carter Burwell, Phillip Ludwell
1752-55 Benjamin Waller, Carter Burwell, Ed. Champion Travis
1756-58 Benjamin Waller, Joseph Morton, Ed. Champion Travis
1758-61 Benjamin Waller, Lewis Burwell, Ed. Champion Travis
1760-61 Benjamin Waller, Lewis Burwell, John Ambler
1761-65 Phillip Johnson, Lewis Burwell, E. C. Travis
1766-68 Robert C. Nicholas, Lewis Burwell, John Ambler (dec.), Edward Ambler.
1769   Robert Carter Nicholas, Lewis Burwell
1769-71 Robert Carter Nicholas, Lewis Burwell, Champion Travis
1772-74 Robert Carter Nicholas, Lewis Burwell, Champion Travis
1775-76 Robert Carter Nicholas, William Nowell, Champion Travis

BURGESS FROM SUSSEX

1754   Gray Briggs, John Edmunds, John Ruffin
1755   Gray Briggs, John Edmunds
1756-58 Gray Briggs, John Edmunds
1758-61 John Edmunds, David Mason
1761-65 John Edmunds, David Mason
1766   John Edmunds, David Mason
1766-68 John Edmunds, David Mason
1769   John Edmunds, David Mason
1769-70 John Edmunds, David Mason

1770   David Mason, James Bell (in place of Edmunds, dec.)
1772-74 David Mason, Richard Blunt
1775-76 David Mason, Michael Blow

BURGESS FROM SOUTHAMPTON

1753   Robert Jones (in place of Thomas Jarrell, dec.) Ethelred Taylor
1754   Joseph Gray, Ethelred Taylor
1755   Joseph Gray, Ethelred Taylor
1756-58 Joseph Gray, William Taylor, Ethelred Taylor
1758-61 Benjamin Simmons, William Taylor
1761-65 Benjamin Simmons, Joseph Gray
1766   Benjamin Simmons, Joseph Gray
1766-68 Benjamin Simmons, Joseph Gray
1769   Menry Taylor, Edwin Gray
1769-71 Henry Taylor, Edwin Gray
1772-74 Henry Taylor, Edwin Gray
1775-76 Henry Taylor, Edwin Gray

ORDER BOOK

SURRY COLONIAL MILITIA

(V.M. 23, p. 208)

May 15, 1764.   William Allen qualified as Colonel.
Christopher Mooring and Thomas Bailey as militia officers

June 19, 1764.   James Rodwell Bradby, Captain
Nicholas Faulcon, Jr., Lieutenant

SURRY REVOLUTIONARY MILITIA

(P. 210)

May 23, 1775.   William Allen, County Lieutenant.
William Browne, Lieutenant Colonel
Allen Cocke, Colonel
William Simmons, Major
Nathaniel Harrison ⎫
Nicholas Faulcon ⎬ Captains
Josiah Wilson ⎭

June 27, 1775.   John Hartwell Cocke, Captain
William Browne, Jr. ⎫ Lieutenants
Jacob Faulcon ⎭
John Wilkins, Ensign

March 25, 1777.   James Kee, Ensign
John H. Cocke ⎫
Nicholas Faulcon ⎬ Captains
William Seward ⎭

(P. 207)

November 24, 1778.   James Belsches, Captain; Alexander Belsches, 2nd. Lt.; and James Belsches, ensign, qualified. (That is presented their commissions as officers of militia and took the required oaths.)

December 28, 1778.   Certificate that Mildred Williams is widow of Lewis Williams, a soldier who died in service, leaving her five small children. Same as to Martha, widow of John Thorn, who died in service leaving her four children. Same as to Hannah, widow of Samuel Moody, who died leaving her three small children. Same as to Hannah, widow of John Ealey who left one child. Same as to Elizabeth Price, a widow, whose son Francis Price is now a soldier.

February 25, 1779. The County Court recommended: John Lucas, Captain; Stephen Coller, 1st Lt.; Benjamin Putney, 2nd. Lt.; William Collins, ensign; James Davis, 2nd Lt., Joseph Holt, ensign.

June 2, 1779. Henry Crafford and John Lucas, Captains. James Davis, Benjamin Putney, and Stephen Collier, 2nd. Lt., William Collins and Hardwood Calcott, ensigns; qualified.

March 28, 1780. Jacob Faulcon, Captain, William Edwards, 1st Lt.; John Wesson, ensign in Captain Nicholas Faulcon's company, qualified.

May 23, 1780. William Edwards, Captain of company of which Henry Crafford (resigned) was Captain. William Blow, 1st Lt., both qualified.

(P. 211)
August 26, 1777. Stephen Collier, 2nd Lt., Benjamin Putney, ensign in Captain John Cocke's company, John Pitt, 2nd Lt. and Nathaniel Berriman, ensign, in Captain Seward's company; James Nicholson, 2nd. Lt., Alexander Belches, ensign, in Captain Short's company; William Browne, 2nd Lt., Captain John H. Cocke's company; Randolph Prince, 2nd. Lt., and James Davis, ensign in Captain Faulcon's company; William Spratley, 2nd Lt. and William Evans, ensign, in Captain Gray's company; James Kee, 2nd Lt., and Sterling Hill, ensign in Captain Lemuel Cocke's company; Jesse Warren, 2nd. Lt. and Thomas White, ensign in Captain Wilson's company.

February 21, 1778. Recommended: William Hart, Captain, Vice Ethelred Gray, resigned, and William Spratley, 1st Lt., William Evans, 2nd Lt., and James Judkim, ensign in said company.

March 24, 1778. William Hart, Captain qualified.

May 28, 1778. James Nicholson, 2nd Lt., William Evans, 2nd Lt., and James Judkim, ensign, qualified.

July 26, 1778. William Short recommended as Major in room of William Simmons, dec., whereupon he produced a commission and qualifier.

Recommended: James Belsches, Captain, Vice William Short, James Nicholson, 1st Lt., Alexander Belsches, 2nd Lt., James Belsches, ensign.

June 26, 1781. John H. Cocke, Major; William Bailey, Captain; William Browne, Jr., John Watkins, and John Wesson, Lieutenants, qualified.

Recommended: William Blow, Captain, in place of William Edwards removed out of the county; Nathaniel Berriman, 1st Lt., and William Simmons, ensign.

SHERIFFS

1706—Thomas Holt	1714—Robert Ruffin
1707—	1715— " "
1709—Joseph John Jackman	1716—Robert Wynne
1710—Ethelred Taylor	1717—Stith Bolling
1711— " "	1718—William Gray
1712—Henry Harrison	1719— " "
1713—William Edwards	1721—Thomas Collier

MEMBERS OF THE COUNCIL FROM SURRY

1611	Ralph Hamor
1614	John Rolfe
1619	Samuel Maycock
1620-29 d.	Roger Smith
1621	George Sandys
1626	Edward Blaney
1630	John Utie
1631	William Pierce, Surry
1634	Henry Browne, Surry
1640	William Browne, Surry
1659-60 d.	Thomas Swann, Surry
1698-1713 d.	Benj. Harrison, Surry
1713-27 d.	Nathaniel Harrison, Surry
1730-32 d.	Henry Harrison, Surry

COUNTY COURT CLERKS

Geo. Watkins	Nov. 17 to Nov. 27, 1652	10 days
Robert Stanton	1652-53	1 year
Nicholas Meriwether	1652	?
William Edwards I	1653-1673	20 years
William Edwards II	1673-1698	25 years

Francis Clements	1698-1708		10 years
John Allen	1708-1751		43 years
C. A. Claiborne	1751-1754		3 years
William Nelson	1754-1781		27 years
Jacob Faulcon	1781-1801		20 years
John Faulcon	1801-1829		28 years
Walter J. Booth	1829-1839		10 years
William P. Underwood	1837-1869		30 years

In Reconstruction days William P. Underwood was removed, April 1869 by Gen. Canby, J. C. Underwood was appointed in his place but left the State a few months afterwards. He was succeeded by John Fomock(?) who served until April 1870.

J. R. Kitchell(?)	1870-1871	dec.	1 year
A. S. Edwards	1871-1922		51 years
H. B. Barham	1922		

(Names from here to the end of the book are shown in alphabetical order and do not appear in the index.)

SURRY LAND GRANTS 1624-1679

The grants, 1624 to 1666, shown below, are taken from Mrs. Nugent's *Cavaliers and Pioneers* which contain abstracts of all land patents for Virginia up to June 1666. Land grants 1666 to 1679 are taken from patent book No. 6 in the Commonwealth Land Office. The abstracts in *Cavaliers and Pioneers* often contain much information of a vital nature, such as, the location of the land and the names of the grantee's wife and family. Grants prior to 1652 were located on the south side of the James River in James City County.

An * before a name indicates that the patent was obtained jointly with some other person.

Name	Acres	Year	Name	Acres	Year
Allen, Arthur	200	1649	Bland, Edward	2000	1644
Allen, Arthur, Mr.	1000	1665	Bland, Edward	300	1648
Allen, Arthur	350	1669	Bland, Jane, Mrs.	4300	1652
Allen, Arthur	300	1678	Blow, George	600	1663
*Allen, Arthur	554	1678	Blow, Richard	635	1675
*Allen, Arthur	432	1678	Braddy, John	180	1662
Awborne, Rich	605	1669	Braddy, John	300	1668
Baker, Lawrence, Capt.	350	1665	Bridger, Jos., Col.	432	1673
*Baker, Lawrence	500	1650	Browne, Henry, Capt.	900	1637
Baker, Law., Capt.	2050	1667	Brown, John	600	1666
*Barham, Charles	850	1666	Burtcher, Geo.	200	1635
Barker, John, Jr.	600	1657	Burcher, Geo.	200	1637
Barker, John, Jr.	600	1657	Burcher, Geo.	300	1648
Barker, John	916	1667	Bushy, Thos.	1170	1667
Barrow, John	386	1653	Busby, Thos.	760	1672
Bartley, Patrick	100	1666	Bushell, Ed.	400	1666
Batt, William	128	1648	Butler, Wm.	700	1643
*Bell, Richard	500	1637	Butler, Wm.	590	1673
Binns, Thomas	343	1653	*Carter, John	500	1655
Binns, Eliza, Mrs.	777	1669	Carter, Wm.	700	1636
Binns, Thos.	974	1671	Carter, Wm.	1000	1638
Bishopp, Henry, Col.	1200	1646	Cary, John	230	1669
Bishop, John	150	1638	Caufield, Wm., Capt.	1230	1656
Bishop, John	300	1651	Caufield, Wm., Capt.	550	1656
*Bishop, John	50	1653	Caufield, Wm., Maj.	550	1662
Bishop, John, Jr.	300	1658	Caufield, Wm., Maj.	1230	1662
Blackborne, John	100	1652	Clarke, Phillip	200	1638
Blackborne, John	151	1652	Clarke, Phillip	300	1642

Name	Acres	Year	Name	Acres	Year
Clarke, Thos............	300	1650	Greene, Peter...........	200	1656
Clement, Jeremiah.......	500	1635	Greene, Peter...........	350	1663
Clements, Jeremiah.......	500	1639	Greenwood, Edward......	281	1651
Clement, Jeremiah........	200	1643	Grey, Jeremiah..........	150	1642
Clements, John..........	350	1667	Gualtney, Thos...........	200	1666
Cockerham, Wm., Lt......	1230	1656	Hacker, John............	150	1638
*Cockerham, Wm., Capt....	850	1666	Harris, William..........	850	1668
Corker, John............	1150	1657	Harrison, Benj...........	600	1637
Crafton, Thomas.........	670	1646	Harrison, Benj...........	500	1643
Creed, Ralph............	750	1666	Harrison, Ben., Jr........	500	1649
*Cooksey, Henry..........	350	1639	Harrison, Benj...........	600	1672
Dampert, Lancelot.......	50	1639	Hart, Henry.............	350	1635
*Davies, John............	100	1671	Hart, Thomas...........	100	1648
*Davis, Rice.............	1080	1648	Heath, Will.............	378	1669
Davis, Wm..............	200	1638	Hill, Thomas (Gent.)....	3000	1643
Delke, Roger............	100	1663	Homwood, John.........	300	1650
Dickinson, Jeremiah......	500	1638	Holt, Randall............	400	1636
Diston, Thos............	386	1662	Holt, Randall............	400	1639
Dixon, Adam............	200	1627	Holt, Randall............	710	1642
Doll, Benj. (negro)......	300	1656	Holt, Randall............	1622	1650
Drew, Richard...........	800	1667	Holt, Randall............	1450	1679
Drew, Richard..........	250	1672	Howse, Robert...........	250	1666
*Duchase, Chas...........	100	1671	Hirby, Sam..............	500	1655
Dunston, John...........	850	1636	Hutton, Eliz.	136	1654
Dunston, John...........	250	1639	Hunt, Thomas...........	836	1666
Dunston, John...........	600	1639	Huniford, Phillip........	800	1666
*Dunston, Peleg..........	300	1663	Jarratt, Richard..........	345	1667
Dunston, Ralph..........	350	1656	Jennings, John...........	211	1648
Edmonds, Samuel........	350	1636	Jennings, Wm.	251	1655
Edmonds, Samuel........	350	1637	Jennings, Wm.	350	1657
Edmonds, Samuel........	400	1638	Jordan, Francis..........	100	1652
*Edwards, William........	1080	1648	Jordan, George, Lt. Col....	690	1675
Edwards, Wm............	490	1656	Kempe, John............	500	1639
Edwards, Wm.	1800	1662	King, John..............	480	1653
Edwards, Wm.	605	1678	Kindred, John...........	554	1670
Edwards, Wm.	605	1679	Knott, Wm.............	112	1653
Egebrow, Wm.	500	1647	Knott, Wm..............	200	1653
Egbrough, Wm.	300	1653	Knott, Wm., Jr...........	312	1666
Egbourne, Wm...........	500	1650	Lawrence, Wm...........	300	1643
Ewen, Wm.	1400	1648	Lawrence, Wm...........	300	1647
Flood, John, Capt........	1100	1650	*Lawson, Chris	500	1637
Fludd, John.............	2100	1638	Lawson, Chris...........	400	1638
Francis, Henry..........	150	1676	Lee, George.............	300	1675
Ford, Charles...........	250	1638	Lewis, Chris............	400	1649
Gapin, Wm.............	140	1643	*Lawther, Robert........	50	1639
Gaping, Wm.	250	1651	*McJuinney, Michael......	330	1667
Gaping, Wm.	50	1657	*Marriott, Matthias........	338	1672
George, John............	900	1635	Marriott, Wm., Maj.......	1460	1669
Gray, Thomas	558	1635	Mason, Francis..........	300	1678
Gray, Thomas	550	1638	Mason, James	60	1648
Gray, Thomas	400	1639	*Mason, James	50	1653
Grey, Thomas	100	1642	Meriwether, Nicholas, Mr..	430	1666
*Grey, John.............	800	1678	Meriwether, "	650	1667
*Grey, Wm.	800	1678	Mills, Wm.	350	1637
Goring, John............	574	1670	Minter, Edward..........	250	1635
Goring, John............	974	1673	Minter, Ed.	300	1636

Name	Acres	Year
Minter, Ed	300	1638
Moore, Thos.	400	1666
Mudgett, Thos.	520	1663
Neale, Henry	850	1643
Newet, Eliz.	170	1672
Nichols, Roger	150	1649
Nichols, Roger	300	1650
*Newman, John	432	1678
Newsum, Wm.	850	1678
Newsum, Wm.	350	1636
Newsum, Wm.	550	1643
Osborne, John	300	1638
Oliver, John	300	1650
Owen, Barth.	648	1673
Pace, George	400	1628
Parish of Southwarke	700	1666
Parker, Rich.	314	1673
Pawley, John	600	1639
Pawley, John	500	1639
Perry, Isabelle	200	1628
Pettaway, Edward	500	1635
Pettaway, Ed.	700	1666
Pierce, Wm., Capt.	200	1635
Pilkington, Wm.	200	1638
Pilkington, Wm.	200	1635
Plomer, Thomas (Plummer)	400	1638
Porter, Will.	432	1667
Proctor, William	600	1667
Prosser, Wm.	50	1676
Quiney, Richard	300	1649
Rawlins, Gregory	476	1653
Rawlings, Gregory, Jr.	326	1654
Rawlings, Gregory	476	1663
*Rawlins, John	330	1667
Regan, Daniel	200	1667
Reynolds, Nicholas	1000	1637
*Robinson, Andrew	300	1663
Rogers, John	200	1666
Rookins, Wm.	150	1638
Rookins, Wm.	100	1636
Roote, Abraham	50	1634
Ruffinn, Robt.	850	1678
Russell, John	250	1632
Sandys, Geo.	300	1624
Saynes, ?, John	250	1648
Senior, John	150	1651
Senior, John	800	1652
Seward, Wm.	300	1664
Sessum, Nicholas	550	1679
Shepard, Robert	300	1635
Shepard, Robert, Capt.	1000	1650

Name	Acres	Year
Skynner, Rich.	50	1671
Smith, John	670	1642
Sowerby, Francis	211	1666
Sowerby, Francis	80	1666
Sowerby, Francis	455	1672
Spencer, Robert, Capt.	300	1672
Spencer, Robert, Mr.	300	1666
Spencer, Wm.	250	1632
Spencer, Wm.	1100	1635
Spencer, Wm. (Gent.)	550	1637
Spencer, Wm.	1350	1637
Spiltimber, John	100	1649
Spiltimber, Anthony	460	1666
Stamp, Thomas	500	1639
Stephens, Thomas	100	1656
Stephens, Mary (Widow)	150	1656
*Stephenson, Edward	350	1639
Swan, Samuel	248	1668
Swan, Thomas	300	1638
Swan, Thomas	1200	1638
Swan, Thos., Lt. Col.	900	1655
Swann, Thos., Col.	900	1658
Swann, Thos.	248	1664
*Taylor, James	300	1644
*Taylor, James	500	1650
Thompson, Henry	150	1637
Thomson, Wm.	230	1666
Twy, John	200	1648
Travis, Edward	900	1637
*Travis, Edward	900	
Utye, John, Ensign	100	1624
Wall, John	1791	1643
Warradine, Jas.	350	1637
Warren, John	180	1671
Warren, Robert	300	1649
Warren, Thos.	290	1648
Warren, Thos.	200	1667
Warren, Thomas	450	1669
Watkins, Geo.	917	1666
Watkins, Geo.	200	1667
Watkin, Geo.	105	1670
Watkins, John	150	1638
Watkins, John	150	1638
Webb, Stephen	250	1638
Webb, Stephen	500	1639
Webb, Stephen	500	1642
White, Henry	200	1649
Williams, Nicholas	200	1652
Williams, Nicholas	200	1662
*Woodhouse, Thos.	200	1648

SURRY LAND GRANTS 1676-1714

Grant Bk.	Page	Name	Year	Acres
9	572	Achison, Richard....	1703	82
8	365	Allen, Arthur.......	1662	
7	109	Allen, Maj. Arthur..	1681	200
8	127	Allen, Maj. Arthur..	1691	200
8	219	Allen, Maj. Arthur..	1692	1000
7	298	Audreios, Robert....	1683	140
10	160	Audros, Robert	1714	165
10	151	Audrews, Thomas Jr.	1714	225
8	90	Atkins, Richard & Bagley, Peter.....	1690	274
10	57	Atkins, Thomas.....	1711	440
7	371	Baker, Henry.......	1684	200
7	131	Baldwine, William..	1682	275
7	376	Baldwin, William & Dues, John.......	1684	2600
8	366	Baldwin, William...	1694	100
7	189	Barker, John	1682	240
8	7	Barker, Jethro	1089	261
7	575	Bayly, Edward......	1687	220
7	183	Bennet, Richard.....	1682	630
7	670	Bently, Thomas Jr...	1688	300
9	497	Blow, George.......	1702	65
7	134	Brashear, John......	1682	420
8	127	Brecey, William	1691	721
7	375	Brett, John, Jr......	1684	720
10	150	Briggs, Samuel......	1714	790
10	175	Briggs, Charles	1714	275
8	155	Bullock, Richard....	1691	160
7	216	Busby, Thomas	1682	475
7	68	Byneham, John	1681	215
7	718	Campbell, Hugh	1688	500
7	509	Carpenter, William..	1686	450
7		Canfield, Robert	1682	2250
8	247	Chambers, William..	1693	50
7	377	Clark, Hohn........	1684	410
7	703	Clement, Francis....	1689	450
9	725	Clements, Francis ...	1706	1000
7	441	Clement, John......	1685	42
9	439	Cocke, William.....	1702	45
9	720	Cocke, William.....	1706	580
7	369	Collins, John.......	1684	950
7	511	Collins, John.......	1688	1550
7	371	Coker, John........	1684	400
7	670	Cotton, Walter & Cotton, Thomas....	1688	314
7	280	Cotton, Thomas.....	1683	335
7	6	Davies, Arthur......	1671	161
8	6	Dennis, Nathaniel...	1689	140
7	699	DeBerry, Peter.....	1688	100
7	179	Drue, Thomas......	1682	390
8	101	Edwards, John......	1690	950

Grant Bk.	Page	Name	Year	Acres
7	67	Edwards, William...	1680	590
7	408	Edwards, William...	1684	920
7	648	Edwards, William...	1683	290
8	101	Edwards, William...	1690	950
8	204	Edwards, William...	1684	410
8	213	Edwards, William...	1691	750
8	5	Evans, Abraham	1689	472
8	154	Evans, Abraham	1691	190
9	663	Evans, Benjamin	1705	300
9	622	Everis, John........	1694	300
8	219	Foreman, William ..	1692	240
7	183	Francis, Henry......	1682	580
7	299	Giffins, Thomas.....	1683	400
7	297	Grantham, Edward ..	1683	300
7	27	Gray, William......	1680	680
10	175	Guillam, Hinshea ...	1714	550
10	175	Guillam, Hinshea ...	1714	550
7	190	Harrison, Benjamin..	1682	450
7	363	Harryson, Benjamin .	1684	620
7	573	Harryson, Benjamin .	1687	330
9	259	Harrison, Benjamin .	1700	115
10	171	Harrison, Henry	1704	350
7	576	Hart, Henry........	1687	285
9	637	Hart, Robert	1704	1000
7	595	Hartwell, Henry	1687	1960
8	412	Heath, Adam.......	1695	386
9	676	Heath, Adam.......	1705	681
7	111	Hill, Sion..........	1681	420
8	5	Hunt, Thomas......	1689	150
7	467	Jenkins, Samuel & Jenkins, Robert...	1685	200
7	70	Jordan, Arthur......	1681	150
7	373	Jordan, Arthur......	1684	250
7	374	Jordan, George & Jordan, River.....	1684	200
9	423	Jordan, George	1701	670
7	369	Jordan, Richard.....	1684	260
7	691	Jordan, Richard.....	1688	200
8	4	Jordan, Richard.....	1689	568
7	191	Jordan, Thomas.....	1682	265
7	372	Jordan, Thomas.....	1684	235
7	120	Kae, Robert	1682	300
7	473	Kae, Robert	1685	1
7	671	King, John.........	1688	117
8	377	King, John.........	1694	100
8	365	King, John.........	1694	44
9	724	King, Thomas	1706	180
7	184	Lane, Thomas	1682	400
7	297	Loveday, George....	1683	100
8	6	Lucas, William	1689	213
10	62	Minge, James.......	1712	540

Grant Bk.	Page	Name	Year	Acres
8	87	Meazell, Luke	1690	150
7	603	Morring, John	1687	697
7	135	Macloode, John	1622	270
10	178	Nickells, John	1694	
8	3	Owen, Robert	1689	743
7	669	Page, Thomas	1688	290
8	127	Parker, Richard	1697	39
7	374	Parsons, John, Jr...	1684	290
7	376	Parsons, John, Jr...		740
7	377	Pettaway, Edward ...	1684	480
7	296	Phillips, David	1683	85
7	370	Plow, Samuel	1684	240
7	463	Potter, Capt. Roger..	1685	380
8	4	Potter, Capt. Roger..	1689	268
9	718	Procter, Joshua	1706	50
2	366	Pyland, Richard	1684	580
8	6	Rawlins, John	1689	455
8	220	Rawlins, John	1692	220
8	5	Ray, William	1689	314
9	724	Rhodes, William	1706	150
7	669	Roberts, Nathaniel & Proctor, Joshua ...	1688	566
7	247	Rogers, Joseph	1683	1025
7	463	Rogers, William & Proctor, Joshua ...	1685	900
8	202	Rookings, William ..	1699	296
10	116	Rookins, William ...	1713	418
9	109	Rookins, William ...	1697	400
10	126	Rookins, Wm	1714	106
10	161	Rookins, Wm	1714	94
7	439	Ruffin, Robert	1685	2250
7	569	Ruffin, Robert	1687	422
7	136	Savage, Charles	1682	570
7	28	Senior, Thomas	1680	113
7	368	Sessum, Nicholas ...	1684	1050
8	155	Sessums, Nicholas ...	1691	260
9	631	Simons, John	1704	350
10	142	Simmons, John	1714	230
7	475	Symonds, William ...	1685	800
9	32	Symmons, William & Symmons, John ...	1695	500
8	316	Smith, Nicholas	1694	150
9	723	Smith, Nich	1706	200
7	368	Smith, Richard	1684	230
7	367	Smith, Thomas	1684	200
7	43	Soresby, Thomas ...	1680	620
7	432	Swann, Mary (Mrs.)	1684	1
7	717	Stanford, Alice	1689	1400
10	97	Stead, Francis	1713	100
8	156	Stuart, John	1691	275
7	539	Thompson, Samuel ..	1686	350
8	7	Thompson, Samuel ..	1689	278
7	182	Thompson, William .	1682	
7	370	Thompson, William .	1684	150
7	408	Thompson, William .	1684	150
7	544	Thompson, William & Chilton, Edward ..	1686	1160
7	670	Tyas, Thomas	1688	500
8	87	Vincent, John	1690	287
7	373	Wall, Joseph	1684	900
10	11	Wall, Joseph Jr	1711	217
10	11	Wall, Joseph Jr	1711	200
7	133	Waller, Thomas	1682	420
7	367	Warren, Thomas ...	1684	200
9	573	Warrich, John	1703	95
7	165	Washington, Richard.	1682	330
8	88	Washington, Richard.	1690	772
7	186	Watkins, James	1682	100
8	366	Watkins, John	1694	966
8	89	Wilkinson, John ...	1690	189
8	312	Wilkinson, John ...	1683	100
7	600	Williams, George ...	1687	150
7	447	Williams, John & Brocone, John ...	1685	1200
9	623	Williams, George ...	1704	200
10	152	Williams, George ...	1714	260
7	690	Williams, Roger ...	1688	150
8	88	Wray, William	1690	200

SURRY LAND GRANTS 1710-1740

These grants were south of the Blackwater in what is now Sussex County.

Grant Book	Name	Year	Acres
13	Allen, John	1720	115
11	Anderson, James	1723	100
11	Andrews, William	1723	100
10	Atkinson, Chris	1715	100
13	Atkinson, William	1727	150
11	Bagley, Peter	1723	100
12	Bailey, Phil	1725	145
10	Baker, John	1714	100
10	Barker, Joel	1716	170
12	Barker, Joel	1724	170
10	Barker, Jethro	1717	165
11	Barker, Jethro	1723	180
13	Barker, John	1727	100
10	Barrow, Edmund	1718	100
10	Barrow, Thomas	1711	128
11	Bell, John	1723	135

Grant Book	Name	Year	Acres
9	Bently, Thomas	1706	150
10	Binam, James	1714	330
10	Binam, James	1714	140
12	Blackgrove, Samuel	1724	150
10	Bland, Richard	1717	800
9	Blow, George	1702	65
12	Blow, Richard	1724	300
10	Blunt, Thomas	1714	320
13	Bolling, Alex	1730	250
11	Bolling, Robert	1722	1150
10	Booth, George	1715	100
11	Booth, George	1723	90
13	Bradley, William	1727	150
11	Briggs, Charles	1723	200
11	Briggs, Charles	1723	100
12	Briggs, Charles	1724	230
10	Briggs, Charles	1714	550
10	Briggs, Sam	1714	290
13	Brimm, William	1727	220
12	Brittle, William	1724	215
12	Brown, John	1724	200
10	Brown, Marmaduke	1715	200
10	Brown, William	1714	250
10	Brown, William	1719	500
13	Bush, Nicholas	1728	100
12	Cahill, Thomas	1725	345
11	Callaham, Nicholas	1723	350
11	Cargill, John	1722	250
11	Cargill, John	1722	350
12	Carter, Joseph	1724	63
11	Chappell, ——	1722	150
12	Clanton, Edward	1725	150
10	Clarke, Sam	1715	250
10	Clary, William	1715	100
9	Clements, Francis	1706	1000
10	Clements, Francis	1714	184
10	Cocke, Nicholas	1715	130
9	Cock, William	1706	380
12	Collyer, Joseph	1724	350
11	Cooke, William	1722	175
13	Cook, William	1727	190
13	Cook, William	1727	175
13	Cain, James	1727	100
12	Cooper, Benjamin	1725	100
12	Corbies, Nathaniel	1724	640
12	Crips, William	1724	300
13	Davidson, William	1727	200
11	Davis, John	1723	100
12	Doby, John	1725	235
12	Dunn, Thomas	1724	125
10	Edmunds, William	1713	830
11	Edmunds, William	1723	170
13	Edmunds, William	1727	280
12	Edmunds, Howell	1724	230
10	Edwards, William	1715	350

Grant Book	Name	Year	Acres
10	Eldridge, Thomas	1714	370
10	Eldridge, Thomas	1718	190
10	Ellis, Jeremiah	1714	150
12	Evans, John	1725	200
11	Fellows, Robert	1722	125
12	Feltz, Richard	1725	140
10	Fitzpatrick, Richard	1717	215
10	Freeman, John	1714	300
11	Gee, Charles	1722	425
10	Giddeon, Benjamin	1717	200
10	Gillum, Charles	1715	100
11	Gillium, John	1723	240
10	Glover, William	1714	160
10	Golitely, Hugh	1715	200
10	Goodwyn, Thomas	1717	425
10	Green, Lewis	1719	375
11	Green, Lewis	1720	200
11	Green, Lewis	1720	195
11	Green, Lewis	1720	425
11	Green, Lewis	1723	135
12	Green, Lewis	1724	400
10	Groves, John	1715	100
12	Groves, John	1725	145
13	Hall, Isaac	1727	200
12	Hamilton, George	1724	135
12	Hamlen, William	1725	235
11	Hamlin, Thomas	1723	145
11	Hancock, John	1723	250
11	Hargrove, Samuel	1723	190
12	Harper, William	1724	200
13	Harris, William	1727	250
9	Harrison, Benjamin	1706	100
10	Harrison, Benjamin	1717	1530
12	Harrison, Benjamin	1724	200
12	Harrison, Benjamin	1724	470
12	Harrison, Benjamin	1724	340
10	Harrison, Henry	1714	350
10	Harrison, Capt. Henry & Sidwell, Philip	1714	6365
10	Harrison, Henry	1717	100
10	Harrison, Henry	1719	500
12	Harrison, Henry	1725	430
10	Harrison, Nathaniel	1714	570
10	Harrison, Nathaniel	1714	1720
11	Harrison, Nathaniel	1723	2450
12	Harrison, Nathaniel	1725	550
10	Harrison, Thomas	1713	180
10	Harrison, Thomas	1713	180
11	Hatley, John	1723	125
10	Heath, William	1717	325
12	Higgs, John	1724	100
12	Higgs, John	1724	100
11	Hill, Richard	1723	200
12	Hollyman, John	1724	78
10	Holleman, Thomas	1714	220

Grant Book	Name	Year	Acres
10	Horton, Thomas	1715	145
13	Houseman, Stephen	1730	16
10	Hunnicutt, Robert	1715	100
10	Hunt, William	1711	190
10	Hunt, Maj. William	1711	140
10	Hunt, Maj. William	1711	190
10	Hunt, William	1718	1120
10	Hunt, Thomas	1714	200
11	Hynes, William	1723	90
12	Inman, Robert	1725	150
10	Ivy, John	1715	100
10	Jackson, John	1715	140
13	Jarrard, Nich	1727	150
11	Jecreys, John	1722	100
13	Johnson, Henry	1727	80
11	Johnson, William	1722	225
10	Jones, Henry	1713	250
9	Jones, James	1702	634
13	Jones, James	1727	150
10	Jones, John	1713	330
10	Jones, John	1714	170
11	Jones, John	1723	95
12	Jones, John	1725	435
11	Jones, Phillip	1723	180
10	Jones, Robert	1713	120
13	Jones, Robert	1727	100
13	Jones, Robert	1727	190
11	Jones, Thomas	1722	2119
10	Jones, Thomas	1715	320
10	Jones, William	1714	280
10	Jones, William	1718	100
12	Jones, William	1725	450
13	Jones, William	1727	375
12	Jones, William	1725	400
12	Judkins, Charles	1725	375
11	Judkins, Robert	1719	175
10	Kerney, James	1715	80
12	King, Richard	1725	190
10	Lashley, Walter	1714	280
11	Leath, Charles	1722	170
13	Leath, Charles	1727	400
12	Lee, William	1724	300
11	Lester, Andrew	1723	150
12	Lester, Andrew	1725	145
12	Loftin, Cornelius	1725	200
10	Ludwell, Phillip	1714	6305
10	Ludwell, Phillip	1714	930
11	Ludwell, Phillip	1722	415
12	Magee, Robert	1725	285
13	Maggett, Nich	1727	380
11	Malone, William	1723	195
10	Malone, Nathaniel	1715	215
10	Marker, John	1718	446
11	Massingall, John	1723	350
10	Mason, John	1715	80

Grant Book	Name	Year	Acres
10	Mason, John	1716	200
10	Mathews, James	1716	140
11	Maybury, Charles	1723	250
12	Mayberry, Charles	1725	145
11	Maybury, George	1723	115
10	Mayberry, Francis	1713	125
11	Mitchell, Henry	1723	150
13	Mitchell, Henry	1727	100
14	Mitchell, Henry	1732	200
14	Mitchell, James	1731	380
11	Mitchell, John	1722	150
11	Mitchell, John	1723	290
11	Mitchell, John	1723	440
13	Mitchell, John	1727	640
15	Mitchell, John	1734	175
15	Mitchell, John	1734	300
10	Mitchell, Peter	1717	220
11	Mitchell, Robert	1723	320
11	Mitchell, Robert Jr.	1723	100
11	Mitchell, Thomas	1723	135
18	Mitchel, Thomas	1739	375
10	Moore, John	1715	130
10	Nichols, John	1714	270
13	Norcross, Richard	1726	100
10	Parker, Richard	1715	540
11	Pasmore, John	1722	100
10	Pasmore, George	1714	150
10	Patridge, Nich	1715	100
12	Patridge, Nich	1725	350
13	Peebles, William	1727	200
12	Pennington, Edward	1725	485
11	Peters, Thomas	1722	130
13	Peters, Thomas	1727	430
13	Pettiway, William	1727	350
12	Phillips, Nathaniel	1725	95
10	Phillips, Nathaniel	1713	100
11	Phillips, William	1723	150
10	Pitman, Thomas	1714	200
10	Pitman, Thomas	1714	250
12	Pittman, William	1724	240
11	Poythress, David	1723	250
10	Poythress, John	1717	267
10	Poythress, Thomas	1715	180
10	Proctor, Robert	1717	80
13	Rainey, William	1727	240
10	Rayney, William Jr.	1713	250
12	Rawlings, Gregory	1725	250
10	Rayburn, John	1715	80
12	Read, William	1724	100
12	Richardson, John	1724	75
12	Rogers, Robert	1725	100
10	Rogers, William Jr.	1714	220
13	Rogers, William	1728	100
11	Roberts, John	1723	235
11	Robertson, Chris	1722	80

Grant Book	Name	Year	Acres
13	Robinson, Nathaniel....	1729	200
12	Rose, John	1724	165
12	Rose, William	1724	130
10	Rose, William	1715	100
11	Saunders, William	1723	90
10	Savidge, Charles	1714	120
11	Shands, William	1722	250
13	Shands, William	1727	270
12	Simes, William	1724	95
12	Simmons, John	1724	240
12	Simmons, John	1724	500
10	Sledge, Charles	1716	150
10	Sledge, Charles	1716	100
11	Smith, William	1723	190
10	Stanton, James	1712	700
10	Stanton, James	1718	130
10	Stead, Francis	1713	100
12	Stokes, John	1725	250
10	Stokes, Silvanus	1717	200
11	Stokes, Silvanus	1723	500
11	Stokes, Sylvanus	1723	365
10	Sturdivant, Mathew	1717	100
13	Sturdivant, Mathew	1727	230
13	Tatum, Sam	1729	80
13	Taylor, Thomas	1727	285
12	Tell, Lambert	1725	220
13	Threewit, John	1727	375
10	Thorp, John	1719	175
11	Thrower, John	1723	295
10	Thrower, Thomas	1725	125

Grant Book	Name	Year	Acres
11	Tines, Amos	1723	100
11	Tomlinson, John	1723	145
12	Tomlinson, John	1725	70
10	Tomlinson, Thomas	1716	195
10	Tomlinson, Thomas	1722	200
12	Topley, Adam	1724	75
12	Tucker, Dan	1725	215
11	Underhill, Giles	1720	133
11	Vincent, Peter	1723	125
10	Wall, Joseph	1711	200
10	Wall, Joseph	1715	200
10	Waller, Thomas	1713	340
10	Warrin, Robert	1713	65
12	Webb, Charles	1725	145
10	Webb, Robert	1717	280
11	Webb, Robert	1723	205
12	Whitehead, Robert	1724	100
10	Wiggins, Thomas	1714	350
12	Wiggins, Thomas	1725	150
10	Wilkison, Thomas	1715	100
10	Williams, William	1715	295
13	Williamson, John	1727	175
10	Winfield, Jarvis	1715	150
10	Worsden, John	1726	375
12	Woodrope, Richard	1724	250
12	Woodrope, Richard	1724	655
11	Wyche, George	1722	115
10	Wyche, George	1713	400
10	Wyche, William	1716	150
11	Wynne, Robert	1723	475

CENSUS OF TITHABLES IN SURRY COUNTY, VIRGINIA, IN 1668, 1678, 1688, AND 1698

BY W. A. GRAHAM CLARK

"Until after the Revolution, taxes in Virginia were imposed chiefly according to the number of tithables in each county. The tithables consisted of all male natives of the county, and imported free persons, above sixteen; and all male and female negro and Indian servants, whether above or under sixteen. The population was generally estimated at four times the tithables." (W. & M., Vol. 8, p. 160.)

In the Surry County Records on file at Surry, Virginia, there are included the lists of tithables in that county in the years 1668, 1669, 1670, 1674, 1675, and in each year from 1677 to 1703 inclusive. Each census was taken by four prominent men, usually two for Southwark Parish and two for Lawnes Creek Parish, and each census was taken on or near June 10th.

The tithables lists for 1668, 1678, 1688, and 1698 have been rearranged alphabetically to show all male whites over sixteen, and are given herewith. The spelling is as shown on the original lists and includes such names as "Richard Whichpatrick" (evidently Richard Fitzpatrick) and "James Horsenails" (evidently James Hosnell) but in most instances there is little doubt as to the names intended even though there is variation in spelling from one list to another. In a few instances a question mark has been added after a name when the handwriting was such that there was uncertainty as to the name intended.

The following is a condensed record, for each of the four years listed, of (a) the total tithables, white, black, and Indian, including females who worked in the fields, (b) the total white males over sixteen, and (c) the total number of white family names (for instance, listing "Smith" as one surname, irrespective of whether those bearing this name were or were not related).

Year	Total tithables (white, black, & Indian)	Total white males over sixteen	Total surnames of whites
1668	433	216	182
1678	482	425	297
1688	582	476	337
1698	674	509	317

Odds and Ends

"The 25th day of March was the beginning of the year according to the Jewish computation; and the same rule was observed in England until by statute it was declared that beginning with 1752, the year should begin January 1. The statute was rendered necessary by the adoption in England of the reformed calendar of Pope Gregory XII, made in the year 1572. Most of the nations of Europe had adopted the Gregorian or 'New Style Calendar,' as distinguished from the Julian or 'Old Style' calendar, before the English." (Hening's *Statutes at Large of Virginia*, Vol. 1, p. 393.)

The title "junior" as used in the colonial and revolutionary periods does not necessarily signify "son of," as it is usually interpreted today. In this early period the term "junior" conveyed the thought of the "younger" of two men, but it does not signify that the man styled "junior" was the son of the man styled "senior." (By George H. S. King in *Tyler's Quarterly*, Vol. 21, 1939-1940, p. 280.)

SURRY COUNTY TITHABLES (WHITE) IN 1668

Mr. Arthur Allen
Alberte Albatson
Tho. Andrews
Hen. Applewhaite
(Richd.) Atkins
Capt. Law. Baker
Mr. Charles Barham
Mr. John Barker
Patrick Bartley
Walter Bartley
Wm. Batt.
Mathew Batle
John Beasley
Marmaduke Beckwith
Jonas Bennet
Tho. Bentley
John Bineham
Mr. (Tho.) Binns
John Bird
John Blast
Jno. Booth
Henry Braderton
John Brady
Mr. Hen. Brigs
Richd. Briggs
John Browne

Capt. Wm. Browne
Hezekiah Bunell
Maurice Burcher
Robt. Burges
Mr. Tho. Busby
Mr. (Edwd.) Bushell
Mr. Wm. Butler
Cornelious Cardenpaine
Wm. Carpenter
Robt. Carthrage
Mr. John Cary
Richd. Case
Tho. Causby
Mr. Robert Caufeild
Maj. Wm. Caufeild
Wm. Chambers
John Clarke
Henry Clarke
Mr. Tho. Clarke
Wm. Clarke
Tho. Clary
Tho. Clay
John Clemens
Capt. Wm. Cockerham
John Collyer
Geo. Corke

Capt. (Wm.) Corker
Samuel Cornwell
Nicholas Craford
Ralph Creed
Thomas Crews
Francis Davis
Roger Delke
Robt. Dennis
Amara Dolores
Richd. Drew
Peleg Dunston
Timothy Easwell
Edwd. Ellis
Jerrimy Ellis
John Emerson
Antho. Evans
Robert Evens
Capt. Tho. fflood
Wm. Foreman
Geo. Foster
Tho. Forscraft
Henry ffrancis
Henry Freeman
James Furbush
Tho. Gibson
Henry Gord

[1] Probably Gerardt Gronwadt who so signed as witness to 1672 will of Samuel Judkins.

Mr. John Goring
ffrancis Gray
Tho. Gray
Jarratt Greenewalt[1]
Mr. Peter Greene
Tho. Greene
John Gregory
Capt. (John) Grove
Roberte Gyles
Edw. Hale
Wm. Hancock
Wm. Hare
John Harlow
Richd. Harris
Mr. Ben. Harrison
Tho. Harte
Wm. Heath
Hermon Hill
Wm. Hill
John Hode
Xpher Holliman
Mr. Rand. Holt
Edmond Howell
Wm. Howell
ffran. Howgood
Robt. House
Austin Hunicutt
John Hunicutt
Tho. Hux
Wm. Hux
Tho. Ironmunger
Richard Jarratt
Tho. Jarrell
Edward Joanes
Richard Joanes
Tho. Joanes
Martin Johnson
Mr. Arthur Jordan
Lt. Coll. (Geo.) Jordan
Wm. Judson
James Kilpatrick
John Kindred
John King
Joh. Kippin
(Wm.) Kite
Mr. Nath. Knight

Robt. Laine
Tho. Laine
Henry Lathrid
John Legrand
Gopher Lewis
Tho. Lilicrop
Arthur Long
Samll. Magget
Mr. Mathias Marriott
Maj. Wm. Marriott
Mr. Nich. Merriwether
Wm. Mills
Geo. Midleton
Michaell Micqaney
Luke Mizell
John Moring
Edwd. Morth
Mr. Moulson
James Murrey
Edward Napkin
Wm. Newitt
James Nibley
Mr. Wm. Norwood
Tho. North
Phillop Oberry
(John) Orchard
Mr. Bartho. Owen
Wm. Oldis
(Richd.) Pace
Law. Peach
Geo. Petters
John Phillops
Wm. Prosser
Capt. (Thomas) Pitman
Obedia Pit
Mr. (Edwd.) Pitway
Sam. Plaw
Roger Potter
Edw. Ramsey
John Rawlings
Roger Rawlings
James Redick
Daniell Regan
Francis Reynolds
Robt. Reynolds
Andrew Robinson

Ralph Rochell
John Rogers
Joseph Rogers
Richard Rogers
Mr. Wm. Rookings
Wm. Rose
Mr. John Salloway
Tho. Sanders
Wm. Scarbrough
Wm. Seward
John Sheppe[2]
Wm. Shorte
Mr. Wm. Simmons
John Skinner
Richd. Skinner
Richd. Smith
Tho. Smith
ffran. Sorsby
Tho. Sowersby
Antho. Spiltimber
Mr. Robt. Spensor
Wm. Spring
Tho. Stephens
Mathew Swann
Coll. Tho. Swann
Vincent Shutleworth
Tho. Taylor
Edward Tanner
Mr. (Wm.) Thomson
Wm. Tooke
Michael Upchurch
Ellis Vauter
Chr. Vaughan's Sonn
Timothy Walker
Edward Warren
John Warren
Mr. Tho. Warren
Wm. Warren
Geo. Watkin
Tho. Wicks
John Whitson
David Williams
Harebottle Wms.
Tho. Williams
Roger Wms.
Wm. Winter.

TOTAL 216

[2] Probably intended for John Shepperd (Sheppard).

Note.—Given names in brackets not shown in 1668 list of tithables but added from other records, mostly from the 1669 list of tithables.

The tithables for 1674—1683—1694 and 1702 were inserted in between Mr. Clark's lists in order to show the census at approximately five-year intervals. (J. B. B.)

A LIST OF TITHABLES TAKEN JUNE 10, 1674

Southwark Parish   238
Lawnes Creek Parish   182

Total   420

(Records 1671-84, pp. 95-98)

The numbers in brackets after each name refer to other persons who were tithables on same plantation or in household. These tithables were often partners, sons, or servants sixteen years, or over, in age. These numbers are shown for years 1674-1683-1694-1702. Persons who have "O" after their name were in household of person of same number who carries a numeral after his name such as: "Arthur Allen (50) 7."

Albriton, Albert		1	Bread, Richard		1
Allen, Stephen		1	Briggs, Mr.	(8)	3
Allen, Arthur	(50)	7	Briggs, Henry	(45)	3
Amry, Thomas		1	Briggs, Richard	(45)	3
Amry, Charles	(30)	6	Browne, Major	(29)	6
Amry, Edward	(30)	0	Browne, Berkeley	(29)	0
Anderson, David	(27)	3	Broxey, Nath.	(38)	0
Anderson, David	(27)	0	Bunnell, Hezekiah	(5)	2
Archer, Rog	(33)	0	Burgess, Robert		3
Armstrong, Henry		0	Busby, Thomas		2
Arnold, George	(3)	2	Carpender, Wm.		2
Atkins, Richard		1	Cartwright, Robert		1
Atkins, William	(22)	0	Case, John		1
Avery, Richard		1	Case, John		1
Baker, Capt. Law.	(37)	9	Chambers, William		2
Baker, Henry	(37)	0	Charles, John		1
Baker, John	(37)	0	Chrisdemfolke, Ham	(33)	0
Baker, Henry	(40)	0	Clarke, Henry		1
Baly, ——	(14)	0	Clarke, John		1
Baley, Edward		1	Clarke, John		1
Baly, Henry	(4)	2	Clarke, Thomas		2
Barham, Charles		4	Clay, Thomas		1
Barker, John		3	Clay, William		1
Bartlett, Walter	(33)	4	Clements, John		1
Barnes, John	(36)	3	Clinch, Chris		2
Barton, John	(37)	0	Cogan, William	(42)	2
Beck, Thomas	(30)	0	Conick, Anthony		0
Benett, John	(17)	0	Cooper, Hance	(43)	
Bentley, Thomas		1	Corker, Capt.	(21)	4
Bidelcome, John	(24)	0	Cornewall, Samuel		1
Binam, John		2	Cotten, Tom		1
Bird, Thomas		2	Craft, John		1
Bishop, John	(43)	0	Crewes, Thomas		1
Bishop, John		1	Culledge, Thomas	(50)	0
Blackbone, Wm.	(5)	0	Car, John	(41)	2
Bluett, Lenard	(37)	0	Dargett, John	(28)	0
Blunt, William	(18)	0	Davis, Arthur		1
Blunt, Thomas	(8)	0	Davis, Thomas	(24)	0
Bradford, Thomas	(29)	0	Dawkes, John	(8)	0

Deanes, Edward	(31)	0
Deleforce, Peter	(48)	0
Delke, Rog.	(32)	2
Draper, William		1
Drew, Richard	(38)	3
Drew, Thomas	(38)	0
Dunfield, John		1
Edmunds, Thomas	(22)	0
Edwards, William	(24)	4
Ellis, Jeremiah		1
Essell, George		1
Essell, Timothy		1
Evans, Abraham		1
Evans, Anthony		1
Everett, Tobias		1
Ewers, John	(9)	2
Farlo, Joseph	(40)	0
Foscraft, Thomas		1
Foreman, William	(14)	3
Foster, George	(19)	2
Foster, Kit	(9)	0
Frost, George	(17)	0
Frances, Henry		1
Furbush, James		1
Gary, John	(25)	0
Gibbons, Charles		1
Gray, Francis		1
Gray, Henry	(44)	2
Gray, John	(44)	0
Gray, John		1
Gray, Thomas	(12)	2
Gray, William	(43)	3
Gregory, John		1
Greene, John	(32)	0
Greene, Richard	(10)	0
Goard, Henry		1
Goring, John		3
Gorrell, Eseken	(39)	0
Gulatt, Robert	(25)	0
Gusten, James	(40)	2
Hall, Anthony		1
Hancock, William		1
Harris, John		1
Harris, Richard	(46)	3
Harrison, Benjamin		2
Harry, Welsh	(7)	0
Harvey, William		1
Heath, Adam		1
Heath, William		1
Hide, Richard		1
High, Thomas	(15)	0
Higgs, Thomas	(17)	0
Hill, Mr.	(24)	0
Hill, Harmon		1
Hill, Sion	(42)	0
Hoges, John		2
Hogwood, Francis		2

Hollyman, Xpher		1
Holt, Randall		2
Holten, Ralph	(36)	0
House, Robert		1
House, Robert, Jr.		1
Howell, Edward		1
Hunicutt, Austin		1
Hunicutt, John		1
Hunt, Thomas		1
Hunt, Thomas		0
Hurd, Thomas		1
Hux, Thomas		2
Hux, William	(26)	0
Ironmonger, Thomas	(26)	3
Ironmonger, John	(26)	0
Jarrell, Thomas		1
Johnson, George	(25)	0
Johnson, Martin		1
Jones, Edward		1
Jordan, Ar.	(1)	3
Jordan, James	(1)	0
Jordan, George	(3)	8
Jordan, Thomas	(3)	0
Jordan, Richard		1
Judkens, Saml.		1
Kindred, John		1
King, John		1
King, Thomas		1
Kilpatrick, James		1
Kitto, William		1
Knight, Dr.	(10)	4
Lacy, Robert	(32)	3
Laczis, James		1
Lane, Thomas		1
Leake, Francis	(45)	0
Lee, Robert	(6)	3
Legreate, John		1
Lewis, Henry	(39)	0
Lewis, Thomas		1
Little, William		1
Long, Ar.		1
Lucus, William		1
Maggatt, Samuel		1
Magnus, Math	(11)	0
Marriott, Mat	(16)	3
Mason, Francis	(15)	10
Mason, Francis		2
Merick, Owen		1
Merewether, Nic	(10)	7
Merewether, Francis	(10)	0
Midleton, George		1
Miller, Richard	(48)	0
Mincard, John		1
Moss, John		1
Moss, John	(47)	0
Morris, Richard	(37)	0
Mucano, Muche		1

Name		Value
Negell, Lawrence	(46)	0
Nelson, James		1
Newhouse, Thomas		1
Newitt, William		2
Newman, William	(45)	0
Newsum, William		4
Nichols, Roger		2
Nicholson, James	(11)	0
Norwood, William		2
Nunce, William		2
Oldens, William		2
Orchard, John		1
Owen, Bar.		1
Parker, Richard		2
Pecock, William	(50)	0
Pellwine, Robert	(39)	0
Pettway, Edward	(18)	3
Pettway, William	(18)	0
Phillips, John		1
Phillip, John		1
Phillips, John		1
Pickerell, William		1
Pittman, Capt.		1
Plow, Samuel		1
Potter, Roger		1
Price, John		4
Prince, George		0
Proctor, William	(25)	4
Prosser, William	(34)	2
Puliston, John		3
Ratchell, Ralph		1
Rawlings, Roger		2
Reading, Thomas	(1)	0
Redick, James	(39)	5
Regan, Daniel		1
Renalls, Richard		1
Richards, William	(30)	0
Robinson, Andrew		2
Robinson, Cotten	(27)	0
Rogers, John & son		2
Rodgers, Richard		1
Rogers, John	(36)	3
Rones, Danl.	(3)	0
Rookings, William		3
Ross, William	(29)	0
Rowles, James	(30)	0
Scarbro, William		1
Seat, Thomas		2
Seeth, Richard		1
Senior, Thomas	(23)	0
Sessums, Nic		1
Seward, William		2
Shaw, Robert		1
Sheife, Stephen	6(20)	0
Sheppard, John	(32)	2
Shorce, William		1
Sidway, ——		3
Simonds, William		5
Skiner, John		1
Skinner, Richard		1
Small, William	(14)	0
Salway, John	(28)	2
Sowerby, Francis		1
Sowerby, Thomas		1
Smith, Xpher	(35)	2
Smith, John		1
Smith, John		1
Smith, Richard		2
Smith, William	(49)	2
Spenser, Alan	(20)	2
Spensor, John	(30)	0
Spenser, Robert	(17)	5
Speroate, Abe	(6)	0
Spiltember, John		1
Spring, William		1
Stock, John		1
Stringfellow, James	(36)	0
Summer, Francis		1
Swann, Mathew		1
Swann, ——	(48)	3
Swett, William	(15)	0
Taylor, Francis	(34)	0
Taylor, John		1
Taylor, Walter	(47)	2
Thorne, Martin	(35)	0
Tias, Rich	(19)	0
Tooke, William		1
Towers, John	(31)	0
Vaus, Henry	(13)	2
Vinsent, John	(21)	0
Viveon, Joseph	(32)	0
Wadkins, William		1
Wall, Joseph		1
Waller, Thomas	(35)	0
Warren, Edward	(7)	2
Watkins, Edward		3
Watkins, James		1
Watson, Thomas	(13)	0
Wausell, Thomas	(23)	3
Weeks, Stephen		1
Weeks, Thomas	(12)	0
Welbanck, Edward	(32)	0
Welbeck, Richard		1
White, John	(17)	0
White, William	(49)	0
Whitson, John		1
Wilcocke, George	(39)	0
Williams, Danl		1
Williams, David		1
Williams, Lewis		1
Williams, Richard	(33)	0
Williams, Roger	(22)	3
Willis, Charles		1
Witherington, Nic	(16)	0

SURRY COUNTY TITHABLES (WHITE) IN 1678

Peter Adams
Wm. Alderson
Mr. Ar. Allen
Jno. Allen
Stephen Allen
Wm. Allin
Samll. Alsebrooke
Rob. Altoff
Jacob Aminges ?
Cha. Amry
Rich. Anderson
David Andrews, senr.
David Andrews, junr.
Rob. Andrews
Tho. Andrews, senr.
Tho. Andrews, junr.
Tho. Andrews
Tho. Andrews' son
Dan. Anslo
Henry Armstrong
Geo. Arnold
Wm. Arnold
Rich. Atkins
Robert Austin
Rich. Avery
Tho. Badge
Capt. Baker
Hen. Baker
Jno. Baley
Jno. Ballard
Capt. Charles Barham
Mr. Jno. Barker
Jno. Barnes
Jno. Barton
Wm. Barton
Walter Bartley
Jno. Bashaw
Jno. Battle
Danll. Bayley
Jos. Beale
Tho. Beale
Bluit Beaumont
David Beard
Tho. Bee
Jonah Bennett
Tho. Bentley
Jno. Berry
Jno. Binam
Tho. Binns
Jno. Bird
Jno. Bishop
Jno. Bishop
Roger Blackborne
Wm. Blackborne

Ri. Blow
Tho. Blunt
Wm. Blunt
James Bohon
Jno. Bolton
Phill. Bolton
Tho. Boobe
Tho. Boulton
Tho. Bouth (Booth?)
Francis Bowman
Wm. Bowman
Jno. Boy
Henry Braderton
Tho. Bradford
Rich. Bread
Ed. Bridgman
Mr. Hen. Briggs
Bartho. Britle
Andrew Browne
Edwd. Browne
Jno. Browne
Maj. Wm. Browne
Hezikiah Bunnell
Robert Burgis
Jno. Burnett
Mr. Tho. Busby
Edwd. Canot
Cor. Cardingpan
Wm. Carpinder
Wm. Carpenter
John Cary
Tho. Carr
Jno. Case
Mr. Robt. Caufield
Wm. Chambers
James Chesset
Wm. Chivers
Jno. Clarke
Jno. Clarke
Rich. Clarke
Mr. Tho. Clarke
Wm. Clarke
Tho. Cley
Jno. Clements
Christ. Clinch
Jno. Cockerin
Jno. Collins
Sam. Cornewell
Anthony Cornish
Tho. Cotten
Tho. Cottrell
Patrick Coulter
Charles Covee
Tho. Crews

Lewis Crow ?
Wm. Crudge
Ar. Davis
Ar. Davis
Edwd. Davis
Solomon Davis
Cha. Dennis
Wm. Draper
Mr. Ri. Drew
Tho. Drew
Wm. Drew
Jno. Dun
Jno. Dunford
Peleg Dunstone
Jno. Edwards
Tho. Edwards
Tho. Edwards
Mr. Wm. Edwards
Wm. Eliot
James Ellis
Jer. Ellis
Geo. Essell
Mich. Essell
Thy. Essell
Tim. Essell
Abraham Evans
Anthony Evans
ffra. Evins
Robt. Evans
Jo. Farloe
Tho. Farmer
Rob. Fellows
Humph. Felps
Jno. Fenly
Bartho. Figures
Tho. Fleare
Jno. Flood
Tho. Flood
Wat. Flood
Joseph Foard
James Forbes
Wm. Foreman
Tho. Foscraft
Chr. Foster
Geo. Foster
Hen. Francis, senr.
Hen. Francis, junr.
(Tho.) Futerell
Tho. Gibbons
Roger Gilbert
Jno. Golledge
Wm. Goltney
Wm. Goodman
Mr. Jno. Goring

Zekell Gorrell
Henry Gray
Jno. Gray
Jno. Gray
Fra. Gray
Tho. Gray
Wm. Gray
Wm. Gray, junr.
Jesper Gransom
Edwd. Greene
Rich. Greene
James Griffin
Jno. Griffin
Jno. Grigory
Ustace Grimes
Bo. Gullick
Corne. Hall
Wm. Hancock
Geo. Harris
Jno. Harris
Rich. Harris, senr.
Rich. Harris, junr.
Wm. Harris
Mr. Benj. Harrison
Wm. Harvy
Adam Heath
Wm. Heath
Geo. Henton
Jno. Hicks
Rich. Hide
Tho. High
Harmon Hill
Sion Hill
Hen. Hollinsworth
Mr. Rand. Holt
Ralph Holton, senr.
Ralph Holton, junr.
Ni. Hoskins
Robert House, senr.
Rob. House, junr.
Edmund Howell
Geo. Howell
Jno. Hulett
Van Humphry
Austin Hunicutt, junr.
Jno. Hunicutt
Wm. Hunt
Phy. Hunyford
Tho. Hux, senr.
Tho. Hux, junr.
Tho. Hyard
Jno. Ironmonger
Tho. Ironmonger
Tho. Jarrell
Cha. Jarrett
Rich. Jelkes
Geo. Jennings

James Johnson
Martin Johnson
Nicho. Johnson
Wm. Jones
Mr. Arthur Jordan
Lt. Col. (Geo.) Jordan
Geo. Jordan
James Jordan
Ri. Jordan
Rivers Jordan
Robert Judkins
Samll. Judkins
Rob. Kae, senr.
Rob. Kae, junr.
Mr. Jno. King
Tho. King
Tho. Kite
Wm. Kite
Wm. Kitto
Wm. Knott
Robert Lacy
Rob. Lancaster
Tho. Lane, senr.
Tho. Lane, junr.
James Largoe
Patrick Lashley
Tho. Last
Mr. Geo. Lee, senr.
Geo. Lee, junr.
Jno. Lee
Rich. Leech
Wm. Lile
Samll. Linn ?
Ar. Long
Wm. Littall
Wm. Lucus
Jno. Macarter
Danll. Maclode
Hugh Magee
Samll. Magett
Mr. Malden
Owen Marko
Cha. Marrett
Math. Marriott
Jno. Marshall
Peter Martin
Mr. Fra. Mason
Ni. Mason
James Mathews
Samll. Mathews
Jno. Mathewson
Tho. Mathis
Marco Mechino
Dennis Medeare
Mr. Meriwether
Geo. Midleton
Owen Midleton

Tho. Midleton
Pe. Miller
Solomon Miller
Tho. Milton
Law. Mizle
Luke Mizell
Jno. Miniard
Owen Mirick
Mr. Moring
Jno. Morgan
Geo. Morrell
Rich. Morris
Allin Muget
Jno. Muget
Ja. Murry
Wm. Nance
Edwd. Napkin
Samll. Newell
Wm. Newitt
Wm. Newsum
Roger Nicholls
Ja. Nicholson
Robt. Nicholson
Mr. Wm. Norwood
Jno. Oneale
Rob. Paddant
Ben. Pane
Tho. Parrett
Wm. Peacocke
Rich. Peirce
Ni. Perry
Ja. Petegree
Edwd. Pettway
Wm. Pettway
David Phillips
Jno. Phillips
Jno. Phillips
Wm. Phillips
Jno. Pittford
Capt. (Thomas) Pittman
Tho. Pittman
Wm. Pittman
Samll. Plaw
Samll. Pollett
Lt. Roger Potter
Jno. Price
Geo. Prince
Rich. Prince
Geo. Procter
Wm. Prosser
Jno. Pulestone
Mr. (Jno.) Randolph
Dennis Raphden
Ab. Ratcliffe
Jno. Rawlings
Roger Rawlings
Roger Rawlins

Wm. Reade
Danll. Regan
Hen. Reynolds
Robert Reynolds
Jo. Richardson
Ja. Riddick
Andaro Right
Jno. Roberts
Na. Roberts
Jno. Rodwell
Danll. Rogers
Jno. Rogers, senr.
Jno. Rogers, junr.
Jo. Rogers
Wm. Rogers
Wm. Rogers
Danll. Rome
Wm. Rose
Ed. Rowell
Wm. Rugsby
Mr. Robt. Ruffin
Wm. Sadler
Henry Sanford
Jos. Seate
Tho. Senior
Ni. Sessums
Wm. Seward
Jno. Sharpe
Phy. Shelly
Jno. Shepard
Jno. Shugar

Tho. Sidway
Mr. Wm. Simons
Christo. Smith
Jno. Smith
Ri. Smith
Francis South
Fra. Sowerby
Tho. Sowerby
Alex. Spensor
Capt. (Robt.) Spensor
James Stringfellow
Mathew Swann
Col. (Thomas) Swann
Capt. Samll. Swann
Wm. Swet
Edwd. Tanner
Edwd. Tayler
Fra. Tayler
Jno. Tayler
Walter Taylor
Wm. Temple
Jno. Thompson
Jno. Thompson
Samll. Thompson
Mr. Wm. Thompson
Matt. Thorne
Tho. Tias
Ri. Tias
Ri. Tias, junr.
Tho. Turner
Jno. Turvet

Mich. Upchurch
Walter Vaughan
Isack Very
Jno. Vincent
Thy. Walker
Jo. Wall
Tho. Waller
Ab. Wallis
Jno. Warring
Tho. Waring
Ri. Washington
Hen. Watkins
Ja. Watkins
Jno. Watkins
Chas. White
Geo. White
Jno. White
Wm. White
Jno. Wiggenden
Jno. Wilkeson
Chas. Williams
Geo. Williams
Lewis Williams
Roger Williams
Tho. Williams
Cha. Willis
Ni. Wilson
Ni. Witherington
Tho. Wright
Tho. Young

TOTAL 425

A list of tithables belonging to Lawnes Creeke Parish in Surry County taken 12th of June, 1683 by Robert Caufield.

A list of tithables taken the 9th of June 1683 within the precincts of Lower Chipoaks and Blackwater in Lawnes Creek Parish by Robert Ruffin.

A list of tithables above Upper Sunken Marsh taken June 10th, 1683 by Benjamin Harrison.

A list of tithables taken June 9, 1683 by Samuel Swann.

A list of tithables taken by order of Court by James Dykes June 9, 1683.

Taken by Robert Caufield	122
" " Robert Ruffin	90
" " Benjamin Harrison	115
" " Samuel Swann	110
" " James Dykes	71
Total	508

(Book 1671-1684, pp. 524-528)

Adams, Peter		1	Browder, Edward	(21)	2
Adkins, Thomas	(37)	0	Browne, And	(6)	0
Allen, Maj. Arthur	(23)	7	Browne, Thomas	(42)	0
Allen, John	(33)	0	Browne, Col. Wm.	(78)	8
Allen, William	(9)	0	Bruton, James		1
Allen, Thomas	(88)	3	Bullock, Richard	(48)	0
Alsobrook, Sam	(77)	7	Bunnell, Hez		1
Andrews, Thomas Sr.	(76)	3	Busby, Thomas	(48)	3
Andrews, Robert	(76)	0	Byneham, John	(44)	2
Andrews, Barth	(76)	0	Byneham, John	(44)	0
Andrews, David	(63)	3	Byneham, James	(45)	0
Andrews, Richard	(80)	0	Cane, James	(84)	2
Andrus, Thomas		1	Carr, Thomas		1
Ashley, Thomas	(31)	0	Carpender, William	(84)	0
Avery, Richard	(59)	2	Carpender, William	(32)	3
Baggott, John	(62)	0	Case, And	(50)	0
Bagly, Hue			Case, John		1
Bagly, Peter		1	Case, John	(1)	2
Bags, Thomas	(73)	3	Cartright, Richard		
Baker, Henry		1	Caufield, Robert	(24)	10
Baker, Mrs. Elizabeth		4	Cawwood, John	(92)	0
Bamer, John		3	Chapman, Will	(63)	0
Barber, Peter		1	Chissell, James		1
Barefoot, Noah	(43)	0	Chivers, William		1
Barker, John		2	Clarke, John		1
Barten, William	(94)	0	Clarke, John	(60)	0
Bartlett, Walter	(19)	3	Clarke, Thomas		1
Battell, Thomas	(33)	0	Clary, Thomas	(1)	0
Battle, John	(30)	0	Clary, William	(4)	0
Bayley, Anselm		1	Clemons, John		1
Bayley, Edward		1	Cockerham, William	(6)	2
Bennett, Jonas	(83)	0	Cockerham, Thomas	(14)	0
Beale, Joseph		1	Cogan, William	(17)	0
Beck, Lawrence		1	Coker, John		1
Bently, Thomas	(28)	2	Combe, John	(17)	0
Bently, Thomas	(28)	0	Conish, Anthony		1
Binns, Thomas	(91)	6	Cook, John	(43)	0
Bird, Thomas		1	Cooke, Thomas	(8)	0
Biton, Ri		1	Cooper, Thomas	(82)	0
Blackborne, William		1	Collier, John	(58)	0
Blow, Rich	(72)	0	Collins, John	(20)	0
Blunt, Thomas	(47)	3	Collins, John		1
Bookey, Edward	(25)	0	Cotten, Thomas		1
Bowen, Arthur	(24)	0	Crawford, Robert	(41)	2
Boy, William	(42)	0	Creede, William	(78)	0
Boy, John	(87)	0	Crews, Thomas	(74)	
Braderton, Hen	(18)	0	Crews, William	(74)	
Bradford, Pat	(17)	0	Crouch, William	(11)	0
Bradford, Thomas	(59)	0	Cutt, Edward	(93)	0
Briggs, Henry	(29)	4	Davis, Arthur		1
Briggs, Francis	(29)	0	Deberry, Peter		1
Briggs, Charles	(29)	0	Deerehim, Thomas	(40)	10
Briggs, Henry Jr.	(47)	0	Delke, Roger		1
Brittell, Bart		1	Dennis, Nathaniel		1
Broadrib, William	(67)	0	Dennis, William	(36)	0

Judkins, Robert	1	O'neale, John .... (61)	0
Kelby, John .... (93)	0	Ostin, Robert .... (32)	0
Killingworth, William .... (30)	0	Owen, Robert .... (71)	0
Kersey, Thomas .... (33)	0	Page, John .... (77)	0
Killpatrick, James .... (24)	0	Pallett, Sam .... (35)	
Kindred, John .... (10)	0	Pancost, Edward .... (19)	0
King, John .... (25)	3	Pane, Benjamin .... (39)	0
Kington, John .... (38)	0	Parson, Ph. .... (7)	0
Kito, William	1	Pearce, Ri .... (3)	0
Kitto, William	1	Pecock, William	1
Knott, William	1	Petway, Edward .... (89)	2
Lacy, Robert .... (9)	2	Pettway, William	1
Lancaster, Robert	1	Phillips, David	1
Lane, Ri. .... (25)	0	Phillips, John Sr. .... (90)	
Langford, Thomas .... (77)	0	Phillips, John Jr. .... (90)	
Lashley, Pat .... (49)	2	Pittford, John	1
Law, Thomas .... (16)	2	Pittman, Capt. Thomas	1
Lee, George .... (35)	3	Pittman, Thomas Jr.	1
Little, John	1	Plow, Sam	1
Little, William	1	Potter, Capt.	1
Long, Arthur .... (21)	0	Proctor, James	1
Lother, John .... (75)	0	Prosser, William	1
Loveday, John .... (37)	2	Puleston, John .... (95)	3
Lucas, William	1	Rainolds, Hen	1
Lyle, William	1	Rainolds, Robert	1
Macknia, Merco .... (45)	2	Rawlings, John	1
Maddox, Thomas	1	Reede, William	1
Maggott, Samuel	1	Regan, Danl .... (56)	3
Maldew, James .... (80)	4	Regan, Francis .... (56)	0
Man, John .... (15)	0	Reithdew, Dennis .... (6)	0
Marriott, Charles .... (54)	0	Rice, Da. .... (41)	0
Mason, Francis	2	Richardson, John	1
Mason, Francis .... (96)	7	Riddick, James .... (10)	2
Martin, John	1	Rivers, John	1
Martin, Peter .... (53)	0	Roberts, John	1
Meker, Thomas	1	Roberts, Nathaniel .... (65)	0
Midleton, George .... (46)	1	Robinson, John	1
Midleton, James .... (46)	1	by Mrs. Rob. Parke.	
Miniard, John	1	Rogers, John .... (51)	0
Mirick, Owen	1	Rogers, John	1
Mizle, Luke .... (64)	2	Rogers, James .... (42)	5
Mizle, Law .... (64)	0	Rogers, William .... (71)	2
Moore, John .... (19)	0	Roome, Danl .... (38)	2
Morgan, Abel .... (48)		Rose, William .... (85)	0
Moring, John .... (53)	3	Rosefield, Ni. .... (15)	2
Moring, Xto .... (53)	0	Rowell, Edward .... (18)	2
Morrell, George	1	Rowland, William	1
Morrice, Richard	1	Rugsby, William .... (93)	0
Myles, John .... (77)	0	Ruffin, Robert .... (43)	6
Newbre, Edward .... (7)	0	Rutherford, John .... (14)	2
Newbre, Ri .... (7)	0	Sanford, Hen .... (12)	0
Newton, Samuel	1	Savage, Charles	1
Nurgan, James .... (13)	0	Savage, Robert	1
Napkin, Edward	1	Scidmore, William .... (63)	0
Nicholson, Robert .... (34)	2	Seagood, Stephen .... (11)	0
Nicholson, George .... (34)	0	Sesile, Rich .... (66)	0
Norwood, Mr.	1	Seate, John	1

Senior, Thomas	(96)	0	Tias, Thomas		1
Sessoms, Ni		1	Tias, Rich	(70)	0
Seward, William		1	Upchurch, Mich		1
Shaw, Thomas	(81)	0	Vincent, James	(69)	2
Shelley, Phil		1	Wadlois, Thomas		1
Sherman, John		1	Walker, Tim.		5
Shuger, John	(2)	2	Wall, John		1
Sidway, Thomas		2	Waller, Thomas		1
Simons, William	(27)	3	Warpoole, John	(65)	2
Smith, James		1	Washington, Rich.	(47)	0
Smith, Ni		1	Watkins, James		1
Smith, John	(73)		Watkins, John	(57)	3
Smith, Richard	(72)	2	Watson, John	(75)	0
Smith, John	(61)	2	Warren, John	(52)	0
Smith, Xptr	(20)	2	Warren, Robert	(88)	0
Sowerby, Francis	(69)	0	Weaver, John	(56)	0
Sowerby, Thomas	(58)	2	Welldon, William		1
Spitles, Robert	(86)	0	Wheeler, William	(26)	0
Swann, Sam	(62)	2	White, Ch		1
Swett, William	(91)	0	White, Thomas	(42)	0
Tanner, Edward		1	Wiggins, Thomas	(51)	2
Targett, John		1	Wilham, George		
Taylor, Edward	(6)	0	William, Ni	(17)	4
Taylor, Francis, Dr.		1	Williams, Char	(3)	2
Taylor, Thomas	(73)	0	Williams, Roger		1
Taylor, Walter		1	Willice, Charles		1
Temple, John	(26)	2	Wincome, William	(89)	0
Temple, William	(79)	0	Winklen, Rich	(35)	0
Thompson, John	(75)	4	Witherington, W.	(86)	2
Thompson, Sam	(81)	3	Woodruff, Sam.	(54)	0
Thorne, Martin		1	Wray, William	(55)	0
Thorpe, John	(27)	0	Wright, Thomas	(18)	0

SURRY COUNTY TITHABLES (WHITE) IN 1688

Richd. Adkins	Joell Barker	Tho. Bird
Tho. Adkins	Mr. Jno. Barker	Jno. Bishup
Major Ar. Allen	Tho. Barker	Wm. Blackburn
John Allen	Jno. Barnes	Honr. Blake
Samll. Alsobrook	Humphry Barney	Bennett Blewit
David Andrews, senr.	Walt. Bartlett	Geo. Blow
David Andrews, junr.	Wm. Barton	Mr. Tho. Blunt
Rob. Andrews	Jno. Battle	Ed. Bookey
Tho. Andrews, senr.	Tho. Battle	Jno. Bov
Tho. Andrews, junr.	Peter Bayly	James Boyce
William Arnall	Jno. Bennett	Geo. Branch
Jno. Askew	Jonas Benett	Charles Briggs
Jno. Atwood	William Bennitt	Hen. Briggs
Geo. Avery	Tho. Bentley, senr.	Richd. Brighton
Jno. Ayres	Tho. Bentley, junr.	Jno. Brittaine
Tho. Bage	Wm. Bentley	Batt. Brittle
Hugh Bagly ?	John Berryman	Thomas Broome
Henry Baker	Jno. Bineham, senr.	Jno. Browne
Ed. Baly	Jno. Bineham, junr.	Coll. Wm. Browne
Noah Barefoot	Tho. Binns	John Browne
Jethro Barker	Jno. Bird	James Bruton

Wm. Bruton
Wm. Bullock
Daniell Bulltee
Hezekiah Bunell
Phillip Burrow
Jeffrey Busby
Mr. Tho. Busby
James Bynham
Wm. Carpinder
Robt. Cartright
John Case
Mr. Rob. Caufield
Wm. Chambers
James Chessett
Wm. Chivers
John Clarke
John Clarke
Henry Clarke
Tho. Clary
Wm. Clary
John Clemens
Tho. Cockerham
Wm. Cockerham
Wm. Cockin
John Coker
Jno. Collier
Tho. Collier
John Collins
James Cooke
Samll. Cooke
Tho. Cooke
Anthony Cornish
Tho. Cotten
Walter Cotten
Edward Cottrill
Jno. Coward
Robt. Craford
Tho. Crewes
Wm. Crewes
Wm. Crudge
Ed. Cutt
Ar. Davis
Arthur Davis
Nichol. Davis
Tho. Davis
Peter Debenry
Roger Delk
Nath. Denis
Wm. Denis
Cha. Denisson
Tho. Derham
Charles Digby
Jno. Dikes
Richard Dorman
Rob. Dowling
Wm. Draper
Edward Drew

Jno. Drew
Tho. Drew
Jno. Duce
Mr. Jno. Edwards
Tho. Edwards
Mr. Wm. Edwards
Wm. Ellett
James Ellis
Jer. Ellis, senr.
Jer. Ellis, junr.
James Ely
Abra. Evins
Anthony Evans
Edward Evans
Geo. Ezell
Michaell Ezell
Timothy Ezell, senr.
Tho. Farmer
Tho. Fallwell
Rob. Fellows
Humphry ffelphs
Bartho. Figgers
John Finly
Forlough Fitzpatrick
Peter Fiveash
Robt. fflake, junr.
Law. Fleming
Mr. Tho. Flood
Mr. Walt. Flood
Tho. fforbush
Jos. Ford
Wm. Foreman
Jno. Fort
Xo. Foster
Geo. ffoster
Wm. ffoster
Hen. Francis
Thomas Futrell
Jeffre Gerney
Phillip Gibbs
Banja. Giddion
Roger Gilbert
Hintia Gilliam
Wm. Goard
Jno. Golledg
Wm. Goodman
Gesper Gransom
Ed. Granthum
Jno. Grey
Richd. Gray
Wm. Gray
Wm. Gray
Ed. Greene
Jno. Greene
Jno. Greene
Richd. Greene
Rob. Grice

Saml. Gridley
Fra. Grigory
James Griffin
John Griffin
Euistice Grimes
Rob. Gully
Cha. Guttrich
Wm. Gwaltney
Nath. Hales
Wm. Halsoe
John Hancock
Wm. Hancock
Wm. Hare
Tho. Harebottle
Bray Hargrave
Lamuell Hargrove
Richd. Hargrove
Wm. Harrington
Wm. Harris
Benja. Harrison
Nath. Harrison
Henry Hart
Robt. Hart
Tho. Hart
Wm. Harvey
Rob. Hathen ?
Adam Heath
John Heathfield
Tho. Hiard, senr.
Tho. Hiard, junr.
Jno. Hickes
Jonah Hickman
Richd. Hide
Rob. Hill
Sion Hill
Tho. Hill
Wm. Holeford
Jno. Holt
Wm. Holt
Ralph Holton
Tho. Homes
Wm. Hooker
Tho. Horton
James Hosnell
Wm. Hougens
Charles Houlsworth
Walt. Houlsworth
Rob. House, senr.
Rob. House, junr.
George Howell
Wm. Howell
Evan Humphreys
Augustine Hunnicutt
Jno. Hunicutt
Tho. Hunt
Wm. Hunt
Hugh Hunyford

Tho. Hux
Rob. Inman
John Ironmunger
Tho. Ironmunger
Tim. Isard
Richd. Jackson
Wm. Jackson
Tho. Jarrell
Cha. Jarrett
Richd. Jelkes
James Jolly
Tho. Jolly
Martin Johnson
John Johnson
Jno. Johnson
Richd. Jones
Ar. Jordan
Geo. Jordan
James Jordan
Jno. Jordean ?
Richd. Jordan, senr.
Richd. Jordan, junr.
Nathan Joyce
Charles Judkins
Rob. Judkins
Samll. Judkins
Jno. Kersey
Jno. Kiketan
Wm. Killingsworth
Ja. Kilpatrick
Mr. Jno. King
Jno. Kindred
Wm. Kitto
Wm. Knott
Xo. Lacey
Rob. Lacy
Rob. Lancaster
Jos. Lane
Tho. Lane, senr.
Tho. Lane, junr.
Pat. Lashley
Hen. Lather
Jno. Little
Wm. Little
Robt. Littleboy
Ar. Long
Geo. Long
Jno. Lovett
Wm. Lucas
Col. (Phillip) Ludwell
Jno. Mackletosh
Marco Mackmey
Samll. Magett
(Nich.) Magett
Jno. Manor
Mack. Mansell
Math. Marriott

Jno. Martin
ffra. Mason
Tho. Mathers
Wm. Meades
Law. Meazell
Luke Meazell
David Meleanie
Fra. Meriwether
Nichol. Meriwether
Chas. Merrit
Jno. Midleton
Geo. Midleton
Tho. Midleton
John Miles
Owen Mirick
Edward Moolio
Ja. Moony
Xo. Moreing
Jno. Moreing
Jno. Morgan
Tho. Morgan
Abraham Morris
Richd. Morriss
Nathaniel Munger
Geo. Murrell
Ed. Napkin
Wm. Nash
Edward Newby
Wm. Newitt
Geo. Newsom
Mr. Wm. Newsum
Jarvis Newton
Samuel Newton
Roger Nicholls
Geo. Nicholson
Robt. Nicholson
Hen. Norton
William Norwood
Morgan Ocanada
Robt. Ostin
Rob. Owin
John Page
Gesper Parker
Richd. Parker
Jno. Parton
Tho. Partridg
Nicholas Pasfield
Wm. Peacock
Tho. Peddington
Richd. Peirce
Tho. Peirce
Jno. Pestle
Geo. Peters
Mr. Ed. Pettway
Wm. Pettway
David Phillips
Jno. Phillips, senr.

Jno. Phillips, junr.
John Phillops
Wm. Phillops
Wm. Pickerell
John Pittford
Tho. Pittman, senr.
Tho. Pittman, junr.
Wm. Pittman
Sam. Plaw
Wm. Pope
James Porch
Capt. (Roger) Potter
Tho. Preston
Joshua Prockter
Wm. Prockter
Wm. Prosser
John Puliston
Rob. Randall
Roger Rawlings
Wm. Rawlings
Ja. Reddick
Rob. Reddick
Danll. Regan
Fra. Regan
Rob. Reynolds
David Rice
Jos. Richardson
Tho. Right
Jno. Rivers
Wm. Rivers
Jno. Roberts
Nath. Roberts
John Robinson
Richd. Robinson
Jno. Rodwell
Jno. Rogers
Jos. Rogers
Wm. Rogers
Jno. Rollings
Jno. Rolph
Richd. Rose
Wm. Rose
Edward Rowell
Wm. Rowland
Robt. Ruffin
Henry Sanford
Charles Savidge
Rob. Savidge
Ed. Scarbrough
Wm. Scarbrough
Fra. Sealoe
Joseph Seate
Nichol. Sessums
Jno. Seward
Wm. Seward
Jno. Sharp
Richd. Shaw

Richd. Shockey
Fra. Shrosby
Jno. Shrosby
Tho. Sidway
Wm. Simons
Xo. Smith
Jno. Smith
Nicholas Smith
Richd. Smith
Richard Smith
Tho. Sowersby
Randall Spensor
Rob. Spittless
Wm. Spragg
Roger Squire
Jno. Sugar
Mathew Swann
Maj. (Samll.) Swann
Tho. Swann
Rob. Swett
William Swett
Geo. Symes
Edward Tanner
Edward Taylor

Walter Taylor
Mr. Jno. Thompson
Martin Thorne
Jno. Thornall
Joseph Thorpe
Walt. Tomkins
Tho. Tarver
Jno. Tooke
Henry Tooker
Tho. Tyus
Micaell Upchurch
Jno. Vincett
Danll. Wade
Mr. Tim. Walker
Jos. Wall
Tho. Waller
Jno. Wapoole
Tho. Ward
Jno. Warick
Tho. Warr
Allen Warren
Jno. Warren
Rob. Warren
Tho. Warren

Wm. Warren
Richd. Washington
Wm. Waterman
Tho. Watson
James Wattkins
Jno. Wattkins
Richd. Whelehouse
Jno. Wheler
Wm. Wheler
Nich. Wheskin
Charles White
Tho. White
Tho. Wiggins
Jno. Wilkinson
Chas. Wms.
Geo. Williams
Roger Williams
Jno. Williamson
Nichol. Witherington
Tho. Woalves
Josias Wood
Wm. Wood
John Woolly

TOTAL 476

A LIST OF TITHABLES TAKEN JUNE 10, 1694

Southwark Parish   373
Lawnes Creek Parish   269

646

(Deed Book 1694-1709, pp. 21-23)

Allen, Maj. Arthur .... (73) 16	Bagly, Peter .... (19) 1	
Allen, John 1	Baker, Hen .... (79) 3	
Allsbrooke, Samuel 1	Baker, Hen .... (79) 0	
Adcock, Eliza .... (21) 0	Baker, Wm. .... (79) 0	
Adkins, Thomas 1	Barham, Robert .... (98) 0	
Alcock, Thomas .... (13) 0	Barber, William 1	
Amry, Edward .... (45) 0	Barker, Joel .... (17) 2	
Amory, Thomas .... (2) 0	Barker, George .... (18) 2	
Anderson, David .... (34) 3	Barker, John 2	
Andrews, Thomas 1	Barrow, Edward .... (33) 0	
Andrews, Robert 1	Battle, John .... (20) 2	
Andrews, Bat 2	Battle, Thomas .... (9) 0	
Archer, Benjamin 1	Bartlett, Walter .... (94) 2	
Atkinson, William .... (78) 0	Bayly, E. 1	
Austin, Robert 1	Beighton, Rich 1	
Austin, Rich .... (4) 0	Bennett, James 1	
Barefoot, Noah 1	Bennett, Jonas 1	
Bage, Thomas .... (37) 3	Bennett, William 1	
Bage, John 1	Bentley, Thomas .... (11) 2	

Bentley, James	(11)	0	Collins, James	(5)	0

Bentley, James ....(11) 0
Bently, Thomas ....(4) 4
Berryman, James 1
Binns, Thomas ....(52) 3
Bishop, John 1
Blackshire, John ....(71) 0
Blackbourne, Wm. 1
Blow, George ....(33) 2
Blunt, Thomas ....(21) 3
Bly, Chris 1
Booky, Edward ....(41) 2
Brodstone, James 3
Briggs, Charles 1
Briggs, George ....(18) 0
Briggs, Henry ....(14) 2
Briggs, Henry ....(14) 0
Brittle, Bar 1
Browne, Edward ....(80) 0
Browne, John 1
Browne, Col. Wm. ....(42) 13
Browne, Wm. ....(42) 0
Browne, Hen. ....(42) 0
Bruton, William 1
Bunnell, Hez. 1
Burnett, Dav. ....(50) 0
Burrow, Phill 1
Busby, Thomas ....(28) 2
Busby, Jeffry ....(28) 0
Byneham, John 1
Byneham, James 1
Caps, John ....(80) 2
Carpinder, Wm. ....(24) 4
Cartright, Robert ....(27) 0
Case, John 1
Caufield, Mrs. Eliz 7
Chambers, William ....(84) 2
Chisell, James 1
Christian, Mathews ....(93) 0
Clarke, John ....(62) 2
Clary, Thomas ....(52) 0
Clary, William 2
Clement, John Sr. ....(53) 2
Clement, John Jr. ....(53) 0
Clement, Capt. John 7
Cock, Walter ....(110) 5
Cock, William ....(110) 0
Cocker, John ....(101) 2
Cocker, William ....(101) 0
Cockerham, Wm. 1
Cockerham, Thomas ....(83) 0
Cockerill, Edward 1
Cogin, William 1
Cooke, James 1
Cooke, Sam 1
Cooke, William 1
Cooke, Thomas 1
Collins, John ....(5) 2

Collins, James ....(5) 0
Cornish, Art ....(92) 2
Cornish, Robert ....(92) 0
Cotton, Thomas ....(1) 2
Cotton, Walter 1
Collyer, Thomas 2
Cornwell, Samuel 1
Crafford, Robert ....(78) 2
Crews, Thomas 1
Crips, William ....(42) 0
Crotch, William ....(13) 2
Crouch, William ....(65) 0
Davis, Art 1
Davis, Art Jr. 1
Davis, Thomas ....(36) 2
Davison, John ....(81) 0
Deloch, William ....(94) 0
Dennis, Math 1
Digby, Charles 1
Doll, John ....(76) 0
Doll, Sambo ....(32) 0
Doorkin, Thomas 1
Dowling, Robert 1
Draper, William 1
Drew, Edward 1
Drew, John 1
Drew, Thomas 1
Dyer, Henry 1
Dykes, James 1
Edmons, Howell ....(17) 0
Edwards, John ....(50) 3
Edwards, Thomas 1
Edwards, William ....(49) 13
Edwards, Wm. Sr. 2
Elliott, Danl 1
Elliott, William 1
Ellis, Edward 1
Ellis, James 1
Ellis, Jere. Jr. ....(9) 2
Ellis, Jere. Sr. ....(9) 0
Elmes, Mathews 1
Ely, James 1
Essell, George ....(91) 1
Essell, John ....(91) 1
Essell, Mich 1
Essel, Tim. ....(2) 3
Evans, Anthony 1
Fellows, Robert ....(67) 2
Felks, Hump. 1
Fenly, John 1
Ferribe, Benjamin ....(39) 0
Figgars, Bart 1
Fiveash, Peter 1
Fleming, Lawrence 1
Flood, Thomas 1
Flood, Walter ....(39) 5
Ford, John 1

Ford, James		1	Hiard, Thomas		1
Foreman, William	(32)	3	Hickman, Jonah		1
Fort, Eliza		1	Hide, Rich	(26)	2
Fort, George		1	High, John	(40)	2
Foster, William		1	Hill, Robert		1
Foster, George	(100)		Hill, Sion		1
Gardner Zeph	(25)		Hilliard, William		1
Gibbons, John		1	Hodges, James	(62)	0
Gilbert, Rog		1	Hogwood, George	(34)	0
Gilliam, Hin.	(23)	2	Hogsworth, Walter		1
Good, John		3	Hollingsworth, Hen		1
Goodman, William		1	Holt, John		1
Gorney, George	(69)	0	Holt, Thomas		1
Gransum, Jasper	(8)	2	Holt, William	(58)	4
Grantham, Ed. Sr.	(47)	2	House, Robert		1
Grantham, John	(47)	0	Howell, William		1
Gray, John		1	Huggins, William		1
Gray, William		1	Humphry, Evan	(63)	2
Gray, William Jr.	(30)	0	Huniford, Hugh		1
Gray, William Sr.	(30)	2	Huniford, William		1
Greene, John	(76)	2	Hunnicutt, Austin	(65)	2
Greene, Rich		1	Hunicutt, John	(51)	2
Grice, Robert		1	Hunnicutt, William	(51)	0
Griffin, James	(85)	3	Hunt, William	(8)	3
Griffins, James	(85)	0	Huson, Thomas		1
Griffin, John	(85)	0	Hux, Thomas		1
Gregory, John	(81)	0	Ingram, John		1
Grimes, Eustice		1	Inman, Robert		1
Gullage, John		7	Jackson, William		1
Gully, Robert		1	Jarrell, Thomas Sr.	(88)	2
Gualtney, William	(97)	2	Jarrell, Thomas Jr.	(88)	0
Gualtney, Thomas	(97)	0	Jarrett, Charles		1
Halso, William		1	Jelks, Rich		1
Hancock, John		1	Johnson, John		1
Harding, Nic	(66)	0	Johnson, Martin Jr.	(59)	0
Harbotle, Thomas	(73)	0	Johnson, Martin, Sr.	(59)	4
Hargrove, Bray	(72)	0	Johnson, William	(59)	0
Hargrove, Lemuel	(87)	0	Johnson, John	(59)	0
Hargrove, Rich		1	Johnson, William		1
Harrington, John	(58)	0	Johnson, William		1
Harris, Rich		1	Jones, Arthur	(12)	2
Harris, John		1	Jones, Richard	(12)	0
Harrison, Benj.	(27)	19	Jones, James		1
Harrison, Nathaniel	(27)	0	Jordan, Richard, Sr.	(48)	3
Harrison, Daniel		1	Jordan, Charles	(48)	0
Harrys, Arthur		1	Jordan, Richard Jr.		1
Harrys, William	(89)	2	Jordan, Arthur		2
Hart, Hen	(72)	2	Jordan, James		1
Hart, Robert	(98)	2	Jordan, George		2
Hart, Thomas	(77)	2	Jordan, River		1
Hassell, James		1	Judkins, Charles		
Harvey, William	(3)	2	Judkins, Sam		1
Haynes, Thomas	(27)	0	Keeper, John	(34)	0
Heath, Adam		1	Kersey, John		1
Heathfield, Thomas		1	Kindred, John		1
Heward, John		1	King, Thomas	(38)	0
Hewson, George	(55)	0	Knight, John	(1)	

Knott, William		1
Lacy, Robert		1
Lacy, Robert, Jr.	(86)	0
Lacy, Robert, Sr.	(86)	2
Lancaster, Robert	(74)	3
Lanceaster, Robert	(74)	0
Lancaster, Samuel	(74)	0
Lane, Joseph		1
Lanier, Robert	(48)	0
Lane, Thomas Sr.		1
Lane, Thomas Jr.		1
Lane, William		1
Lashley, Pat	(22)	2
Lashley, Walter	(22)	0
Lewis, Tom		1
Little, John		1
Little, William		1
Littleboy, ——		1
Long, Arthur		1
Long, George		2
Lother, John		
Ludwell, Col.		17
Lyle, William		1
Mainor, John	(99)	0
Mangham, John		1
Mason, Fra		2
Mason, Fra	(57)	7
Mason, James	(57)	0
Mason, James		1
by Elizabeth Judkins		
Mathars, Thomas		1
Mayfall, Mach	(19)	
Mead, James		1
Meade, William		1
Merritt, Charles		1
Midleton, George	(9)	0
Midleton, John		1
Mirick, Owen	(16)	2
Mirick, Thomas	(16)	0
Moreland, Edward	(93)	2
Morgan, John	(7)	0
Moring, C.		1
Moring, John	(46)	4
Morrell, George Sr.	(70)	2
Morrell, George Jr.	(70)	0
Morris, Richard		1
Moss, John		1
Munger, Nathaniel		1
Nash, William		1
Napkin, Edward		1
Nicholson, Robert		1
Nicholson, Thomas	(75)	0
Nicolls, Roger Sr.	(74)	2
Nicolls, William	(74)	0
Newbee, Edward		1
Newett, William	(99)	2
Newsum, John	(100)	1

Newsum, William	(87)	3
Newton, Samuel		1
Norton, Henry		1
Norwood, William Sr.	(43)	2
Norwood, George	(43)	0
Oliver, John		1
Orandia, Morgan		1
Osborne, Humph	(7)	0
Owen, Robert		1
Parker, Richard		1
Pasfield, Nich		1
Patridge, Samuel		1
Peacock, William		1
Peirce, Rich		1
Peters, George		1
Petway, William		1
Phillips, David		1
Phillips, John Jr.	(60)	0
Phillips, John Sr.	(60)	2
Phillips, John		1
Phillips, William	(61)	0
Pickerell, William		1
Pidington, Thomas		1
Pittford, John		1
Pittman, William		1
Pitt, Thomas	(96)	2
Pittman, William Jr.	(96)	0
Plaw, Samuel	(56)	0
Potter, Capt. Roger		1
Price, William	(84)	2
Proctor, Joseph		1
Prosser, William		1
Pulistone, John	(55)	2
Rachell, William	(26)	0
Rachell, William	(7)	0
Randall, Capt.		5
Rawlings, John	(6)	2
Rawlings, Roger		1
Regan, John		1
Rice, David		1
Richardson, Joseph	(95)	2
Rivers, John	(7)	2
Rivers, William		1
Robards, John		1
Robinson, James	(36)	0
Rogers, John		1
Rogers, Joseph	(81)	3
Rogers, Rich	(46)	0
Rogers, William		1
Rogorr, William	(37)	0
Rookings, William		1
Rose, Rich		1
Rose, William		1
Rowland, William	(71)	2
Rowell, John		1
Rowell, Edward		1
Ruffin, Mrs. Eliz.	(61)	7

Rutherford, Sam		1
Sandago, James	(15)	0
Savage, Charles		1
Savage, Henry		1
Savage, Robert		1
Scarboro, John	(29)	0
Scarboro, Edward	(10)	2
Scarboro, William	(10)	0
Scogan, Richard	(9)	2
Seale, Joseph	(82)	2
Seale, Robert	(82)	0
Senior, John	(46)	0
Seward, John	(86)	6
Seward, William		1
Sharpe, John		1
Shelley, Phil	(6)	2
Sheppard, William		1
Shippey, Rich	(6)	0
Short, William		1
Shugar, John		1
Sidway, Thomas		1
Simons, William	(15)	4
Sims, George		1
Smith, John		1
Smith, Nic	(32)	2
Smith, Rich	(35)	2
Smith, Silas	(27)	0
Smith, Thomas	(32)	2
Smith, Thomas Jr.	(32)	0
Smith, William	(49)	13
South, John		1
Sowerby, Fra.	(45)	2
Sowerby, John		1
Sowerby, Thomas		1
Sowerby, Thomas		1
Sowerby, Thomas	(44)	0
Squier, Roger		1
Stanton, James	(8)	
Stringfellow, Ri.	(63)	0
Swann, Math	(66)	2
Swann, Thomas Jr.		2
Swett, William	(54)	2
Swett, Robert	(54)	0
Sugar, James		2
Tall, Anthony		1
Tanner, William	(77)	0
Tayler, Edward	(90)	2
Taylor, Rich		1
Thompson, John		4
Thorne, Martin		1

Thorpe, John		
Thorpe, Joseph	(68)	4
Thorpe, T.	(68)	0
Thorpe, Robert	(68)	0
Tias, Thomas		1
Tooker, Capt. Hen.		6
Tonor, Thomas	(75)	2
Tuke, John		1
Twyford, John	(35)	0
Twyking, Walter	(41)	0
Twying, Richfl	(46)	0
Upchurch, Mich	(64)	2
Upchurch, Ni.	(64)	0
Vaughan, Stephen	(40)	0
Vincent, John	(44)	2
Walker, Tim		5
Wall, Joseph		1
Wallis, Thomas		1
Ward, Rich		1
Ward, Thomas	(68)	0
Ward, Thomas		1
Ward, William	(95)	0
Wapole, John	(25)	2
Warren, Allen		1
Warren, John		1
Warren, Robert		1
Warren, Robert		1
Warren, Thomas	(56)	2
Warren, William		1
Warrike, John		1
Washington, Rich		1
Watkins, John		3
Webb, Robert	(4)	0
West, Fra.	(23)	0
White, Charles	(29)	2
Wheeler, William	(20)	0
Wiggins, Thomas		1
Wise, Ni.	(90)	0
Witherington, Nic.	(31)	2
Wilkinson, John	(8)	3
Wilham, Andrew		1
Williams, Rog.	(31)	0
Williams, Charles		1
William, George		1
Williams, John		1
William, Thomas		1
Williamson, Rog.		2
Woolly, John		1
Wood, George		1
Wright, Thomas	(69)	2

SURRY COUNTY TITHABLES (WHITE) IN 1698

Jno. Abbott
James Adkinson
Albert Alburson
Jno. Aldee
Maj. Arthur Allen
John Allen
Wm. Alsoe
Barth. Andrewes
David Andrewes
Robert Andrewes
Tho. Andrewes
Thomas Arnall
Tho. Atkins
Wm. Austin ?
John Avery
Thomas Bage
Henry Baker, senr.
Henry Baker, junr.
John Baker
Anselm Baley
John Baley
Noah Barefoot
Robt. Barham
Jethro Barker
Joell Barker
Mr. Jno. Barker
Henry Barnes
Edward Barrow
Thomas Barrow
Water Bartlett
Wm. Barton
Jno. Battle
Peter Bayley
Walter Bayley
Jno. Bell
George Benbridge
James Bennett
John Bentley
Thomas Bentley, senr.
Thomas Bentley, junr.
John Berriman
James Bineham
Jno. Bineham
Mr. Tho. Binns
Jno. Blackburne
Wm. Blackburne
Jno. Blackshire
Jno. Blewer ?
George Blow
Mr. Tho. Blunt
Christopher Bly ?
Edward Bookey
Mr. Tho. Bowman
Henry Bridges (Briggs?)
Charles Briggs

Samll. Briggs
Edward Bright
Edward Browne
Mr. Henry Browne
Jno. Browne
Jno. Browne
Col. Wm. Browne
Mr. Wm. Browne
Jno. Bruce
James Bruton
Wm. Bruton
Richd. Bullock
Hezekiah Bunnell
Phillip Burah ?
David Burnett
Richd. Busby
Wm. Carpenter
Jno. Carrell
Tho. Carsey
Robt. Cartridge
Jno. Case
Jno. Case
Roger Case
William Chambers
James Chessett
Mathew Christian
Tho. Clare
Henry Clarke, senr.
Henry Clarke, junr.
John Clarke
Sampson Clarke
Tho. Clary
Wm. Clary
Capt. Francis Clements
Jno. Clements, senr.
Jno. Clements, junr.
Christopher Clinch
Mr. Walter Cock
Mr. Wm. Cock
Tho. Cockerham
Wm. Cockerham
Richd. Cockin
Wm. Coggin
Jno. Coker
Wm. Coker
James Kook (Cook?)
Samll. Cooke
John Collier
Joseph Collier
Tho. Collier
John Copeland
Samll. Cornell
Anthony Cornish
Robt. Cornish
Tho. Cotten

Walter Cotten
Robt. Crafford
Wm. Cripps
Wm. Crudge
Arthur Davis, senr.
Arthur Davis, junr.
Arthur Davis
John Davis
Nich. Davis
Peter Davis
Robt. Davis
Tho. Davis
Charles Digby
James Dikes
Nathll. Dennis
Robert Dowlen
Wm. Draper
Edward Drew
Tho. Drew
Wm. Drew
Melchisideck Duche
Charles Dun
Howell Edmunds
Wm. Edmunds
Mr. Jno. Edwards
Mr. Tho. Edwards
Edward Ellis
James Ellis
James Ellis
Jeremiah Ellis, senr.
Jeremiah Ellis, junr.
Wm. Ellitt
John Ellson
Wm. Elfert ?
James Ely
Tho. Emerley
Edward Emery
Anthony Evans
Abraham Evans, junr.
Wm. Ezell
Wm. Farmer ?
Humphrey Felps
Wm. Felps
Benj. Ferreby
Barth. Figures
Jno. Fitchett
Richard Whichpatrick
Robert Flake
Lawrence Fleming
Jno. Flood
Thomas Flood
Water Flood
Joseph Ford
Benj. Foreman
Mr. Wm. Foreman

Elias Fort
George Fort
Jno. Fort
Christopher Foster
Wm. Foster
Zephaniah Gardner
Robert Garrett
Richard Gilbert
Hinshaw Gilliam
Wm. Glover
Tho. Goltney
William Goltney, senr.
Wm. Goltney, junr.
Mr. Jno. Good
William Gootage
George Gourney
Jasper Gransom
Edward Grantham
John Grantham
Jno. Gray
Mr. Wm. Gray
Wm. Gray, junr.
Wm. Gray, junr.
Edward Green
John Green
Jno. Green
Richard Green
Francis Gregory
Samll. Grigory
Robert Grice
James Griffin, senr.
James Griffin, junr.
John Griffin
John Griffin
Eustace Grimes
Robt. Gulley
Richd. Ham
John Hancock
Tho. Harebottle
Bray Hargrove
Lemuell Hargrove
Mr. Richd. Hargrove
John Harris
Wm. Harris
Mr. Benjamin Harrison
Danll. Harrison
Mr. Nathl. Harrison
Henry Hart
Robert Hart
Tho. Hart
William Harvey
Adam Heath
Wm. Heath
Tho. Heathfield
John Henden
Jonah Hickman
Jno. Higgs

Robt. Hill
Sion Hill, senr.
Sion Hill, junr.
Wm. Hilliard
James Hoge
Jno. Holt
Tho. Holt
William Holt
Richd. Horne
James Horsenails (Hosnell)
Tho. Horton
Edward Hoskins
John Hosskins
Wm. Howell
Robt. Howes
Wm. Huggins
Evan Humphrey
Agustin Hunnicutt
Wm. Hunnicutt
Hugh Hunniford
Wm. Hunniford
Lawrence Hunt
Tho. Hunt, senr.
Tho. Hunt, junr.
Wm. Hunt
Wm. Hurdle
Tho. Hux
Tho. Hyard
Richard Hyde
Jno. Ingram
Robt. Inman
George Isell
Michl. Isell
William Jackson
Tho. Jarrell
Tho. Jarrell
Charles Jarrett
Ferdinando Jarrett
Hen. Johnson
John Johnson
John Johnson
Martin Johnson
Martin Johnson
Thomas Johnson
Tho. Johnson
Wm. Johnson
Wm. Johnson
James Jones
James Jones
Richard Jones
Mr. Arthur Jordan
George Jordan
Richard Jordan, senr.
Richard Jordan, junr.
River Jordan
Charles Judkins
Samll. Judkins

Wm. Judkins
Jno. Kersey
Jno. Kicotan
Terrence Kiggin
Wm. Killingsworth
John Kindred
Tho. King
Jno. Knight
Wm. Knott
Robt. Lacy
Robt. Lancaster, senr.
Robt. Lancaster, junr.
Samll. Lancaster
Joseph Lane
Thomas Lane
Thomas Lane, junr.
Jno. Laneere
Benja. Langley
Patrick Lashley
Walter Lashley
Jno. Later (Lather?)
Mr. John Lees ?
Morgan Lewis
Francis Little
Jno. Little
Wm. Little
William Little
Robert Littleboy
Arthur Long
George Long
William Loyle
Wm. Lucas
Nich. Maggett
Maximilian Mansell
Luke Marco
Jno. Marner ?
Wade Marner ?
Thomas Martin
Mr. James Mason
Ezekiall Mathis
Tho. Mathers
James Mice
George Midleton
John Miles
Owen Mirick
Tho. Mirick
Machth. Mongo
Edward Moreland
Mr. Christopher Moring
Mr. Jno. Mooreing
George Morrell, senr.
George Morrell, junr.
Humphrey Morrell
Tho. Morrell
Richd. Morris
Henry Morton
Wm. Moseley

Alexr. Musslewhite
Edward Newby
William Newitt
Robt. Newsum
William Newsum
Mr. Samll. Newton
Geo. Nicholls
Roger Nicholls
Tho. Nicholls
Wm. Nicholls
James Nicholson
Mr. Robt. Nicholson
George Norwood
Richd. Norwood
Wm. Norwood
John Owen
Robert Owen
John Page, senr.
John Page, junr.
Richard Parker
Nich. Pasfield
Wm. Peacock
Jno. Pengaly
John Person, junr.
George Peters
Wm. Pettaway
Tho. Pettingtune
Jno. Phillips
Jno. Phillips
William Phillips
Wm. Phillips
Wm. Pickerell
Richd. Peirce
John Pittford
Thomas Pittman
William Pittman
Wm. Pittman
William Plater
Mr. Saml. Plaw
Francis Porch
Jno. Price
Wm. Price
Joshua Proctor
Robt. Proctor
Jno. Pulistone
Capt. Randall
Francis Regan
Jer. Regan
Phillip Regan
Nich. Reynolds
Robert Reynolds, senr.
Robert Reynolds, junr.
David Rice
Joseph Richardson
George Riddick
Wm. Rivers
George Rochell

Jno. Rochell
John Rodwell
Wm. Rogers, senr.
Wm. Rogers, junr.
Wm. Rogers
John Rollins
John Rollins
Wm. Rookins
Richard Rose
Wm. Rose
Edward Rowell
Wm. Rowland
Wm. Rowland
Robt. Ruffin
Charles Savage
Edward Scarburgh
William Scarburgh
Jno. Scoggin
Richard Scoggin
Joseph Seate
Robt. Seate
Nicholas Sessums
Tho. Sessums
Mr. Jno. Seward
Mr. Wm. Seward
Jno. Sharpe
Phillip Shelley
Richard Shok
Jno. Short
Wm. Short
Jno. Simonds
Christopher Smith, senr.
Christopher Smith, junr.
Jno. Smith
George Smith
Nich. Smith, senr.
Nich. Smith, junr.
Nicho. Smith
Richard Smith, senr.
Richard Smith, junr.
Tho. Smith
Tho. Smith
Jas. Snow
Fra. Sowerby
Jno. Sowerby
Tho. Sowerby
Roger Squires
Arthur Stampe
Jno. Stampe
Mr. James Stanton
Jno. Steward
Joseph Steward
Richd. Stringfellow
Jno. Sugar
Mathew Swann
Capt. Tho. Swann
Wm. Swett, senr.

Wm. Swett, junr.
George Syms
Edward Tanner
Tho. Tarver
Edward Taylor
Richard Taylor
Jno. Thompson
Nicholas Thorne
Jno. Thorpe
Joseph Thorpe
Timothy Thorpe
Walter Tomkins
Jno. Tooke
Capt. Henry Tooker
Arthur Truse ?
George Tutur ?
Jno. Tyas
Thomas Tyas
Stephen Vaughan
Jno. Vinson
Timothy Walker
Joseph Wall, senr.
Joseph Wall, junr.
Tho. Waller
John Ward
Jno. Wappell
Jno. Warr
Tho. Warr
John Warren
Robt. Warren
Mr. Tho. Warren
William Warren
Wm. Warren
Jno. Warrick
Richard Washington
Mr. Jno. Watkins
Robt. Webb
Francis West
Charles White
Thomas Wiggins
John Willis
Charles Wilkins
John Wilkinson
Mathew Wilkinson
Charles Wms.
George Wms.
John Williams
Roger Williams
Roger Williams
Thomas Williams
William Williams
Edmund Windum
Nich. Witherington
Geord Wood
Wm. Wray
Nich. Wyatt
Tho. Wight TOTAL 509

A LIST OF TITHABLES IN SOUTHWARK PARISH IN SURRY COUNTY TAKEN JUNE 10, 1702 BY WILLIAM BROWNE AND IN LAWNES CREEK PARISH BY THOMAS HOLT

To the County—total 479.

(Surry Deed Book 1694-1709, pp. 256-259)

Andrews, Bartt		2	Bonely, Thomas	(47)	5
Adkins, Rich.		1	Bonner, Fra.	(55)	0
Adkins, Thomas		1	Bookey, Edward	(23)	3
Adkinson, James		4	Bostock, Lancaster	(121)	0
Adams, Thomas	(52)	0	Brantings, John Sr.		1
Adams, Thomas	(52)	0	Branton, Thomas	(74)	0
Andrews, Robert	(134)	2	Bridgeman, Thomas	(24)	0
Allen, Maj. Art.	(109)	19	Briggs, Charles		1
Andrews, Dav.	(9)	3	Briggs, Hen.		1
Andrews, Rich.	(9)	0	Briggs, Sam.		1
Andrews, Thomas		1	Broadrib, Thomas		3
Atkins, William	(85)	0	Browne, Col.		2
Austin, William	(21)	0	Browne, Col.		7
Avery, John	(61)	0	Browne, Edward		1
Avon, Thomas	(56)		Browne, John		1
Bagly, Peter		1	Browne, John		1
Bailey, Anselen		3	Browne, William Jr.		6
Bailey, John		1	Bruton, James		3
Bailey, Robert	(116)	2	Bruton, William		1
Bailey, William	(116)	0	Bunnell, Hez.		1
Baker, John			Burnett, David	(13)	1
Baker, Hen.		1	Burrough, Phil Sr.	(46)	2
Baker, John Sr.	(33)	4	Burrough, Phil Jr.	(46)	0
Baker, John	(33)	0	Byton, Rich.		1
Barefoot, Noah	(24)	2	Caps, John		1
Barham, Robert	(131)	2	Carrington, Isack	(37)	0
Barker, Jetho		1	Carroll, Thomas		1
Barker, Joel		1	Carroll, William	(?)	0
Barks, Oliver	(22)	0	Casey, Pat	(21)	0
Barnes, Hen.		1	Castle, Phil	(109)	0
Barrow, Edward	(80)	2	Carry, Fran	(114)	0
Barrow, Thomas		1	Cary, Charles	(121)	0
Bas, Charles		2	Chesset, John		1
Battle, John		1	Chessett, James		1
Benbridge, George		1	Chinn, Walter	(29)	0
Bennett, James		1	Cholmoley, William	(5)	0
Berryman, John		1	Christian, Math		1
Bineham, John		1	Clare, Thomas		1
Binham, John		1	Clarke, Henry Jr.	(11)	0
Blackburn, William Sr.	(60)	3	Clarke, Henry Sr.	(11)	3
Blackburn, John	(60)	0	Clarke, John	(11)	0
Blackburn, William Jr.	(60)	0	Clarke, John	(130)	3
Blake, William		1	Clarke, Samuel		1
Blow, George		1	Clarke, Thomas	(94)	0
Blunt, Thomas		7	Clary, Thomas	(79)	0
Boddit, William	(94)	0	Clements, John Jr.	(12)	0
Bonely, John	(50)	2	Clements, John Sr.	(12)	5

Gualtney, Thomas		1
Hales, Fra	(109)	0
Hancock, John		1
Hancock, William		1
Hardgrove, Rich	(133)	0
Hardgrove, Sam		1
Hargrove, Bray		1
Hart, Henry	(84)	4
Hart, Robert	(94)	4
Hart, Thomas		5
Harris, John	(119)	
Harris, Micall	(9)	0
Harris, William	(76)	2
Harris, William	(130)	0
Harris, Thomas		1
Harrison, Bart		1
Harrison, Col. Benjamin	(1)	25
Harrison, Capt. Nath		13
Harvey, William		1
Harsh, John		1
Hathfield, Thomas	(78)	0
Heath, Adam Sr.	(57)	3
Heath, Adam Jr.	(57)	0
Heath, William	(57)	0
Hide, Rich		1
Hide, Rich	(39)	2
Higgs, John	(133)	0
Higgs, John	(6)	2
Hill, John	(38)	0
Hill, Robert		1
Hill, Sion Sr.	(19)	3
Hill, Sion Jr.	(19)	0
Hill, Richard	(19)	0
Hilyard, William		1
Hodges, Charles		1
Hogwood, George		1
Hoole, Fra		1
Holly, Nath		1
Holt, John	(74)	10
Holt, John Jr.	(74)	0
Holt, William	(83)	5
Holt, Thomas	(122)	6
Hollyman, Rich	(108)	2
Hollyman, William		1
Honiyford, William	(73)	3
Honycutt, John	(13)	1
Honycutt, Thomas	(13)	1
Honycutt, Young Wm.	(14)	0
Hopkins, Edward	(39)	0
Horne, Rich		1
Horton, Thomas Sr.	(41)	2
Horton, Thomas Jr.	(41)	0
Hunnicutt, August	(117)	3
Hunnicutt, August Jr.	(117)	0
Hunt, Law		1
Hunt, William Sr.	(21)	4
Hunt, William Jr.	(21)	0
Hunt, Thomas Sr.	(17)	2
Hunt, Thomas Jr.	(17)	0
Hugins, William	(70)	2
Hudson, Thomas	(121)	0
Humphrey, Evans	(103)	2
Humphrey, Evans Jr.	(103)	0
Hurdle, William		10
Hyr, John	(10)	0
Hyr, John	(12)	0
Hyard, Thomas		1
Hux, Thomas	(65)	0
Ironmunger, Tom	(132)	0
Jackson, William		1
Jackson, William		1
Jackman, Joseph John	(121)	23
Jarrett, Charles	(91)	2
Jarrett, Richard	(91)	0
Jarrett, Ferdinand		1
Jarrell, Thomas Jr.		1
Jeffris, John		1
Jelks, William	(122)	0
Johnson, Hen		1
Johnson, John		1
Johnson, John		1
Johnson, Martin		1
Johnson, Martin Jr.	(129)	0
Johnson, Thomas	(127)	0
Johnson, Thomas	(20)	0
Johnson, William	(33)	0
Johnson, William	(130)	0
Johnson, William		1
Jordan, George		3
Jordan, Richard	(44)	2
Jordan, Robert	(44)	0
Judkins, Sam Sr.	(51)	2
Judkins, Sam. Jr.	(51)	0
Judkins, William	(34)	0
Judkins, Charles		1
Kindred, John		1
King, Thomas		1
Kitchen, John	(12)	0
Knight, John		1
Knott, William Sr.	(7)	2
Knott, William Jr.	(7)	0
Lanbrook, Sam	(1)	0
Lancaster, Robert		1
Lancaster, Sam	(113)	0
Lancaster, Robert Jr.	(113)	2
Land, Curtis		1
Lane, Abraham		1
Lane, Joseph		1
Lane, Robert		2
Lane, Thomas	(126)	2
Lane, Rich	(126)	0
Lane, Thomas		1
Lasley, Pat	(30)	2
Lasley, Walter	(30)	0

Lennger, William	(1)	0
Lencord, John	(67)	2
Lenoard, Clemon	(67)	0
Lewis, Morgan	(1)	0
Lewis, Richard	(1)	0
Little, John	(92)	3
Little, Fra	(92)	0
Little, Robert	(92)	0
Little, William	(101)	0
Littleboy, Robert	(96)	2
Long, Edward	(121)	0
Long, George		1
Loo?, Ralph	(47)	0
Lothar, Chris	(29)	2
Loogin, John		1
Loogin, Richard		1
Lorie, Phil	(105)	0
Lucius?, William	(2)	3
Lulpork?, Robert		0
Lyle, William	(68)	2
Lyle, John	(68)	0
Lyle, William	(22)	0
Mackdaniel, Dane	(110)	0
Macklemore, Leonard		1
Maggett, Richard	(22)	3
Makare, Thomas	(114)	0
Mansell, Max	(28)	0
Marriott, William		1
Marriott, Vinsent	(20)	0
Marro, Luke	(124)	0
Martin, Robert	(121)	0
Martin, Thomas	(74)	0
Mason, Mrs. Eliz.		2
the elder, 2 negroes		
Mason, Mrs. Eliz.	(14)	6
Matthews, Eze	(96)	0
Mathews, Thomas		1
Mays, Thomas	(62)	0
Midleton, George		1
Midleton, Martin	(38)	0
Mied, James		1
Mills, John		1
Moore, Ralph	(109)	0
Moreing, John	(132)	3
Moreland, Edward	(88)	3
Morris, John	(38)	0
Morris, Richard	(128)	2
Morris, Richard Jr.	(128)	0
Morroll, George	(86)	4
Morroll, George Jr.	(86)	0
Morroll, Hump	(86)	0
Morroll, Thomas	(86)	0
Moseley, William		1
Moss, William		1
Mounger, Nath		1
Myrick, Owen Sr.	(27)	2
Myrick, Owen Jr.	(27)	0
Nelson, John		1
Newsons, Robert	(85)	2
Newsons, William		1
Newton, Samuel		
Newitt, William	(127)	5
Nicholls, John	(56)	
Nicholas, Rog.	(120)	2
Nicholas, Rog. Jr.	(120)	0
Nicholas, William	(124)	2
Nicholas, Thomas		1
Nicholson, James	(6)	0
Nicholson, Robert		4
Norris, Robert	(76)	1
Norton, Elias	(82)	0
Norton, Henry		1
Norwood, George	(63)	3
Norwood, Richard	(63)	0
Norwood, William		1
Osburne, Eliz		1
Owen, Robert		1
Piddengton, Thomas	(40)	4
Piddengton, Edward	(48)	1
Piddengton, Thomas	(48)	1
Pittford, John		1
Pittman, Thomas Jr.	(108)	0
Pittman, Thomas		1
Pittman, William		1
Pittman, William		1
Pittman, William		1
Parke, Robert		1
Parke, Thomas		1
Parker, Daniel	(55)	0
Parker, Nicho	(36)	2
Parker, Richard	(36)	0
Parks, Willima	(47)	0
Parrott, Edward	(1)	0
Parson, John		1
Pasfield, Rich		1
Parting, Robert		1
Peacock, William		1
Petteway, Robert		1
Phelps, Hump Sr.	(26)	3
Phelps, Hump Jr.	(26)	0
Phelps, William	(26)	
Phillips, John	(81)	0
Phillips, William	(64)	0
Phillips, Thomas	(50)	0
Phobo,? Lork	(77)	0
by Thomas Wright		
Pipe, Nich	(23)	0
Ponson,? William	(121)	0
Pottor, Capt. Roger	(104)	0
Potors, George		1
Portor, Edward	(74)	0
Price, John	(122)	0
Pride, William		1
Prime, John	(75)	0

Proctor, John		1	Sharpe, John		1
Proctor, James	(45)	2	Shelley, Phil	(106)	3
Proctor, Robert	(45)	0	Shelley, Phil Jr.	(106)	0
Pulford, John	(18)	0	Shelley, John	(106)	0
Pulistone, John		1	Shivors, Thomas	(49)	0
Rachell, John	(54)	3	Short, Richard	(74)	0
Rachell, George	(54)	0	Short, William	(35)	3
Rawlen, Arthur	(16)	0	Simons, Ed.		1
Rawlin, William	(38)	0	Sims, George		1
Rawlings, John Jr.		1	Simons, John	(28)	4
Ray, John		1	Smith, George		1
Rays, William		1	Smith, John		1
Reddicke, Robert	(88)	0	Smith, Nich	(101)	2
Regan, Fra	(62)	3	Smith, Nich Sr.	(69)	2
Revell, Rr.		1	Smith, Nich Sr.	(69)	0
Reynolds, Robert		1	Smith, Richard		1
Reynolds, Robert Jr.		1	Smith, Thomas		1
Rhine, Phil.	(118)	0	Smith, Richard		1
Richardson, Jos.		1	Smith, Thomas		1
Riddick, George		0	Smith, Thomas Sr.		1
Ridley, Thomas	(121)	0	Smith, Thomas Jr.		1
Rives, David		1	Smith, William	(131)	0
Roades, William		1	Smoot, William Sr.	(4)	2
Robbin, Tom	(121)	0	Smoot, William Jr.	(4)	0
Robertson, Fra.	(121)	0	Snow, Joseph		1
Roger, Thomas		1	Sowerby, John		1
Rogers, William Sr.		1	Sowerby, Fra		1
Rogers, William Jr.		1	Sowerby, Thomas		1
Rookings, William		1	Stamp, Art	(25)	0
Read (?) Rood, William	(38)	0	Stamp, Art	(25)	2
Ros, Thomas	(102)	0	Steward, John		1
Rose, Richard		1	Steward, Joseph	(100)	0
Rose, William		1	Stringfellow, Richard		1
Rowell, Edward	(111)	2	Stanton, James	(34)	2
Rowell, Edward Jr.	(111)	0	Suggar, John		3
Rowland, William		1	Swan, Mac	(119)	4
Ruddy, Richard		1	Tanner, Edward		1
Ruffin, Robert		0	Tanner, William	(79)	0
and			Tarvor, Thomas	(115)	2
Ruffin, William		0	Tarvor, Saint	(115)	0
by			Taylor, Rich	(102)	
Ruffin, Mrs. Eliz.	(125)	9	Taylor, Edward	(75)	2
Rutherford, Sam	(134)	0	Taylor, John	(75)	0
Sanderson, Estor		1	Thompson, Richard	(83)	0
Savage, Charles		1	Thompson, Samuel	(133)	11
Savage, Henry		1	Thorpe, James	(81)	3
Savage, Levely		1	Thorpe, Tim	(78)	2
Seat, Joseph	(87)	2	Tomkins, John	(132)	
Seat, Joseph Jr.	(87)	0	Tooke, John	(114)	3
Seat, Robert		1	Tooker, Maj. Hen	(110)	7
Sesams, Thomas		1	Tyas, John	(65)	2
Sessams, Nich	(98)	4	Tyas, Thomas		1
Seward, William	(123)	2	Vaghan, John		1
Seward, William Jr.	(123)	0	Vaghn, L	(65)	0
Scarborougs, Ed.		1	Wilkson, Matt	(58)	0
Scarborough, William		1	Walker, Benjamin	(71)	0
Sharpe, John		1	Walker, Tim	(121)	0

Wall, Joseph .... (97) 2	West, William .... (109) 0
Wall, Richard .... (97) 0	Wigh, George 1
Waller, Thomas .... (112) 2	Wigh, Hen .... (72) 2
Waller, Thomas Jr. .... (112) 0	Wigh, William .... (72) 0
Walters, John 1	Wigins, Thomas .... (42) 2
Wappes, John .... (64) 2	Wigins, Richard .... (42) 0
Ward, John 1	White, Charles .... (135) 2
Ward, Thomas 1	White, John .... (135) 0
Ward, William .... (80) 0	White, Thomas 1
Warren, Allen .... (36) 2	Whetstone, James .... (52) 2
Warren, John 1	Wild, Robert .... (121) 0
Warren, Robert .... (10) 2	Windham, Edward 1
Warren, Thomas Sr. .... (40) 4	Williams, Charles .... (79) 3
Warren, Thomas Jr. .... (40) 0	Williams, Roger 1
Warren, Sam .... (40) 0	William, Roger Sr. 1
Warrick, John 1	Williams, Roger Jr. .... (66) 5
Washington, Richard .... (15) 3	Williams, Willima .... (99) 2
Washington, George .... (15) 0	Williams, George .... (99) 0
Watkins, John .... (35) 4	Williamson, Batt .... (54) 3
Watkins, Robert .... (35)	Williamson, George 1
Watt, John .... 81) 0	Williamson, George 2
Watt, Joseph Jr. 1	Witherington, Nich 1
Webb, Robert .... (16) 2	Woodrift, John .... (121) 0
Welsh, John .... (109) 0	Young, Alex .... (53) 0
West, Fra 1	

SURRY COUNTY MILITIA IN 1687

List of those reported as qualified in either estate or person to find and maintain a man and horse or to go themselves when occasion shall require.

(*William and Mary Quarterly*, Vol. II, p. 81)

Jno. Allen	Blewit Beaumont	Wm. Carpinter
Rich. Adkins	Rich. Beighton	Jno. Casse
Tho. Adkins	Jno. Berryman	Wm. Chambers
Wm. Also	Jonah Bennett	Jno. Clarke
Bat. Andrews	Tho. Bentley junr.	Jno. Clarke
Daniel Andrews	Tho. Binns	Tho. Clary
Robt. Andrews	Wm. Blackborne	Wm. Clary
Tho. Andrews junr.	Wm. Blith	Jno. Clements
Robt. Austin	Geo. Blow	Wm. Cocke
Tho. Bage	Tho. Blunt	Wm. Cockersham
Hen. Baker	Edw. Booky	Tho. Cockersham
Noah Barefoot	Cha. Briggs	Jno. Collier
Jethro Barker	Henry Briggs	Tho. Collier
Joell Barker	Jno. Brown	Ja. Cooke
Jno. Barker	Tho. Browne	Samll. Cooke
Jno. Barnes	Ja. Bruton	Tho. Cooke
Walter Bartlet	Wm. Bruton	Nath. Cornish
Jno. Battle	Hez. Bunnell	Tho. Cotten
Tho. Battle	Jeoffrey Busby	Walter Cotten
Anselm Bayley	Tho. Busby	Jno. Cowood
Peter Bayley	Ja. Byneham	Robert Craford
David Beard	John Byneham	Wm. Creede

Wm. Crews
Wm. Couch
Ar. Davies Senr.
Ar. Davis junr.
Jno. Davies
Tho. Davis
Peter Deberry
Tho. Deerkin
Rogr. Delke
Nat. Dennis
Wm. Dennis
Cha. Digby
Robert Dolling
Wm. Draper
Edw. Drew
Jno. Drew
Tho. Drew
Jno. Dunfeild
Jno. Edwards
Tho. Edwards
Ja. Ellis
Jer. Ellis Senr.
Jer. Ellis Junr.
Ja. Ely
Geo. Essell
Michael Essell
Tim. Essell junr.
Antho. Evans
Tho. Farmer
Robt. Fellows
Humphrey Felps
Bat. Figgus
Jno. Finley
Jno. Fiveash
Robt. Flake junr.
Law. Fleming
Tho. Flood
Walter Flood
Tho. Forbush
Jos. Ford
Wm. Foreman
Tho. Forver
Xto. Foster
Wm. Foster
Hen. Francis
Tho. Futrill
Jno. Garner
Rogr. Gilbert
Cha. Gillum
Hincha Gillum
Jno. Golledge
Wm. Goodman
Cha. Goodrich
Edw. Grantum
Jno. Gray
Wm. Gray
Wm. Gray

Edwd. Greene
Jno. Greene
Richard Greene
Ja. Griffin
Wm. Gwathney
Nathl. Hales
Wm. Hancock
Antho. Hardwicke
Tho. Harebottle
Bray Hargrave
Wm. Harrington
Wm. Harris
Daniell Harryson
Hen. Hart
Robt. Hart
Tho Hart
Wm. Harvy
Tho. Hayward
Adam Heath
Jonah Hickman
John Higgs
Tho. High
Sion Hill
Jno. Holt
Wm. Holt
Wm. Hooker
Wm. Horniford
Ja. Horsnell
Tho. Horton
Wm. Houlford
Robt. House junr.
Wm. Howell
Ja. Hugate
Evan Humphrey
Austin Hunnicutt
Wm. Hunt
Geo Huson
Tho. Hux
Rich. Hyde
Robert Inman
Tho. Ironmonger
Rich. Jackson
Wm. Jackson
Charles Jarret
Tho. Jarrett
Ja. Jolly
Tho. Jolly
Rich. Jones
Geo. Jordan
James Jordan
Rich. Jordan Senr.
River Jordan
Nathan Joyce
Cha. Judkins
Rich. Judkins Junr.
Robt. Judkins
Samll. Judkins

Tho. Kersey
Ja. Kilpatrick
Jno. Kindred
Jno. King
Wm. Knott
Robt. Lacy
Robert Lancaster
Jos. Lane
Tho. Lane Senr.
Tho. Lane Junr.
Patrick Lashley
Jno. Lathar
John Little
Robt. Littleberry
Wm. Lucas
Col. Phill. Ludwell
Max Mansell
Mr. Francis Mason (J. P.)
Tho. Mathars
Law. Meazle
Luke Mizle
Ni. Meriwether
Cha. Merrett
Jno. Middleton
Owen Mirick
Rich. Moonk
Ja. Morish
Geo. Morrell
Jno. Myles
Edw. Napkin
Wm. Nash
Robt. Nathan
Wm. Newitt
Wm. Newsume
Jarvis Newton
Rogr. Nicholls
Robt. Nichollson
Geo. Nichollson
Hen. Norton
Edw. Nubee
Ja. Omoone
Robert Owen
Jno. Page
Tho. Partridge
Ni. Pasfeild
Wm. Peacock
Tho. Peddington
Rich. Peirce
Tho. Peirce
Wm. Petway
David Phillips
Jno. Phillips
Jno. Phillips Junr.
Tho. Pittman
Wm. Pittman
Ja. Porch
Capt. Roger Potter

Tho. Presson
Jno. Procter
Joshua Proctor
Jno. Pulesson
Mr. Robert Randall (J. P.)
Jno. Rankins
Ja. Reddick
Robert Reddick
Danll. Regan
Fra. Regan
Robt. Renolds
Dennis Rethden
Daniel Rich
Jas. Richardson
Wm. Rivers
Wm. Rivers
Jno. Roberts
Jno. Rodwell
Jno. Rogers
Wm. Rogers
Wm. Rose
Wm. Rowland
Mr. Robert Ruffin (J. P.)
Wm. Rugsbee
Edwd. Runee
Cha. Savage
Joseph Seate

Ni. Sessorms
Wm. Seward
Jno. Sharpe
Rich. Shaw
Phill. Shelley
Jno. Shugar
Tho. Sidway
Wm. Simons
Rich. Smith
Fra. Sowerby
Tho. Sowersby
Jno. Spitless
Rogr. Squier
Jno. Steward
Math. Swann
Maj. Saml. Swann (J. P.)
Edw. Tayler
Walter Tayler
John Thompson
Samll. Thompson
Jos. Thorpe junr.
Tho. Tias
Wm. Tillinsworth
Walter Tompkins
Hen. Tucker
Michael Upchurch
Jno. Vincent

Tim. Walker
Jos. Wall
Tho. Waller
Jno. Wallis
Tho. Ward
Jno. Warpool
Allen Warren
Jno. Warren
Robt. Warren
Tho. Warren
Rich. Washington
Ja. Watkins
John Watkins
Wm. Wheeler
Cha. White
Tho. White
Tho. Wiggins
Jno. Wilkinson
Ch. Williams
Geo. Williams
Rogr. Williams
No. Witherington
Tho. Wolves
Josias Wood
Wm. Wray
Tho. Wright
Hen. Wych

VIRGINIA QUIT RENT ROLLS FOR SURRY COUNTY, 1704

(*From Virginia Historical Magazine,* Vol. 29, p. 18)

	Acres		Acres
Major Arthur Allen	6780	Jno. Clark	100
Bartho. Andrews	375	Robert Clark	400
David Andrews	225	Jno. Clements	387
Robt. Andrews	130	ffran. Clements	600
Tho. Andrews	190	Walter Cocke	875
Tho. Atkins	80	Wm. Cocke	630
Richd. Atkinson	100	Jno. Cocker	900
Jno. Averett	120	Wm. Cocker	100
Jno. Avery	150	Jno. Collier	350
Edwd. Bayley	350	Joseph Collier	40
Peter Bagley	100	Tho. Collier	550
Jno. Baile	250	Elizabeth Cook	200
Col. Henry Baker	850	James Cooper	100
Sarah Baker	50	Tho. Cotten	257
Robt. Barham	650	Walter Cotten	257
Jery Barker	420	Carter Crafort	100
John Barker	1160	Robert Crafort	1000
Joell Barter	100	Arthur Davis	460
Jno. Bell	180	Arthur Davis	50
Geo. Benbridge	200	Nathl. Davis	157
James Bennett	200	Richd. Dean	100
Richd. Bennett	200	Roger Delk	790
Bentley	180	James Dicks	400
Richd. Bighton	590	Edwd. Drew	600
Jno. Bincham	100	Tho. Drew	800
James Bineham	157	Howell Edmunds	200
Wm. Blackburn	150	Wm. Edmunds	100
Wm. Blake	200	John Edwards	470
Sarah Bland	1455	Mr. Wm. Edwards	2755
Christo. Blico	50	Edward Ellis	30
Thos. Blunt	1355	James Ellis	180
Edwd. Bookey	180	James Ellis	170
Phill. Bougher	100	Jere. Ellis	150
Charles Briggs	331	Wm. Ellit	250
Henry Briggs	100	Abrah. Evans	150
Samll. Briggs	300	Anth. Evans	100
Sarah Briggs	300	Geo. Ezell	150
Edwd. Browne	200	Benja. Ferisby	170
Jno. Browne	600	Robt. Flake	200
Col. Wm. Browne	2510	Lawrence Fleming	360
Capt. Wm. Browne	398	Tho. Flood	150
James Bruton	500	Walter Flood	820
Mary Bullock	100	Elias Ford	200
Hezichiah Bunnell	150	Geo. Ford	100
Obedience Candenscaine	200	Anne Foster	200
Thos. Carrell	100	Christo. Foster	500
Wm. Chambers	50	Wm. Foster	100
Benjamin Chapman	500	Hinche Gillham	658
James Checett	50	Wm. Goodman	200

	Acres		*Acres*
Jno. Gray	200	Tho. Lamb	200
Capt. Wm. Gray	1750	Robt. Lancaster	100
Wm. Gray, Junr.	1050	Tho. Lane, Junr.	200
Wm. Gray	100	Mary Lang	77
Edwd. Green	200	Patrick Lasley	520
Richd. Green	260	Jno. Laughter	300
John Griffin	200	Geo. LeNeve	300
Hustin Grimes	100	Wm. Lucas	315
Richd. Gully	50	Col. Phill. Ludwell	1100
Wm. Gwaltney	400	Francis Mallory	147
Wm. Gwaltney	225	Elizabeth Mason	300
Richd. Ham	75	Edwd. Mathew	50
Colin Hancock	60	Matt. Merrett	60
Tho. Harde	900	Tho. Middleton	100
Bryan Hargrove	100	Owen Mierick	250
Wm. Harris	150	Edwd. Moorland	225
Col. Benjamin Harrison	2750	John Moreing	695
Danll. Harrison	70	Geo. Morriel	250
Capt. Nathl. Harrison	2177	Wm. Moss	100
Henry Hart	725	Wm. Newitt	330
Robert Hart	600	Robt. Newsom	250
Tho. Heart	750	Wm. Newsom	225
Adam Heath	200	Geo. Nicholl	150
Robert Hill	200	Robt. Nichols	230
Syon Hill	300	Barefoot Nolway	150
Henry Hollingworth	60	Geo. Norwood	330
Elizabeth Holt	1450	Richd. Norwood	80
John Holt	150	Mary Park	100
Capt. Tho. Holt	538	Richd. Parker	269
Wm. Holt	630	John Persons	830
Richd. Holloman	480	Jno. Pettfort	200
Tho. Holloman	450	Wm. Pettfort	50
Mary Hollyman	290	Elizabeth Pettoway	650
Richd. Horne	100	Humphrey Phelps	100
Wm. Howell	50	John Phillips	270
Evan Humphrey	70	Wm. Phillips	300
Hugh Humfort	150	Tho. Pitman, Junr.	100
Wm. Humfort	50	Jno. Price	340
Wm. Hunt	4042	Joshua Proctor	660
Wm. Hunt	696	Wm. Pully	300
Tho. Hyerd	50	Jno. Pulystone	1400
Mr. Jos. John Jackman	2980	Geo. Rachell (Rochelle)	70
Tho. Jarrell	115	Col. Wm. Randolph	1655
Charles Jarrett	615	Jno. Rowling	476
Ferdo. Jarrett	630	Gregory Rollings	106
John John	350	Wm. Read	450
Wm. Johnson	360	Wm. Reads	150
James Jones	1000	Frances Reazan	200
Geo. Jordan	620	Elizabeth Reynolds	150
Richd. Jordan	350	Robt. Reynolds	150
Samll. Judkins	100	Joseph Richardson	300
Wm. Judkins	100	Wm. Rogers	450
Mary Kigan	200	Wm. Rokings	596
Wm. Killingworth	60	Richd. Rose	100
Wm. Knott	300	Elizabeth Ruffin	3001
Mary Lacey	100	Charles Savage	358

	Acres
Henry Savage	200
Mary Savage	263
Jno. Scagin	100
Edwd. Scarboro	150
Joseph Seat	295
Nicho. Sesoms	800
Anne Sewards	300
Thomas Sewins	400
Tho. Sharp	70
Wm. Short	200
Francis Shrowsbury	820
Joseph Shrowsbury	260
Tho. Shrowsbury	566
Geo. Sims	200
Jno. Simmons	1300
Richd. Smith.	200
Tho. Smith	700
Tho. Smith	380
John Steward	200
Richd. Stockly	100
Richd. Stringfellow	75
Jno. Suger	250
Wm. Swann	1800
Ethelred Taylor	538
Richd. Taylor	77
Samll. Thompson	3104
Joseph Thorp	250
Major Henry Tooker	700
Tho. Tyous	400
Mary Vincent	187
Joseph Wall	150

	Acres
Jno. Waple	300
Tho. Ward	100
Joseph Ward, Junr.	150
Allen Warren	300
Robert Warren	150
Thomas Warren	1040
John Warrick	80
John Watkins	1160
Richd. Watkins	1345
Robert Webb	340
Henry Welch (Wyche)	100
Charles White	136
Tho. Wiggins	300
Mathew Wilkinson	200
Roger Will	78
Roger Williams	150
Charles Williams	100
Wm. Williams	300
Nicho. Witherington	100
Thomas Wright	100
John Young	300
	116,089
New Land allowed p ord^r	3,841
	112,248

April 19th, 1705.

Errors Excepted

p Jos. John Jackman

Sheriff.

Ages of early Surry settlers taken from depositions. The depositions were mainly about domestic issues and servants sometimes testified. The ages are usually followed by the word "thereabouts" and appear to be approximately correct within one or two years.

Year	Name	Age	Year	Name	Age
1675	Adams, Thomas	42	1672	Gray, Thomas	21
1668	Allen, Arthur	60	1653	Gray, Thomas, Sr.	60
1676	Allen, Margaret	28	1666	Gwaltney, Mary	48
1671	Amry, Benjamin	19			
1668	Applewhaite, Henry	25	1668	Hare, William	30
			1668	Hay, Thomas	23
1675	Barlow, Thomas	40	1670	Hayden, Sam	26
1666	Bartlett, Dorothy	50	1615	High, Thomas	78
1666	Bartley, Patrick	40	1672	Hunt, Thomas	21
1661	Biggins, Lawrence	27	1659	Hux, John	46
1652	Blackborn, John	33	1652	Hux, John	40
1683	Blake, George, Sr.	46			
1683	Blake, George, Jr.	22	1659	Jordan, Arthur	32
1675	Braddy, John	74	1677	Jordan, Arthur	50
			1670	Johnson, Martin	30
1677	Carpenter, William	?	1672	Johnson, Martin	33
1654	Carter, Alice	55	1658	Jarrell, Thomas	23
1654	Carter, William, Sr.	54	1670	Kindred, John	35
1672	Case, Isabell	56	1677	King, John	32
1677	Case, Judith	36	1679	King, John	33
1668	Case, Richard	48	1675	Kirtland, Ebenezer	19
1672	Case, Richard	53	1675	Kirtland, Elenor	19
1666	Clarke, John	30			
1672	Clarke, John	20	1674	Lane, Thomas	39
1666	Clarke, Katherine	36	1670	Laine, Thomas	36
1659	Cooper, John	21	1659	Lea, Henry	16
1659	Corker, Dorothy	50	1659	Lucas, Ann	29
1652	Cutler, Thomas	25	1659	Lucas, William	30
1672	Davis, Janet	24	1677	Macon, Thomas	35
1672	Davis, Mrs. Mary	52	1677	Marriott, Alice	32
1658	Davis, William	23	1668	Mason, Francis	21
1677	Delke, Roger	48	1668	Meriweather, Nicholas	37
1668	Dowling, William	50	1652	Mitchell, Christopher	34
			1659	Mizelle, Luke	45
1659	Edwards, William	43	1667	Muggett, Ann	43
1677	Ellis, Jeremiah	34	1652	Murrell, William	40
1678	Ellis, Jeremiah	35			
			1672	Phillips, Eliz.	72
1652	Flood, John	30	1672	Phillips, John	36
1659	Flood, John	44	1675	Pittman, Thomas, Sr.	60
	lived 10 years with		1677	Price, John	27
	Thomas Gray, Sr.		1670	Price, John	21
1677	Flood, Walter	21	1668	Pride, William	30
1678	Francis, Henry, Jr.	18	1660	Rawlings, Roger	26
			1657	Redwood, Anthony	25
1654	Gaping, William	50	1672	Robinson, Cottin	19
1653	Garye, John	50	1652	Rose, William	30
1672	Gray, John .... (over)	21			

Year	Name	Age	Year	Name	Age
1653	Rose, William	30	1674	Taylor, Francis	43
1655	Sawyer, Eliza	24	1672	Taylor, Thomas	35
1668	Senior, John	17	1675	Thompson, Benjamin	30
1677	Sidway, Thomas	22	1668	Thorne, William	25
1677	Simmons, Williams	29	1672	Tooke, William	46
1659	Skelton, Edward	22	1668	Tucker, Daniel	55
1672	Skinner, Mary	40	1677	Tyus, Richard	49
1672	Skinner, Richard	46	1671	Upchurch, Michael	50 odd
1677	Sowerby, James	66			
1657	Sowerbye, Thomas	23	1655	Warner, Richard	20
1677	Sowerby, Thomas	44	1661	Warren, Thomas	40
1660	Spencer, Robert	30	1675	Watkins, Henry	21
1672	Stevenson, Thomas	48	1659	Whitmoald, John	20
1668	Swett, William	25	1667	Wincaster, Margt	24
1667	Tatem, Isaac	31			
1672	Talbot, John	22	1652	Yates, Stephen	46

SOME SURRY MARRIAGES

16 Oct. 1679 Adamson, Andrew and Sally Burn.
21 Dec. 1772 Almond, William and Ann Wilson.
31 Dec. 1789 Anderson, Thomas and Amy Bishop.
11 May 1791 Andrews, Thomas and Rebecca Charity.
11 Mar. 1790 Anthony, William and Lucy Bishop.
12 Nov. 1785 Ariss, John and Patty Newall.

27 June 1780 Barham, Benjamin and Frances Phillips.
12 Aug. 1789 Barham, Burwell and Sylvia Ryland.
10 Mar. 1780 Barlow, George and Mary Lancaster.
23 Feb. 1774 Bee, James and Jane Bailey, orphan of Francis Bailey. Sec. Ethelred Gray.
13 Feb. 1775 Bell, Benjamin and Edith Roane?
16 Apr. 1786 Bell, James and Bramble Pabridge.
8 June 1786 Bishop, Hubbard and Lucy Bishop.
1 June 1786 Bishop, William and Frances Greswit.
25 Nov. 1790 Blunt, Benjamin and Ann Edwards.
13 Mar. 1775 Boykins, Joel and Sarah Grantham, Sec. Thomas Grantham.
24 Dec. 1785 Browne, Benjamin and Anne Cocke.
10 Oct. 1789 Burwell, Lewis and Elizabeth Harrison.
28 Aug. 1790 Butler, Samuel and —— ——.

24 Feb. 1791 Cofer, Frederick and Betty Dewell.
26 Apr. 1791 Charity, Squire and Lucy Elliott.
14 Nov. 1790 Clark, James and Mary Watkins.
14 Nov. 1785 Clark, William and Mary Bristow.
29 Dec. 1777 Clinch, William and Mrs. Rebecca Thompson who writes consent.
23 Jan. 1786 Clinch, William and Sarah Collier.
26 Dec. 1780 Cocke, Jessie and Rebecca Kee (widow). Rebecca Kee gives consent.
12 May 1791 Cocke, Robert and Martha Ruffin Newsom.
27 Dec. 1789 Cocks, Thomas and Polly Berriman.
26 Nov. 1774 Cole, John and Elizabeth Burt.
30 Jan. 1776 Collier, Benjamin and Patty Cryer.
22 June 1779 Collier, Stephen and Viney Hobbs. Robert Hobbs, father of Viney consents.
17 July 1775 Cook, Henry and Betty Lucas. Sec. John Jarrett.
19 May 1777 Crafford, Carter and Sarah Marriott. Sec. Josiah Wilson. Elizabeth Marriott writes consent for her dau. Sally. Wit: Sally Washington, William Marriott.
8 Apr. 1780 Crafford, Henry and Jane White. Sec. John White.
25 Dec. 1777 Crocker, Samuel and Anne Hollman, dau. Arthur Hollman.

31 Dec. 1778 Delk, Moreland and —— Holliman. Joseph Holliman, father.
27 June 1780 Dewell, James and Hannah Stewart, spinster. John Stewarts letter of consent.
21 Dec. 1772 Donnan, David and Amy Davis. Sec. Henry Browne.
5 Nov. 1785 Dowden, Thomas and Esther Bishop.
26 Apr. 1779 Dudley, Edward and Anne Holt. Sec. J. W. Simmons.
14 Jan. 1778 Dunlap, Archibald and Mrs. Lucy Kinson.
25 Mar. 1791 Dunlop, Archibald and Susan Buchanan.

24 Nov. 1785 Edmunds, Charles and Eliza Edwards.
13 May 1791 Ellis, Benjamin and Sarah Jones.
2 Mar. 1786 Ellis, Joseph and Susana Atkins.

1 Oct. 1785	Emory, Peyton and Lucretia Emory.
13 Apr. 1786	Evans, Benjamin and Mary Ellis.
14 Dec. 1779	Evans, William and Miss Rebecca Drew. Sec. William Hart.
17 June 1773	Faulcon, Jacob and Ann Spratley, dau. John Spratley. Sec. William Spratley. Wit: Thomas Fiveash.
14 July 1791	Freeland, Abraham and Mary Anne Barker.
13 Dec. 1777	Gardner, George and Lucy Warren.
8 Jan. 1773	Goosley, William and Miss Ludwell Harrison. Sec. Nathaniel Burwell. Nathaniel Harrison consents.
19 Nov. 1789	Grantham, William and Nancy Bishop.
17 Nov. 1777	Green, Abraham and Miss Elizabeth Browne, orphan of Henry Browne, gent. decd. William Browne consents that Eliza Browne of Surry should marry Abraham Greene of Amelia County. Wit: Henry Browne, Lemmon Still, Benjamin Browne.
20 Feb. 1775	Hamilin, William and Rebecca Faulcon. Sec. Nicholas Faulcon, Jr.
16 July 1785	Hardyman, John and Susanna Harrison.
15 Dec. 1785	Harrison, Henry and Mary Stark Cocke.
9 Nov. 1779	Hart, Joseph and Hannah Bailey. Sec. William Bailey, Jr.
15 Dec. 1785	Hart, William and Sarah Drewery.
20 Dec. 1771	Harwood, Major, and Lucy Watson, dau. James Watson who writes consent.
24 Sept. 1776	Haynes, Thomas of Halifax Co., N. C. and Catharine Allen Bradby. Sec. Allen Cocke.
25 June 1778	Hobbs, Robert and Lucy Walker.
	Holliman, James and Sarah Gwathney, dau. Thomas Gwathney. Joseph Holliman consents for son and Thomas Gwathney for dau.
9 Jan. 1777	Holt, William and Mildred Hargrave.
23 Mar. 1779	Howard, Henry and Betty Bilbro.
15 Feb. 1779	Hunnicutt, Hartwell and Mary Sweard. James Seward consents to dau. marriage.
27 Jan. 1778	Hunnicutt, John and Miss Martha Binns. Sec. Henry Crafford. Robert Hunnicutt consents for his son John's marriage and Eliza Binns as guardian to Martha Binns consents.
4 Jan. 1781	Irby, William and Jane Edmunds, spinster. William Blunt, guardian of Jane Edmunds, consents. Wit: Lemuel Cocke, Nathan Jones.
22 Jan. 1773	Jarrett, John and Rebecca Mooring.
1 May 1791	Johnson, Allen and Elizabeth Perry.
25 Dec. 1790	Johnson, Caesar and Tillie Trust.
18 Jan. 1786	Johnson, Moses and Sally Girl?
6 Dec. 1773	Jones, Daniel and Susanna Hardyman. Sec. William Eaton. Will Green Munford, guardian Susanna consents. Wit: James New, Ann Munford.
2 Feb. 1778	Judkins, James and Lucy Cocks, dau. William Cocks. Sec. Jessie Cocks.
8 Oct. 1774	Judkins, James and Mary Anne Judkins, Sec. Samuel Judkins.
20 May 1780	Judkins, James and Mary Rowell. Sec. Richard Rowell.
22 Nov. 1774	Judkins, Jessie and Sally Simmons.
26 Jan. 1773	Kello, Samuel and Margaret Belsches, orphan of Patrick Belches, Sec. James Belches.
30 Mar. 1786	King, Edward and Rebecca Judkins,
30 Dec. 1789	King, Thomas and Lucy Bailey.
1 June 1786	Land, John and Aggy Briggs.
30 Jan. 1779	Lane, Frederick and Beckey Thompson. Sec. John Judkins.

4 Mar. 1786	Lucas, James and Kiziah Bunkly.
24 Mar. 1779	Lucas, James and Mary Lucas.
10 Oct. 1789	Lucas, John and Mary Simmons.
28 Mar. 1790	Lucas, Samuel and Mary Watkins.
27 Mar. 1786	McKay, Robert and Mary Anne Katherine Randolph.
2 Mar. 1774	Madera, Joel and Lucy Warren.
2 Sept. 1779	Madera, Joel and Anne Cocke Thompson. Sec. Thomas Warren. Ben Putney, guardian Miss Thompson, consents.
5 June 1778	Mangum, Josiah and Sylva Carrell. Sylvia Carrell was born 10th day of May 1755. Silvas and Elizabeth Carrell.
7 Feb. 1773	Mitchell, William and Eliza Hodges.
16 Feb. 1775	Mooring, Henry, Jr., and Mary Smith. Sec. John Janratt. James Smith, writes consent that William Henry Mooring, Jr. marry May Smith, orphan of Henry Smith, decd.
28 Sept. 1785	Mooring, John C. and Martha Lane.
25 Oct. 1774	Nicholson, Washington and Sarah.
1 Dec. 1789	Parker, Benjamin and Dolly Browne.
26 Jan. 1791	Partin, Wyatt and Lucy Dewell.
17 June 1790	Phillips, Young and Sally William.
15 Dec. 1777	Price, Randolp and Lucy Hamlin, Sec. William Drew.
8 June 1774	Price, Randolph and Miss Rebecca Hunnicutt. Sec. Robert Hunnicutt.
7 Feb. 1780	Putney, David and Eliza Goodwin Collins, Sec. Ben Putney. William Collins consents to dau marriage.
23 Dec. 1772	Randolph, William and Mary Kennon. Sec. Allen Cocke. William Ruffin, Jr. guardian of William Randolph consents.
23 Mar. 1786	Robert, Samuel and —— Harrison.
7 Jan. 1778	Roe, James and Hannah Andrews, Sec. John Ellis. Hannah Andrews consents.
3 Jan. 1775	Ruffin, Francis and Hannah Cocke. John Cocke, father, consents. Witnesses, Mary and Thomas Cocke.
19 Nov. 1772	Russell, Samuel and Priscilla Lanier. Sec. Silvanus Gregory.
14 June 1789	Savage, Josiah and Susan Cheatham.
17 Oct. 1778	Schanell, Richard and Silviah Madera.
29 June 1772	Seward, William Canfield and Ann. Sec. William Drew.
10 Nov. 1777	Seward, William C. and Miss Mary Anne Faulcon. Sec. Nicholas Faulcon, Jr.
19 Sept. 1785	Shuffield, Peter and Sally Emory.
23 July 1791	Sinclair, John and Mary J'Anson.
3 Feb. 1791	Slade, Benjamin and Mary Coggin.
21 Jan. 1786	Slade, John and Elizabeth Holloway.
17 Nov. 1789	Slade, John and Sarah Judkins.
12 Dec. 1772	Smalley, John and Penelope Hunnicutt.
17 Oct. 1779	Smith, Michael and Rebecca Bishop.
28 Jan. 1772	Smith, William and Anne Mooring, dau. Henry Mooring. Sec. John Judkins.
24 Mar. 1786	Soloman, George and Lucy Emory.
5 Apr. 1773	Spratley, William and Anne Taylor, dau. of Nicholas Faulcon. Sec. Nicholas Faulcon, Jr.
20 Jan. 1768	Stevenson, Joseph and Martha Newsum, dau. of Joseph Newsum.
27 Jan. 1791	Stewart, William and Celea Bell.
17 Dec. 1789	Taylor, Robert and Elizabeth Ward.
5 June 1776	Thomas, Micajah and Elizabeth Crafford. Sec. Carter Crafford.
16 Feb. 1775	Thomas Samuel and Katharine Carrell. Eliza Carrell consent for her dau.

8 Sept. 1779   Truman, Isham and Mary Gibbons, Sec. William Evans.
22 Dec. 1777   Turner, Benjamin and Rebecca Grantham dau. Thomas Grantham.
19 Dec. 1774   Vick, James and Sallv Nicholson.

1 Aug. 1790   Walden, Drewry and Hannah Scott.
2 Feb. 1778   Waldron, William and Priscilla Banks, dau. John Banks.
29 May 1774   Walker, Robert and Miss Susanna Harrison, Sec. Nathaniel Harrison.
1 Apr. 1790   Wall, Joel and Rebecca Gibbons.
24 June 1780   Wallace, John Owen and Elizabeth Bennett. Sec. Thomas Warren.
8 Sept. 1785   Watson, James and Peggy Wilson.
24 Nov. 1785   Warburton, William and Nancy Morris.
23 Dec. 1790   Warren, John and Jane Davis.
3 Apr. 1790   Warren, William and Elizabeth Davis.
14 Jan. 1786   Wellings, Robert and Sally Wooten.
7 June 1786   White, Samuel and Clary.
14 Feb. 1791   Williams. Thomas and Mary Williams.
28 Dec. 1772   Willis, Augustine and Mrs. Anne Heath, widow of John Heath. Sec. Allen Cocke.
25 Nov. 1777   Willison, James and Mary Janson. Sec. William Short.
28 Feb. 1786   Wills, Nathaniel and Mildred Comer.
3 Dec. 1785   Windham, Reuben and Jane Clements.
4 Oct. 1785   Wooten, Thomas and Mary Tomlinson.

24 Jan. 1775   Yarborough, Richard and Miss Sarah Watkins.

SURRY CENSUS 1782

HEADS OF FAMILIES

	White	Black		White	Black
Adams, Martha	3	7	Bailey, Mary	3	6
Adams, William	1	5	Bailey, John	2	11
Adams, William	5	2	Bailey, Lemuel	5	15
Adamson, Andrew	2	2	Bailey, Benjamin	5	15
Alexander, James	5	7	Bailey, Samuel	6	45
Allen, John	7	0	Bell, Stephen	6	0
Allen, William, Esq.	9	83	Bell, Benjamin	7	4
Andrews, Nat.	8	2	Bell, Silvah	10	7
Andrews, John, Sr.	3	1	Bell, Jacob	5	0
Andrews, John	11	7	Briggs, Benjamin	3	7
Andrews, William	9	3	Bland, Thomas	6	5
Anthony, William	5	0	Barham, Joseph	7	4
Avoris, John	7	5	Barham, Faith	5	1
			Barham, John	6	0
Belsches, James	3	21	Berriman, Mary	4	0
Badgett, John	3	0	Berriman, Nath.	8	2
Bailey, William, Jr.	5	4	Bennett, William	7	3
Bailey, William	4	3	Bennett, Ann	7	0
Burt, Elizabeth	2	6	Binns, Elizabeth	4	14
Buchanan, Susan	1	10	Bryant, James	4	0
Barradall, Robert	5	3	Barlow, James	6	0
Bishop, Benjamin	5	0	Barlow, George	4	0
Bishop, Joshua	6	0	Bell, Robert	7	2
Bishop, James, Sr.	1	6	Bruce, James	8	0
Bagley, Hannah	3	1	Blow, William	2	6
Bilbro, Benjamin	1	1	Banks, John	7	0
Barker, Elizabeth	5	1	Brock, William	8	1
Barker, Lucy	1	1	Bryant, John	3	0
Barker, Lemuel	5	3	Bedingfield, Ann	8	7
Barker, Elizabeth	6	0	Batts, John	11	0
Bishop, David	10	0			
Bishop, James, Jr.	2	1	Cocke, Joh, Esq.	6	30
Bishop, John	7	0	Cheatham, John	8	16
Burgess, John	6	7	Coman, John	2	2
Burgess, Thomas	1	10	Collier, Benjamin	4	3
Bishop, Thomas	8	0	Cunningham, V.	2	3
Byrd, Joseph	6	0	Cocke, Catharine	5	15
Browne, William	10	54	Cheatham, Rebecca	2	5
Browne, William, Jr.	4	23	Chanty, David	4	0
Browne, Ann	3	0	Cary, Martha	6	2
Brown, Benjamin E.	2	8	Cocke, John	4	10
Brown, James	10	0	Cocke, William	2	19
Brown, John	2	0	Collins, William	2	29
Brown, Ed.	6	7	Campbell, Archibald	7	36
Brown, James	7	9	Caseley, Edmund	1	0
Brown, Richard D.	6	32	Cooper, Frederick	4	0
Bage, Thomas, Sr.	2	7	Caseley, Michael	5	4
Bartle, John	3	3	Chanty, Sarah	7	0
Bartle, Thomas	2	2	Caseley, John	2	1

	White	Black
Cooper, John	6	2
Cocke, Lemuel	4	30
Clinch, William, Jr.	5	10
Clinch, William, Sr.	9	26
Clarke, James	3	10
Cryer, Nick	3	2
Carrell, Mary	7	1
Charity, Henry	9	10
Collier, John	5	7
Cocke, Ann	2	17
Collier, Lucy	2	2
Cocke, Rich	8	21
Cocke, John H.	8	27
Coggin, Micajah	8	1
Clarke, Etheldred	9	0
Clarke, William	3	1
Cocks, Jesse	4	6
Cocks, William, Jr.	2	0
Cocke, Thomas	7	45
Cocks, William	7	17
Clarke, Martha	6	2
Cofer, Thomas	10	5
Carter, William	8	0
Cocks, Mary	5	0
Clarke, Jesse	6	0
Cornwell, James	4	5
Crafford, Henry	9	24
Colcote, Harwood	3	4
Crafford, Carter	6	25
Crafford, Mary	1	11
Dunlop, Arch.	1	34
Dewell, Mary	2	0
Dewell, Thomas	6	0
Dewell, Jesse	1	0
Dewell, Littleberry	7	0
Dewell, Drury	1	0
Deelereaux, John	13	0
Dewell, Rich	1	0
Dowden, Thomas	1	0
Dewell, James	6	0
Deelereaux, David	11	0
Davis, Martha	8	3
Davis, James	1	8
Dicken, William	2	0
Degge, Anthony	6	3
Drewry, Rich	3	5
Davis, Thomas	9	5
Davis, John, Sr.	1	5
Davis, James	11	4
Davis, Thomas	4	3
Delke, Lucy	3	2
Davidson, Thomas	6	6
Derring, William	2	6
Degge, Anthony, Jr.	11	32
Davis, Dolphin	3	0

	White	Black
Davis, Francis	7	0
Emery, Charles	8	0
Ellis, Thomas	2	1
Emery, John, Sr.	8	0
Emery, Sarah	4	0
Emery, Howell	5	0
Ellis, Benjamin	4	7
Emery, James	4	0
Ellis, Jonathan	4	0
Evans, William	6	21
Emery, Ruth	6	1
Edwards, Ethelred	8	7
Edwards, James	7	2
Edwards, Hartwell	2	0
Edwards, J. Anson	7	11
Eaton, Rebecca	7	11
Edwards, William Phil	6	5
Edwards, Lewis	0	2
Edwards, William	10	0
Fugler, Mary	4	1
Fletcher, Thomas	2	11
Faulcon, Nich., Sr.	4	17
Faulcon, Jacob	8	16
Faulcon, Nich, Jr.	10	35
Foster, Rich	4	6
Grantham, Stephen	6	0
Grantham, Thomas	5	7
Gilchist, James	3	8
Gilbert, Henry	6	10
Gardner, George	4	4
Gwaltney, Joseph	4	0
Gwaltney, William	4	0
Gwaltney, Benjamin	6	0
Gwaltney, John	7	0
Green, William	4	0
Gwaltney, Thomas	6	17
Goodrich, Charles	6	3
Gray, Henry	5	3
Gray, John	7	0
Gray, James	10	10
Harrison, Nathaniel, Jr.	5	41
Harriss, Thomas	5	10
Harriss, William	6	26
Howard, Henry, Jr.	4	13
Hill, Mary	1	3
Howard, Henry, Sr.	4	12
Howard, Thomas	9	20
Hill, Stirling	6	4
Hamlin, William	5	5
Holdworth, Rebecca	5	11
Holdsworth, John W.	4	16
Hargrave, Hinches	4	0
Holt, William	5	2
Holleman, Joseph, Sr.	10	13

	White	Black
Hargrave, Lucy	6	0
Hargrave, John	1	1
Holleman, Joseph, Jr.	4	5
Hart, Joseph	4	3
Harris, Chapman	9	1
Hargrave, Robert	4	20
Hargrave, Anselm	6	6
Harris, James	9	1
Hart, Hartwell	5	10
Holt, Joseph	6	2
Hutchings, John	11	43
Holt, Thomas	8	1
Holleway, Lazarus	11	0
Holleway, Jesse	7	0
Hart, Bramley	2	4
Harrison, William	7	10
Hartwell, James	8	0
Hart, William	9	35
Hunnicutt, Hartwell	5	0
Harrison, John	4	10
Holt, Archer	5	0
Holt, Elizabeth	6	6
Hunnicutt, Robert	1	10
Hunnicutt, John	2	15
Hunnicutt, Augustine	3	1
Holt, William	6	11
Holt, James	4	4
Ingram, Patience	6	0
Inman, Ann	2	5
Inman, Isham	4	8
J'Anson, Thomas	1	10
Jarratt, John	9	12
Jimm, Rice	5	2
Johnson, Peter, Jr.	9	0
Johnson, Thomas	3	1
Justiss, William	5	6
Johnson, Levy	5	0
Johnson, William	7	0
Johnson, Mary	1	1
Johnson, Peter, Sr.	3	0
Jones, Jane	4	0
Justiss, Elizabeth	4	0
Jones, Nathan	5	30
Jones, Hamilton (Est)	5	18
Johnson, Hartwell	6	0
Jordan, Stephen	7	0
Jordan, Perry	3	0
Judkins, John	1	1
James, Jeremiah	6	4
Judkins, James	4	7
Judkins, Jacob	5	2
Judkins, Elizabeth	2	3
Jordan, Ann	3	1
Judkins, Samuel	9	10
Judkins, Charles	6	5

	White	Black
James, Enos	6	0
Judkins, Martha	6	18
Judkins, Mark	1	0
Judkins, John, Jr.	8	0
Judkins, Jesse	2	0
Judkins, Mary	6	2
Jordan, Ann	4	0
King, Randolph	6	2
King, Mary	3	4
Kee, Robert	4	5
Kee, William	4	5
Kee, James	11	10
Kee, Sarah	3	2
Kee, Charles	9	0
Laughton, William	1	8
Lucas, John	12	27
Lunsford, Swann, Sr.	5	6
Lunsford, Swann, Jr.	1	0
Lane, John	10	6
Little, John, Jr.	4	1
Lane, Micajah	3	1
Little, Jesse	6	0
Little, John	4	1
Lane, Fred	4	6
Logan, John	4	4
Lane, Thomas	6	4
Lane, Lucy	6	0
Long, Hartwell	5	0
Long, David	3	0
Long, Lewis	3	2
Little, John	5	1
Milby, William	5	2
Moring, John	1	0
Moring, Joseph	6	5
Munro, Joseph	6	0
Moring, Benjamin	6	7
Marks, John	4	5
Marriott, Elizabeth	3	12
Macintosh, Robert	7	6
Maddera, Joel	4	6
Moody, Archb.	5	2
Moring, Henry, Jr.	8	9
Maddera, Joanna	1	2
Maddera, Elizabeth	5	0
Maddera, Elizabeth	5	6
Maget, William	4	13
Moreland, Mary	2	0
Moore, Jesse	6	0
Moring, Henry	7	10
Mitchell, William	5	1
Mitchell, Mary	1	3
Norsworthy, John	6	4
Newsum, Littlebery	4	10
Nimmo, Andrew	7	2

	White	Black		White	Black
Newton, Thomas	8	25	Saunders, John	4	6
Nelson, William	9	26	Shuffield, James	8	0
			Scarborough, Mary	2	0
Partin, William C.	1	10	Sledge, Ann	5	6
Peterson, Peter	8	3	Stephens, William	5	1
Putney, Benjamin	9	12	Shuffield, Hardy	6	0
Putney, David	9	4	Sherman, Mary	4	0
Peters, Armstead	15	0	Smith Michael	5	10
Peter, Thomas	5	20	Savidge, Joel	4	0
Peter, Robert	2	4	Smith, Lucy	7	10
Putney, Lewis	1	12	Smith, Nicholas	4	1
Parker, Elizabeth	2	2	Smith, Henry	1	0
Porter, Ed.	10	0	Sprately, Benjamin	4	10
Phillips, Hannah	2	2	Sprately, John	1	8
Pyland, Mary	5	4	Sharp, Burwell	4	13
Pleasants, Thomas	6	0	Sebrell, Nathaniel	10	12
Presson, John	8	7	Smith, William	1	5
Purdy, Lewis	9	1	Sprately, William	6	19
Price, Lucy	4	66	Steward, John	8	0
Pettway, John	8	2	Sewards, William Cofield, Est.	4	11
Pyland, Robert	8	4	Sewards, Britain	7	1
Pyland, Mary	1	2	Sewards, James	3	0
Pyland, Thomas	1	0	Sinclair, Arthur	4	6
Pyland, John	1	0	Savidge, Henry	3	0
Pyland, Ann	6		Slade, John	6	0
Pyland, Obediah	4	1	Savidge, Michael	3	0
Presson, Toomes	6	0	Savidge, John	3	0
Person, Mary	12	4	Savidge, Sarah	7	0
Pitt, John	8	7	Slade, William	8	0
Priclow, Sam	3	29	Skipwith, Peyton	4	26
Pierce, Jeremiah	9	24	Smalley, John	4	5
Price, William	10	3	Smith, Benjamin for		
			Allen Cocke's est.	3	75
Rae, James	4	2	Shelley, James	3	1
Rigan, William	10	0	Scammell, Richard	7	10
Rigan, Benjamin	4	0	Salter, William	4	8
Rispers, Robert	8	0	Smith, Mary	5	5
Rae, William	5	3			
Rose, William	9	0	Tucker, Jane	4	0
Rigan, Jesse	8	0	Tillot, John	5	6
Rogers, William	5	0	Thompson, Ann	3	4
Rhodes, Benjamin	2	0	Thorp, Joseph	4	5
Rhodes, John	5	0	Thompson, William	3	0
Rowell, Richard	6	4	Thompson, William	7	2
Roberts, Joseph	8	0	Thompson, Joel	10	12
			Thompson, Phillip	5	6
Sorsby, Stephen	12	16	Taylor, John	7	0
Simon, Thomas	6	0	Thompson, John	7	3
Stewart, William	3	2	Taylor, James, Jr.	8	1
Sorsby, Thomas	5	11	Taylor, James	6	0
Slade, Benjamin	1	0	Thomas, John	7	0
Simmon, William	10	17	Turner, Thomas	7	0
Scott, Nicholas	9	0			
Stewart, James	6	0	Valentine, Peter	10	0
Short, William	7	49	Verall, John	1	0
Shuffield, Jesse	5	11			
Shuffield, Elizabeth	5	3	Wyatts, Hubbard, Est.	0	6

	White	Black
Walden, Stephen	1	0
Wall, Thomas	6	6
Walden, Sarah	3	2
Warren, John	6	0
West, Phillip	3	17
Watkins, John, Sr.	9	32
Wrenn, Thomas	6	2
Wall, Aron	4	1
White, Benjamin	3	2
Wilson, John	8	0
White, Henry	12	00
White, John	4	35
Wrenn, John	10	4
Wrenn, John, Sr.	2	10
Wrenn, John, Jr.	2	2
Walles, Benjamin	6	11
Warren, Joseph	8	3
Ward, William (for John Paradise)	4	17

	White	Black
Wesson, John	3	5
Warren, Hannah	7	14
Warren, Jesse	5	13
Warren, William	7	6
Warren, John	8	1
White, Thomas	6	15
Warren, Arthur	7	4
Wilson, Willis	7	36
Wright, John	2	0
Wildair, John	7	1
Wright, William	1	3
Williams, Jesse	3	0
Wilson, Thomas	6	0
Williams, Thomas	3	17
Wills, Thomas	11	4
Wills, Mary	3	13

SUSSEX MARRIAGE BONDS

26 Feb. 1760	Adams, James and Ann Harper, widow of Wiatt Harper, Sec. Thomas Huson.
30 May 1776	Avery, John and Ann Hill, widow.
29 Jan. 1765	Barker, John and Lucy Wallace.
20 Apr. 1769	Bell, Silvanus and Mary Johnson, dau. Lewis Johnson.
11 Feb. 1771	Blow, Henry and Rebecca, dau. John Birdsong.
1 Feb. 1766	Belsches, Hugh and Martha Avery, dau. Richard Avery.
28 Feb. 1768	Biggins, William and Molly Biggins, dau. Sarah Biggins, widow.
17 June 1763	Blow, John and Mary Briggs, dau. of George Briggs. Consent of John Thomas, guardian of George Blow who writes John Blow was 21 July 7, 1762.
9 Nov. 1766	Blunt, Benjamin, orphan Richard Blunt and Frances Briggs, Sec. Joseph Rosser.
11 Nov. 1783	Blunt, Thomas and Elizabeth Peete, dau. Dr. Thomas Peete.
17 Dec. 1756	Blunt, William and Ann Nicholson, dau. Robert Nicholson, Sec. Robert Nicholson.
19 Nov. 1764	Blunt, William and Martha Peete, dau. Samuel Peete.
8 Oct. 1776	Bolling, Stith and Charlotte, dau. John Edmunds, dec.
1771-1772	Bonner, Jeremiah and Sally Hall.
9 Feb. 1756	Bonner, John and Mary Briggs, widow, Sec. William Bonner.
13 Nov. 1761	Bowler, Burrell, and Mary Mason.
19 Apr. 1779	Brent, William and Mary Parham.
24 May 1762	Briggs, William and Mary Cooke, dau. Reuben Cooke. Sec. Hinchea Gilliam.
17 Mar. 1758	Brown, Lewis and Martha Richardson, dau. William Richardson.
22 June 1763	Burge, Drury and Elizabeth Dunn.
1771-1772	Burgess, Henry John and Judith Driver.
20 June 1765	Butler, Thomas and Mary Norris, minor
1 Dec. 1762	Cargill, John and Sarah Avery, dau. Capt. Richard Avery.
1 Dec. 1781	Collier, Sampson and Sarah Gilliam, widow, sec. Peter Jones.
21 Sept. 1776	Cocke, John and Lucy Herbert Claiborne, dau. Augustus Claiborne.
27 Dec. 1773	Cocke, Lemuel and Ann Irby, ward of Richard Blunt.
19 Nov. 1768	Cocke, Richard, son of Richard Cocke and Anne, dau. Col. Augustine Claiborne.
11 Apr. 1774	Chambliss, James and Sarah, Dau. Thomas Moore, dec.
5 Nov. 1779	Chappell, Henry and Elizabeth, dau. of Elizabeth Rives.
20 Apr. 1769	Chappell, —— and Sally, dau. William Hines.
17 Mar. 1758	Chappell, John and Mary Hines, dau. Thomas Hines.
1771-1772	Chappell, Thomas and Elizabeth Malone.
27 Jan. 1759	Collier, Charles and Susanna Smith, dau. of William Smith. Leter from her brother Josiah, executor of his father, William Smith, stating that his sister was born in 1737.
15 Sept. 1774	Cargill, John and Ann Eldridge, relict of William Eldridge.
3 Nov. 1769	Clark, Eldridge and Betty, dau. John Hunt, dec.
25 Oct. 1759	Dennis, Joseph and Lucretia Parham, dau. Matthew Parham, Sec. Thomas Young.
21 May 1767	Dixon, Frederick and Nancy Hines, dau. William Hines.
1771-1772	Dunn, Thomas and Sarah Hobbs.
19 Aug. 1757	Edmunds, Henry of Brunswick and Sarah Briggs of Surry. Sec Richard Stark.

20 Nov. 1767	Edwards, Edward and Budd Brookwell.
13 Jan. 1755	Edwards, Nicholas and Mary Nicholson, widow, Sec. John Irby.
30 May 1774	Edwards, William and Susanna Edmunds, dau. John Edmunds, dec. Sec. William Irby.
20 July 1756	Edwards, William of Brunswick and Sarah Edmunds, dau. of Thomas Edmunds. Sec. William Eldridge. Consent of J. Edmunds to marriage of his sister Ward.
18 Sept. 1774	Eppes, Joel and Lucy, dau. Banks Meacham.
21 Apr. 1769	Eldridge, Thomas and Elizabeth Pennington, widow.
7 Feb. 1758	Ford, Joshua of Southampton and Mary Collia Thorp, dau. Joseph Thorp.
24 June 1757	Freeman, Joel and Patty Richardson, dau. of William Richardson, Sec. William Richardson.
15 Aug. 1765	Gary, William and Boyce Gee.
18 Mar. 1773	Gee, Chappell and Rebecca, dau. William Lucas.
16 Mar. 1758	Gee, Henry and Frances Parham, dau. Ephraim Parham.
17 Mar. 1768	Gibbons, Lawrence and Lucy, dau. James Jones.
19 May 1774	Gilham, Thomas and Sarah, dau. Arthur Williamson.
9 Oct. 1758	Green, Abram and Ann Blunt, widow. Sec. John Irby.
Sept. 1777	Gregory, Richard and Mary Broadnax, widow of William Broadnax, dec. Consent of Roger Gregory of Lunenburg father of Richard.
14 Feb. 1756	Hardaway, John and Rebecca Pepper, dau. Richard Pepper.
4 July 1765	Hare, Jesse of N. C. and Betty Renn, dau. James Renn.
18 Feb. 1775	Harrison, Cole, dau. Margaret Hay, dau. John Hay, dec. Signed Peter Cole Harrison. Nathaniel Harrison writes that Peter Cole Harrison is 21. Margaret, dau. of John Hay and Judith his wife, b. 5 Nov. 1751. William Willis, rector.
27 Sept. 1758	Harrison, Capt. Henry and Elizabeth Avery, dau. Capt. Richard Avery.
23 Apr. 1767	Harrison, Thomas and Mary Jenkins.
18 Mar. 1773	Harwood, Phillip and Selah Rochel, dau. John Rochel, dec.
30 Oct. 1780	Heath, Thomas and Selah Rives. Sec. Timothy Rives.
1771-1772	Hines, Allen and Frances Williams.
15 Mar. 1771	Hines, Hartwell and Elizabeth Edmundson. Consent of his father Joshua Hines.
24 Dec. 1754	Hobson, Francis and Frances Judkins, dau. Charles Judkins, Sec. Thomas Dunn Jones.
11 Mar. 1771	Howard, Thomas and Mary, dau. Humphrey Baylis.
9 Jan. 1758	Howell, William and Hannah Wyche, dau. George Wyche, dec. Sec. Benjamin Wyche.
15 Mar. 1756	Hunt, John and Elizabeth Mary Tyus, dau. John Tyus. Sec. John Tyus.
22 Mar. 1765	Hunt, Thomas and Dorothy Vaughan, Sec. Thomas Vaughan.
16 Dec. 1771	Irby, John and Rebecca, dau. George Briggs, Sec. Richard Blunt.
1768	Johnson, Lewis and Mary Horn.
16 Sept. 1772	Johnson, Lewis and Lucy Ezell, dau. Isham Ezell.
20 Feb. 1767	Johnson, William and Agnes Battle, Spinster.
7 Dec. 1762	Jones, Edmund and Rebecca Johnson, dau. of William Johnson.
18 Aug. 1774	Jones, Frederick and Susanna, dau. Aug. Claiborne.
4 July 1774	Jones, Hamilton and Jacobina Willie, spinster.
23 June 1774	Jones, Captain James and Leah Wyche, relict of James Wyche, dec.
19 Oct. 1765	Jones, James and Rebecca, widow of Edward Jones.
14 Oct. 1754	Jones, James Boisseau and Ann Gilliam, dau. ?
16 July 1757	Jones, Jesse and Alice Stagg. Sec. Andrew Froughton ?.
22 July 1758	Jones, John and Elizabeth Binns, dau. of Charles Binns. Sec. John Hay.

22 May 1767	Jones, William and Elizabeth Hunt.
2 June 1767	Justice, John and Sarah, dau. Reuben Cook.
17 Nov. 1766	Kerr, George and Elizabeth Briggs.
17 Apr. 1783	Lanier, Buckner and Rebecca Williamson, widow.
21 Sept. 1778	Lanier, Lewis, son of Sampson and Anne, dau. Thomas Butler.
2 Apr. 1759	Lanier, Richard and Ann Mason, widow. Sec. William Stuart.
16 Feb. 1756	Lee, Peter and Cecelia Pettway. Sec. A. Claiborne and Samuel Lee consents to marriage of son.
3 Feb. 1769	Lessenberry, John and Isabella, dau. Elizabeth Bedingfield.
13 Mar. 1782	Lewis, Enoch and Lucy Barker, widow.
15 Nov. 1779	Mangum, Samuel and Rebecca dau. Richard Cotton.
31 Oct. 1775	Marable, Henry Hartwell and Elizabeth lau. Isaac Mason. Sec. Hartwell Marable.
17 Mar. 1755	Mason, John and Elizabeth Peters, dau. Thomas Peters.
9 June 1760	Mason, John, Jr. and Elizabeth Gee, spinster. Sec. John Mason and Henry Gee.
16 Jan. 1777	Mason, Thomas and Lucy Jones, dau. Capt. James Jones.
16 Oct. 1777	Mason, James and Rebecca. Sec. Richard Parker.
5 Oct. 1782	Mason, Peyton and Patty Peebles.
21 Sept. 1773	Mason, Richard and Mary Burrow, widow.
24 July 1779	Massenburg, John and Elizabeth Eldridge. Letter of consent from Ann Cargill, her mother.
27 June 1771	Mason, William and Mary, dau. William Gilliam, dec.
25 July 1774	Mason, William and Lucy Mason, dau. Major John Mason.
21 Dec. 1781	Meredith, John of Dinwiddie and Elizabeth Pennington.
26 May 1763	Mitchell, Abram and Elizabeth Hines, dau. William Hines.
5 June 1779	Mitchell, John and Scota, dau. William Stewart.
20 May 1762	Moore, John and Mary Smith, dau. Edward Smith, Sec. William Hamlin.
18 Oct. 176–	Moore, William and Elizabeth Flumer? spinster.
15 June 1769	Moss, Joshua and Sarah, dau. John Pennington.
24 Sept. 1757	Nash, Col. John, Sr., of Prince Edward and Elizabeth Fisher, dau. of Charles Fisher, dec. Witness Mary Fisher.
16 Nov. 1769	Nicholson, Harry S. and Susanna, dau. George Briggs.
10 Apr. 1771	Nicholson, James, Jr. and Ely Woodroof, dau. Richard Woodroof.
5 May 1762	Nicholson, Michael and Mildred Cheeseman, dau. of George Cheeseman, dec. Sec. Thomas Young. Letter from John Lamb that Mildred is of age.
25 Feb. 1758	Newsum, Thomas and Alice Stagg, spinster.
23 June 1764	Owen, Robert and Lucy, dau. Silvanus Stokes.
15 Nov. 1764	Parham, Ephraim and Hannah Hill. Sec. Richard Hill.
19 Mar. 1767	Parham, Ephraim and Ruth, dau. Thomas Dunn.
9 Oct. 1758	Parham, Nathaniel and Cecelia Lee, Widow. Sec. Robert Pettway.
10 Feb. 1769	Parham, Nathaniel and Rebecca, dau. William Parham.
18 Oct. 1777	Parham, Robert, son of Nathaniel, and Rebecca, dau. John Berriman.
2 Sept. 1772	Parham, Steth and Lucretia Parham, widow.
1771-1772	Parham, William and Susanna Hunt.
18 Sept. 1755	Parham, William and Mary Stevens, dau. of Edward Stevens, dec.
7 Oct. 1772	Parham, William and Mary, dau. John Kelley.
15 June 1769	Parker, Drury and Mildred Clanton, age 26, dau. Mary Clanton.
9 Feb. 1760	Parker, Thomas and Sarah Parker, dau. of William Parker, Sec. David Jones.
17 Mar. 1768	Parker, William and Mary Peters, dau. Thomas Peters.
27 Dec. 1771	Parker, William and Susanna, dau. Benjamin Hunt, dec.

19 May 1763	Peebles, Thomas and Mary Hancock, widow. Sec. John Harrison.
28 July 1769	Pennington, Marcus and Ann, dau. Solomon Graves.
21 Apr. 1764	Peterson, John of Brunswick and Elizabeth Briggs, dau. of George Briggs of Sussex. Sec. James Machin, Jr.
29 Mar. 1768	Peter, James, son of Thomas Peters and Lucy, dau. William Parker.
15 June 1775	Peterson, Thomas and Elizabeth Claiborne, dau. Augustine Claiborne. Sec. Buller Claiborne.
28 Jan. 1771	Pettway, Edward, Jr. and Susanna, dau. Edward ———. Witness Billey Claiborne.
20 Nov. 1767	Pettway, Hinchea and Mary Parker, witness Herbert Claiborne.
24 Oct. 1765	Pettway, John and Fanny Biggins, dau. Sarah Biggins.
3 Jan. 1760	Pettway, Robert and Phebe Pettway, dau. of Edward Pettway.
24 Feb. 1762	Phillips, Hartwell and Jane Hancock, dau. John Hancock who consents.
27 Nov. 1757	Pride, Halcott of Dinwiddie and Mary Briggs, dau. Capt. Howell Briggs. Sec. Henry Woodcock of Sussex. Howell Briggs letter of consent.
3 May 1756	Raines, Fred and Frances Wyche, dau. of James Wyche, decd. Letter William Johnson, her guardian.
5 Oct. 1762	Raines, John and Amy Mitchell, widow. Sec. Nathaniel Mitchell.
24 Mar. 1768	Renn, Jos. and Ann Zells, widow.
2 July 1759	Rives, Christopher and Elizabeth Mason, spinster. Sec. John Mason.
9 June 1762	Rives, George and Sarah Eldridge, dau. of Thomas Eldridge. Sec. William Eldridge.
16 Dec. 1773	Rives, William and Elizabeth Vaughan, dau. Thomas Vaughan.
19 June 1775	Rives, William and Jemima, dau. William Heath.
4 Feb. 1780	Rives, Timothy and Rebecca Mason.
12 Feb. 1763	Rives, Timothy and Catharine Barker, widow Henry Barker. Sec. William Chamblis.
8 Feb. 1773	Rives, Timothy and Martha Binns.
9 Apr. 1762	Ruffin, William and Sarah Hill, dau. Richard Hill.
18 July 1775	Sammon, John and Lucy Seat, dau. Robert Seat. Sec. Nathaniel Johnson.
25 Oct. 1765	Sanders, Thomas and Ann Harper, widow. Sec. John Bonner.
Dec. 1764	Shands, John and Priscilla Shands, dau. of William Shands and Priscilla his wife.
2 June 1779	Shands, William and Lucy, dau. William Oliver.
17 Feb. 1769	Sisson, Thomas of Brunswick and Martha Parker, dau. of William Parham, dec.
11 Aug. 1767	Smith, Lawrence and Mary Briggs, widow.
18 Aug. 1760	Southall, Holman and Elizabeth Dancy, dau. of William Dancy. Sec. Hugh Belscher.
18 Oct. 1777	Strachan, Dr. Alexr. Glass and Lucy Pride. Consent of Colin Campbell, her guardian.
15 Apr. 1779	Summers, John and Lucretia Jones.
30 Jan. 1773	Tatum, Robert and Amy, dau. Charles Gee.
19 Dec. 1782	Thweatt, David and Rebecca Jones, widow.
10 Feb. 1775	Thweatts, William and Jane Parham, dau. Ephraim Parham. Sec. James Thweatts.
24 Nov. 1759	Tucker, David and Athalia Kezia Hunt, widow. Sec. Thomas Goodwyn.
1771-1772	Tucker, Robert and Mary Ann Parham.
22 Mar. 1771	Tuel, John and Mary, dau. Isaac Mason, dec.
28 Oct. 1754	Verell, John and Susanna Moore, Spinster Sec. Edward Pettway.
11 Nov. 1767	Vinson, Aaron and Sarah, dau. John Ogburn, Jr.

15 Aug. 1771	Walker, Capt. John and Hannah Hunt, widow.
5 Mar. 1781	Ward, Francis and Sarah Webb, dau. Robert Webb.
20 May 1758	Wyche, Benjamin and Elizabeth Peete, daughter of Samuel Peete. Sec. Thomas Peters. Letter of consent from Samuel Peete.
15 Oct. 1761	Wyche, George and Margaret. Sec. Nathaniel Dobie.
26 Sept. 1766	Young, Thomas and Katharine Barlow, widow. Sec. David Mason.

SUSSEX CENSUS 1782

HEADS OF FAMILIES

Whites 2,923   Blacks 3,696

	White	Black		White	Black
Adams, James	7	0	Bell, Silvanus	9	4
Adams, Thomas	7	1	Bendall, Isaac	8	2
Adkins, Lucy	0	23	Berryman, John	6	11
Adkins, Lucy	0	25	Biggins, Sarah	1	11
Adkins, Sarah	2	4	Blizzard, Samuel	8	0
Adkins, Thomas	9	17	Blow, Henry	3	5
Allen, William	14	241	Blow, Col. Michael	9	20
Alsbrook, John	4	4	Blunt, Colin	2	10
Ambrose, Thomas	8	0	Blunt, Collins	2	10
Anderson, Mack	6	2	Blunt, William	5	35
Andrews, Richard	9	18	Bonner, John	10	7
Ashwell, Ann	5	1	Bottom, Samuel	9	0
Armstrong, Robert	10	1	Booth, Michael	4	1
Atkins, Benjamin	3	1	Boiseau, James	3	4
Atkins, John	6	4	Bradley, Elizabeth	2	0
Atkins, Lewis	11	0	Brent, William	5	7
Avent, John	6	6	Brier, John	3	1
Avent, Thomas	10	4	Briggs, Nathan	6	11
			Bullock, Benjamin	5	1
Bailey, Abidon	9	0	Bullock, Joel	6	2
Bailey, Edmund	10	0	Bullock, William	4	0
Bailey, Elijah	4	1	Burrough, Jarrell	9	0
Bailey, Henry	4	1	Butler, Thomas, Jr.	5	6
Bailey, James	4	10	Byshop, Averia	4	3
Bailey, Joseph	6	0	Byshop, Harmon	3	2
Bailey, Joshua	7	4	Byshop, Nathan	10	3
Bailey, Thomas	5	1	Byshop, Morris	5	0
Bailey, Thomas, Sr.	8	0			
Bailey, Phillip	4	1	Cain, Isham	8	4
Bailey, William	4	3	Cain, James, Sr.	6	2
Bain, James	5	0	Cain, James, Jr.	3	0
Bain, John	3	0	Cain, Micajah	4	4
Baird, Benjamin	4	2	Cain, Peter	8	5
Baird, Benjamin	5	2	Cain, William	5	4
Baird, Stephen	7	4	Carrell, Mack	5	3
Baird, William	9	8	Carrell, Nathan	7	0
Barham, Charles	8	6	Carrel, William, Jr.	10	2
Barham, Thomas	3	2	Carrel, William, Sr.	3	2
Barham, William	5	13	Carter, John	3	9
Barker, Benjamin	4	4	Caton, Henry	1	9
Barker, Henry	6	2	Chambliss, James	7	20
Barker, Joanna	8	3	Chambliss, Wm., Jr.	3	3
Barker, Nathan	5	1	Chappel, Howell	9	14
Barker, Nathan	5	1	Chappel, James	8	11
Barker, Nathaniel	2	2	Chappel, John	12	16
Bass, Arthur	9	3	Chappel, Mary	2	12
Belsches, Alex	4	30	Chappel, Thomas	5	7
Belsches, Hugh	8	40	Claiborne, Augustine	9	31
Bell, James	2	1	Claiborne, William	6	35

	White	Black		White	Black
Clark, Eve	6	2	Freeman, Lucy	6	1
Clarey, Capt. Benj.	3	9	Gilbert, William	3	9
Clary, Elizabeth	3	3	Gilliam, Charles	3	20
Clary, James	3	4	Gilliam, William	1	0
Clary, Mary	6	1	Glover, James	7	5
Clemons, Thomas	6	36	Glover, James, Sr.	2	6
Clifton, Samuel	8	5	Glover, Jones	8	9
Cocks, James	10	0	Glover, Mary	7	20
Cocks, John	3	12	Godwin, Christ	4	9
Cocks, Lucy	1	0	Grizzard, Lucy	5	13
Cocks, William	12	6	Grizzard, William	3	6
Cole, John	5	1			
Collier, Jesse	8	2	Hail, Benjamin	6	1
Coman, John, Sr.	3	0	Hail, John	3	2
Cook, Richard	6	10	Hail, Micajah	4	0
Cooks, Joseph	2	0	Hall, Benjamin	2	1
Cooper, James	6	1	Hall, Dixon	6	9
Cornet, Jones	8	0	Hall, Solomon	9	7
Cornet, Selah	3	0	Hall, Willis	6	13
Cosby, William	7	2	Hancock, John	4	5
Cotton, Harris	5	2	Hancock, Nicholas	6	2
Cotton, Nathaniel	2	9	Hancock, Rebecca	6	7
Cotton, William	7	1	Hancock, Thomas	1	1
Cross, Sarah	5	6	Harden, Frances	5	7
Cross, William	3	3	Hardy, William	5	0
Cullom, Thomas	3	1	Harper, Wilkins	6	2
			Harris, Reuben	4	1
Davis, Charles	2	2	Harris, Lewis	4	0
Davis, William	6	0	Harrison, Alex	2	7
Dobie, Mary	1	0	Harrison, Hannah	5	4
Dobie, Nathaniel	7	20	Harrison, Jones	5	5
Duff, Abdon	3	3	Harrison, William	1	34
Dunn, Lewis	4	16	Harrison, William	9	9
Dunn, Morris	11	0	Harwell, Gardiner	1	2
Dunn, Nathaniel	2	20	Harwell, Peter	6	0
Dunn, Thomas	4	1	Harwell, Richard	9	23
Dunn, William, Jr.	2	31	Harwell, Sterling	1	14
Dunn, William, Jr.	6	10	Harwood, Daniel	9	2
			Harwood, Samuel	2	8
Edmunds, Nicholas	0	3	Hawthorn, Joshua	4	2
Ellis, Benjamin	8	4	Hawthorn, Isham	7	5
Ellis, Edwin	8	5	Hawthorn, John	4	7
Ellis, Isaac	3	6	Hay, Balasm	1	0
Ellis, John	3	0	Hay, John	4	1
Ellis, William	10	7	Hay, Richard, Jr.	7	2
Eppes, James	6	6	Hay, Richard, Sr.	4	5
Eppes, Joel	0	9	Hearn, Fred	6	0
Ezell, Abel	3	0	Heath, Adam	6	5
Ezell, Thomas	7	0	Heath, Durham	6	4
			Heath, Henry	3	8
Faison, Henry	8	4	Heath, Nathan	2	9
Felts, Nathaniel	8	0	Heath, Peggy	4	9
Fires, John	3	0	Heath, Wood	6	1
Fort, Fred	10	2	Hight, Ann	7	1
Freeman, Henry	7	1	Hill, Green	6	25
Freeman, John	7	2	Hill, John	5	1
Freeman, John	4	2			

	White	Black
Hill, Mildred	4	4
Hill, Margaret	4	31
Hill, Thomas	6	25
Hines, Fred	4	6
Hines, Hartwell	11	12
Hines, Sarah	2	11
Hitchcock, Russel	3	5
Hite, Thomas	9	0
Hix, James	7	1
Hix, Mary	3	2
Hix, Robert	9	1
Hix, William	4	0
Hobbs, Joseph	8	2
Hobbs, Mary	3	0
Hobbs, Thomas	10	8
Hobbs, William	4	2
Holdsworth, Charles	4	4
Holloway, James	6	0
Hood, Henry	6	0
Hood, John	5	0
Hood, William	4	0
Horn, James	2	0
Horn, Thomas	9	0
Horn, William	8	0
Hubbard, Olive	6	0
Huson, John	6	5
Huson, Thomas	7	4
Hunnicutt, Pleasants	5	25
Irby, John	8	25
Ivey, Daniel	6	4
Ivey, Hugh	3	11
Ivy, Aaron	5	0
Ivy, Adam	7	0
Ivy, David	8	1
Ivy, Ephraim	6	0
Ivy, Peebles	4	0
Jarrat, Faddo	6	6
Jarrott, Henry	8	13
Jarrat, Howell	4	0
Jarrott, Nicholas	9	0
Jarratt, Nicholas, Jr.	6	5
Johnson, Elizabeth	6	5
Johnson, John	8	2
Jones, David	3	2
Jones, David	7	15
Jones, Henry	2	5
Jones, Howell	1	0
Jones, James B.	5	16
Jones, John	5	2
Jones, John	1	4
Jones, Peter	4	15
Jones, Rebecca	3	14
Jones, Samuel	1	5
Jordan, John	1	0
Judkins, John	4	2

	White	Black
Judkins, Robert	4	5
Judkins, William, Sr.	5	0
Judkins, William, Jr.	5	1
Kee, John	5	4
Kelley, John	8	4
Kerr, George	3	15
King, Ephraim	4	0
King, Fathey	6	2
Kitchin, Benjamin	3	0
Knight, John, Sr.	4	5
Knight, Moses	12	5
Lamb, John	4	10
Lamb, John, Jr.	5	4
Lamb, William	11	4
Land, Robert	4	9
Land, Webb	1	0
Lanier, Benjamin	11	27
Lanier, Drury	4	0
Lashley, William	3	5
Leath, John	5	2
Leath, William	7	0
Lessenberry, Elizabeth	3	4
Lewis, Enoch	2	5
Lewis, Capt. William	0	6
Lightfoot, William	0	70
Lilley, Ann	3	2
Lilley, Fred	6	2
Linn, Curtis	4	0
Linn, Robert	6	0
Loyd, Kimmin	3	0
McKinish, John	3	3
McLemore, Burwell	8	2
Mabry, Abel	9	5
Magee, Harmon	3	0
Magee, William	5	2
Maggot, Sam	9	11
Malone, John	8	13
Mangum, Sam	4	11
Marrable, Hartwell	7	17
Massenburg, John	7	16
Massengale, Thomas	4	0
Mason, Capt. David	2	10
Mason, Col. David	7	38
Mason, Capt. John	0	10
Mason, John	6	12
Mason, John	4	18
Mason, John, Jr.	7	36
Mason, John, Jr.	0	13
Mason, Littleberry	1	17
Mason, Richard	8	4
Mason, Thomas	5	18
Maury, Henry	5	0
May, Allen	5	4
Meacham, Banks	8	12
Miscall, Jeremy	2	2

	White	Black		White	Black
Mitchell, Branch	6	2	Pittway, Sterling	4	2
Mitchell, Jacob	9	6	Pittway, Robert	1	29
Mitchell, John	7	8	Pleasant, William	8	1
Mitchell, Samuel	6	3	Porch, Henry	11	1
Mitchell, Thomas	3	13	Porch, Solomon	4	6
Moody, Henry	3	2	Pope, Stephen	6	5
Morgan, Matthew	8	5	Potts, John	4	2
Morris, Lewis	4	0	Powell, Ed. C.	5	6
Moss, Edmund	3	10	Powell, Edward, Sr.	6	9
Moss, Henry, Jr.	7	12	Powell, John	7	4
Moss, Joshua	8	9	Powell, Seymour	8	8
Moss, Thomas	8	3	Poythress, Peter (Est)	4	16
Munns, John	6	0	Presson, Thomas	2	1
Murphy, Charles	7	4	Prince, Nicholas	7	0
Myrick, William	10	29	Prince, William	7	4
Newsum, Joel	2	0	Pritlow, Thomas	1	3
Newsum, Nathen	8	6	Rainey, Will	8	3
Newsum, Peter	4	0	Randall, Peter, Jr.	8	10
Newsum, William	11	5	Randall, Peter, Sr.	10	3
Nichols, Elizabeth	5	5	Raney, Peter	4	8
Nichols, Harris	7	19	Rawlings, Isaac	5	1
Nicholson, John	9	14	Redding, William	7	4
Nicholson, William	4	14	Renn, Ann	5	1
Oliver, William	8	14	Renn, Thomas	3	9
Owen, Elizabeth	5	0	Richardson, William	4	27
Owen, Hannah	4	0	Rives, Elizabeth	5	17
Ozburne, August	2	6	Rives, George	9	43
Ozburn, Nicholas	6	14	Rives, Lucy	6	6
Pare, John	9	0	Rives, Timothy, Sr.	1	3
Parham, Abram, Sr.	2	1	Rives, Timothy	4	21
Parham, Abram, Jr.	5	6	Robinson, Elizabeth	5	1
Parham, Elizabeth	3	19	Robinson, James	3	24
Parham, James	0	2	Robinson, Isaac	5	4
Parham, John	3	0	Robinson, Nathaniel	8	0
Parham, Stith, Sr.	7	30	Roberts, Benjamin	3	15
Parham, Stith	6	12	Roberts, Sarah	4	8
Parkham, Lewis	5	6	Rochell, Richard	6	0
Parkham, Robert	4	8	Rogers, Mary	7	1
Parkhan, George	8	7	Rogers, Rebecca	5	0
Parkham, William	7	6	Roland, Susan	5	0
Parker, Mary	5	14	Rose, William	2	0
Parker, Richard	7	22	Ross, William	11	0
Parsom, Henry	7	7	Rosses, Joseph	7	2
Partin, Drury	7	0	Rowland, John	10	0
Partin, William	6	3	Sammons, Ann	3	0
Partin, William, Jr.	6	3	Sammons, Benjamin	1	0
Patridge, Jesse	4	6	Sammons, James	9	0
Partridge, Nich	4	8	Sammons, Thomas	8	0
Pate, Thomas	11	0	Sammons, William	6	0
Peete, Thomas	7	23	Sands, John	6	12
Pennington, Fred	5	9	Saunders, Thomas	8	11
Pepper, Stephen	7	1	Seaburn, William	8	0
Peters, Mathew	1	9	Seat, Hartwell	5	3
Phillips, Thomas	6	2	Seat, Nathan	3	2
Phipps, Benjamin	8	3	Seat, Robert	3	11

	White	Black
Sledge, August	3	0
Sledge, Jno	6	0
Sledge, Thomas	6	1
Smith, Arthur	8	5
Smith, Drury	9	11
Smith, Edward	3	2
Smith, Joseph	11	0
Smith, Isham	12	16
Smith, Lawrence	5	17
Smith, Sarah	9	5
Solomon, Lewis	2	8
Soot, Samuel	1	3
Spratley, William	5	15
Stacey, Simon	6	4
Stewart, John	4	2
Stewart, Richard	8	24
Stokes, Christopher	3	0
Stokes, Sam	4	0
Sturdivant, Anderson	6	4
Sturdivant, Ann	6	3
Sturdivant, Henry	2	12
Sturdivant, Hollom	21	13
Sturdivant, John, Sr.	4	5
Sturdivant, John, Jr.	5	1
Sturdivant, Richard	4	10
Sturdivant, Thomas	8	9
Sturdivant, William, Jr.	4	3
Sturdivant, William, Sr.	11	15
Sykes, William	4	8
Threewits, Joel	3	7
Thorp, Lewis	5	17
Tillar, Mary	3	0
Tillar, Major	5	11
Tomlinson, Alex	7	2
Tomlinson, John	1	0
Tomlinson, Thomas	5	10
Tomlinson, William	6	2
Tucker, Mary	7	2
Tucker, Robert	6	12
Tuder, Henry	6	1
Turner, Daniel	4	3
Turner, Edm.	1	7
Turner, James	5	8
Turner, James, Jr.	8	
Tyler, William	1	15
Tyler, Benjamin	7	8
Vaughan, James		
Vaughn, Thomas, Jr	6	17
Vaughn, Thomas, Sr.	4	12
Underwood, Abslm	9	0
Underwood, Mark	7	0
Underwood, Lewis		
Underhill, Giles	5	0

	White	Black
Underhill, Howell	7	4
Walker, James	10	6
Wallis, Jesse	10	9
Walpole, Thomas	11	30
Watkins, Joseph	1	0
Weathers, Benjamin	6	3
Weathers, Michael	6	0
Weaver, Henry	6	11
Weaver, Jane	4	3
Weaver, John	4	2
Weaver, William	3	2
Weeks, Thomas	3	0
Wells, Sam	11	0
White, John	9	4
White, James	10	5
Whitehead, Isham	7	0
Whitehead, Robert	9	0
Whitehorn, Edward	4	2
Whitehorn, John	8	1
Whitehorn, Thomas	4	5
Whitfield, Thomas	8	3
Wilkinson, Richard	9	1
Wilkinson, William	5	0
Wilkins, Jeremiah	5	0
Wilkinson, Nathan	7	4
Williams, David	4	2
Williamson, Mary	9	2
Willis, Elizabeth	1	6
Wilson, Capt. Nich.	7	4
Winfield, John	4	12
Winfield, Peter	4	10
Winfield, Robert	9	14
Winfield, William	8	5
Woodland, William	6	11
Wooten, Edward	7	7
Worthington, Nathan	2	7
Worthington, Priscilla	4	12
Wyche, Mary	8	14
Wynne, John, Sr.	4	9
Wynne, Matthew, Sr.	4	3
Wynne, Matthew (son of M.)	5	0
Wynne, Matthew	4	1
Wynne, Robert	10	9
Wynne, Sarah	6	2
Wynne, Will, Sr.	2	6
Wynne, William, Jr.	7	5
Young, Drury	1	4
Young, Joshua	3	2
Zills, Ann	3	0
Zills, Morris	5	3
Zills, Susan	3	0
Zills, William	5	0

THE END.

INDEX

D

Dale, Pet., 109, 110
  Sir Tom., 27, 46, 48, 50
Damfort, Law., 32
Davies, Col., 162
  Jno., 33
  Rob., 63, 64
Davis, Ed., 84, 136
  Kath., 32
  Jas., 19, 34, 171
Joan, 33
  Pet., 151
  Rob., 8, 19
  Tom., 69
  Wm., 165
Day, Jno., 34, 80, 81, 149
  Mrs., 34
Delke, Alice, 49, 103
  Rog., 33, 103, 115
  Rog. Jr., 103, 105
Devil's Woodyard, 64
Devils Old Field, 102
Depwall (Dewell), Tom., 167
Dilke, Clem., 164
Dunsdale, Jno., 34
Doches, Jno., 34
Dodds, Jno., 34, 80
  Jane, 46
Doleman, Tom., 33
Dolphenby, Rich., 30, 31
Dominica, 2, 13
Drake, Hen., 168
  Sir Fr., 6, 7
Draper, Wm., 84
Drew, Eliz., 106
  Jno., 106, 107
  Rich., 86, 110, 144
Drummond, Wm., 123, 133
Duke, Han., 91
  Wm., 92
Dunn, Peter, 34
Dunfield (Dunston), Jno., 144
Dunston, Jno., 30, 93, 98, 144, 166
  Cicely, 98
  Peleg, 98
  Ralph, 98

E

Eaton, Jno., 168
Edmunde, Howell, 156
  Jno., 168, 169

Tom., 167
Edloe Mat, 167
Edwards, Albert S., 99, 173
  Ben., 156
  Ed., 5n.
  J. D., 162
  Jno., 168, 169
  Rob., 80
  Tom., 78, 167
  Wm., 98, 110, 112, 121, 145, 146, 152, 156, 159, 160, 166, 171, 172, 173
Elebeck, Hen., 151
Ellyson, Rob., 167
Eliot, Coe, 162
Elliott, Jno., 30, 31
Ellis, Jere., 126
Elwood, Hen., 33
Elsword, Hen., 30
Emporia, 159
Ealey, Han., 171
  Jno., 171
Evans, Rob., 84, 136
  Wm., 171
Evelin, Geo., 37, 54
  Mjy., 37, 54
Evers, Robt., 34, 35
Every, Fran., 136
Ewen, Wm., 35, 41, 42, 43, 64, 75
  Mary, 43, 44

F

Farrar, family, 89
Fawcett, Tom., 94, 165
Faulcon, Jac., 170, 171, 173
  Jno., 173
  Nic., 170
  Nic., Jr., 161, 167, 170, 171
Felgate, Sara, 43
  Tob., 43, 77
  Wm., 43
Fenley, Jno., 126
Fems, Rich., 30
Filmer, Jno., 34
Finch, Fran., 52
  Wm., 52
Fitch, Enecha, 34
  Mat., 19
  Tom., 34
First Supply, 18
Fitts, Alice, 3d
  Tom., 30